Actors and American Culture, 1880-1920

In the Series *American Civilization*
edited by Allen F. Davis

Richard Mansfield: a grand fusion of ambition and art. COURTESY OF THE BILLY ROSE THEATRE COLLECTION.

Actors and American Culture, 1880-1920

Benjamin McArthur

Temple University Press   PHILADELPHIA

Temple University Press, Philadelphia 19122
© 1984 by Temple University. All rights reserved
Published 1984
Printed in the United States of America

Library of Congress Cataloging in Publication Data

McArthur, Benjamin.
  Actors and American culture, 1880–1920.

  (American civilization)
  Includes index.
    1. Theater—United States—History.   2. Actors—United States.
  3. Theater and society—United States.   4. United States—Popular
  culture.   I. Title.   II. Series.
  PN2256.M39   1984   792′.028′0973   83-24091
  ISBN 0-87722-333-5

Parts of Chapter 3 originally appeared in *Theatre Survey* 23 (November 1982).
The photographs throughout this volume are reproduced by permission of
the Billy Rose Theatre Collection, The New York Public Library at Lincoln
Center, Astor, Linox and Tilden Foundations.

To My Mother and Father

Contents

Preface

*A*merica's most visible industry deals not in objects but in people. The energies of the entertainment media are directed largely at the creation of celebrities. The celebrity phenomenon is so commonplace that it would seem to require no explanation. One is constantly bombarded with a stream of personalities on television, radio, motion pictures and in newspapers and magazines. Celebrities come from many fields, including sports, politics, journalism, and the arts, but they share the feature of a personality thrown into high relief by the media's unrelenting exposure. The glamour and achievement personified in the celebrity have become a source of vicarious satisfaction for the modern individual.

Actors remain the quintessential celebrities. Their lives are dedicated to the creation of images, embodying an excitement and freedom from convention that the ordinary person rarely experiences firsthand. Actors have become an important source of values for many people, both through their stage and screen characterizations and through their personal lifestyles, which have been made a matter of public record. "Life follows art" might be paraphrased "life follows the artist."

Actors have not always enjoyed such a glorified position. Through most of history, until the late nineteenth century, players existed outside the boundaries of respectable society. Between the years 1880 and 1920 actors became significant figures in the American social landscape, and in this era the cult of celebrity had its start. This book deals with actors' efforts at improving their profession's reputation and raising their social status. As an essay in American cultural history it also seeks to relate actors and their work to the wider aspects of American life.

Historians of American entertainment have generally focused on the forms and content of the performance itself.[1] My study concentrates on those who provided the entertainment. This choice was not determined by the mediocrity of the age's dramatic writing, but because the approach seemed especially appropriate for this period. Constance Rourke noted how deeply the theatre was interwoven with the American character in the early nineteenth century.[2] Audiences had a direct and immediate impact on the performances, and the theatre's melodramas embodied the era's democratic values. Likewise, Neil Harris has shown how P. T. Barnum's outrageous showmanship in pre–Civil War America depended upon an active, participatory role by his audience.[3] But this was less true of the later nineteenth century. The theatre became highly centralized, plays being packaged and sent from New York to the rest of the country. Audiences no longer exerted as direct an influence on content or performance. Professional entertainers dispensed amusement to an eager public that generally accepted what was offered. Moreover, the players overshadowed the play. Edwin Booth, Joseph Jefferson, Minnie Maddern Fiske, Maude Adams, David Warfield, E. H. Sothern, the Barrymores: the great players ruled the stage, dwarfing the roles they played. The public needed stars and lots of them. The significant element was no longer the content of the amusement but the personality providing it. Actors became a more telling reflection of cultural values than the play itself.

The time frame for this study, 1880 to 1920, is significant for a number of reasons. These forty years marked the golden age of the American theatre as a national institution. The combination system of traveling companies had reached its complete development by 1880, and over the next thirty years hundreds of theatrical companies left New York annually to tour the nation. Between 1910 and 1920, however, for reasons to be discussed later, the "road" dried up and the commercial theatre became what it is today, primarily a New York institution. A second unity of the era was actors' concern for their social and occupational advancement, given initial institutional form in the founding of the Actors' Fund in 1882 and completed by the Actors' Equity strike of 1919. These years were a time of particular self-consciousness among actors concerning their place in American society. Third, and in a wider sense, these decades witnessed the crucial transformation of the place of entertainment in American society.

I have restricted my study to actors of the legitimate stage. The term "legitimate" meant several different things for actors of the nineteenth century. It sometimes meant drama of the classic authors, such as Shakespeare or Sheridan; at other times it distinguished spoken drama from the musical stage. Its most common usage, however, and the one implied in this book, was a broad one, differentiating full-length dramatic productions from vaudeville, burlesque, minstrelsy, circus, and—later—motion pictures. Performers of the musical operas, forerunners of the modern musicals, were also considered legitimate players. The logic for limiting the study to legitimate actors rests partly in the sense of distinctiveness members of the "legit" felt, whether they were Broadway stars or small-town stock performers, and partly from the special place they had in public esteem. Minstrelsy and vaudeville both had their hour as immensely popular forms of entertainment. But until the advent of the motion picture, the legitimate theatre remained the standard American entertainment. Its performers could claim a lineage tracing far back into European history, and for the American public the stars of the legitimate stage reigned unchallenged in the amusement world.

The theatre was a national institution, but New York City was the capital and must therefore be the focus of attention. A theatrical weekly observed in 1898 that with the rise of combination companies New York had become an "index of coincident conditions throughout the country."[4] Consequently, most of my story is set against Broadway's backdrop. Likewise, while I have attempted to describe all levels of actors from the tent-rep show performers to the Broadway stars, my account is necessarily weighted toward the latter. This preference can be defended, first by the meager information concerning the journeymen players, and second by the nature of the acting profession itself, whose leading members not only dominated the craft but were foremost in the public thinking.

This study covers three major areas. The first describes the workings of the American theatre at its high point in our history, not from the standpoint of its dramatic literature or stage productions, which have received attention elsewhere, but with an eye to the structure of the theatre itself and particularly to the lives of its performers. This side of the theatre has received far less attention from its historians and remains for the most part a story untold.

Second, the study intends to be an occupational history of actors, focusing on players' self-conscious attempts at raising their social status through professionalization. This approach has been recently popular among historians in explaining nineteenth- and twentieth-century occupational history, and through overuse and occasional lack of rigorous definition has risked losing its effectiveness as a conceptual tool. But the ideal of professionalization is crucial for an understanding of actors' institutional ambitions in the later nineteenth century. Moreover, the experience of actors can enrich the scholarship of professionalism by considering the special problems of an artistic occupation, which impeded full professionalization.

Third, my story touches on changes over which actors had no control and which shaped their social role in unforeseen ways. These include cultural changes of far-reaching significance: the legitimization of entertainment in American culture, the beginnings of a mass media, the cult of personality, and a chafing against the restraints of the Victorian age, all of which helped enthrone actors as figures of influence in American culture. Studies of twentieth-century culture have focused on the motion picture to the near exclusion of the theatre. But the theatre and its performers foreshadowed the characteristics of mass culture usually associated with the movies. Through the evolving relationship of actor and society one can glimpse twentieth-century mass culture in the making.

In developing these themes a strictly chronological approach has had to give way to a topical arrangement of chapters. This method involves retracing one's steps at times, but is necessary to display cultural configurations, for values and attitudes do not appear in an orderly, sequential manner. The study can be divided into two parts. The first four chapters and then the final one describe the theatre, actors' lives and work, and their attempts to professionalize. Chapters 5 through 8 explore the broader relationship of theatre and culture and the redefinition of the actor's social role. Although I focus on the American stage and its performers, my research gives conviction beyond all doubt that virtually every trend in the American theatre between 1880 and 1920 can be seen in the English theatre also. I make no claims, therefore, to be describing a uniquely American development. To the contrary, I would suggest that the evolution of the actor's social role was not a function of peculiarly American conditions but was common to western industrial society.

A final caveat: The word "actor" is ambiguous concerning the gender of the person described. I have nevertheless decided that style dictates a generic use of "actor" when referring to both actors and actresses. I have tried to make clear the occasions when "actor" refers only to men.

Acknowledgments

*A*t first glance a theatrical production and a book appear at the extremes of the artistic spectrum, the one representing extensive cooperative endeavor, the other solitary effort. Scholars, however, recognize this distinction to be false. My study, no less than any other, owes whatever merit it possesses to a regiment of people who assisted, advised, criticized, or consoled as the situation warranted. Acknowledging my debt to them provides opportunity for pleasant recollections of acquaintances made over the past several years.

I extend my thanks to the reference librarians at Regenstein Library, the University of Chicago, for their patience and energy. Likewise, Paul Myers and his staff at the Billy Rose Theatre Collection of the New York Public Library at Lincoln Center guided me through their indispensable collection. Louis Rachow, curator of The Players' library, proved a congenial and knowledgable host at what remains—some eighty years after Henry James first described it—"an oasis of quietness and atmosphere." I must also thank librarians at Columbia, Princeton, and the Chicago Historical Society for their assistance.

A number of scholars aided my research and writing. Brooks McNamara graciously made available his private collection of theatrical scrapbooks. Richard Stoddard gave me valuable bibliographic advice. John Cawelti, Allen Davis, Morris Janowitz, Ken Kusmer, Lary May, and Tice Miller read all or parts of the manuscript and commented on it. Thanks also to two readers whose identity is unknown to me, but whose trenchant criticism sparked revision. I would have done well, no doubt, to have taken the advice of all these people more often. My greatest obligation is to Neil Harris, who oversaw this project in its early stages from seminar paper to dissertation.

Dan Meyer and Bob Burger may or may not wish to be associated with these pages, but through many evenings of informal conversation they helped me sort out my thoughts on cultural history. I would be remiss not to mention my undergraduate mentors at Andrews University, particularly Gary Land and Donald Mc-Adams, who provided models of Christian scholarship. A special word of thanks also for Evonne Richards and her staff at Southern College's word processing center. They not only typed the manuscript with remarkable efficiency, but introduced me to the futuristic pleasures of computer editing.

Finally, to my family I extend an earnest thank you. Callie had to live with this project for several years but her enthusiasm for it remained undaunted. My parents have followed its progress even longer. Their support has been crucial throughout. To them I dedicate this book.

Actors and American Culture, 1880-1920

These our actors,
As I foretold you, were all spirits and
Are melted into air, into thin air.

The Tempest IV, i

One *The Theatrical Structure*

A study of American actors begins with an understanding of the theatrical world in which they worked. The American theatre consisted of several levels: itinerant groups, stock companies, and combination companies, the last of which was the most important organizational form from 1880 to 1920. After describing these organizations, I shall consider the theatrical hierarchy, from stars down to extras, then go on to deal with the business side of the actor's life: dramatic agencies, relations with managers and producers, salaries, and the troublesome theatrical contract. Behind the ephemeral moments of entertainment enjoyed by audiences each evening lay an increasingly large and complex organization that controlled the world within which actors moved.

*   1   *

At the bottom of the theatrical ladder were the itinerant acting troupes who brought entertainment to America's hinterland. Often these were theatrical families (the American stage, one recalls, got its professional start with the visiting Hallam family in the 1750s). Two of the most prominent theatrical families were the Drakes, who in the years following the War of 1812 pioneered theatricals in the Ohio River valley, and the Chapmans, a prolific family of troupers who improvised the first showboat in the 1820s and who later barnstormed California's Gold Coast. Throughout the nineteenth century little acting companies tramped across the country. Towns often lacked theatres, so performances took place in meeting halls, dining rooms, and even barns. Conditions demanded versatility. Actors served as their own directors, musicians, stagehands, and publicity agents. Although Joseph Jefferson and Lotta Crabtree, comedians of the first rank, both emerged from this tradition, most strollers remained on the economic fringes of the dramatic world. The success of a tour was closely related to the current prosperity of the region in which it played. A bad crop or low commodity price diminished attendance. The De Angelis family tour met hardship when grasshoppers invaded Kansas in 1874, devouring the crops and devastating theatricals.[1] During bad times players fell back on whatever odd jobs they could find to keep alive. Little is known about most of these "vagabond troupers," who were the nineteenth-century equivalents of the Elizabethan strolling players. But their perseverance and dedication to their craft symbolized for all players the true meaning of the trouper spirit.

This barnstorming tradition was continued down into the early twentieth century by the itinerant repertoire companies, generally called the 10–20–30 theatricals because of their price scale. They originated in the 1880s when H. R. Jacobs and F. F. Proctor launched a circuit of 10–20–30 theatres in a number of eastern cities, presenting one-week stands of melodrama.[2] But dramatic repertoire found its home mainly in small towns and rural areas. In the 1890s nearly every state had companies performing in their small and medium-sized towns. Normally they stayed in a town for a week, giving a matinee and evening performance each day except Sunday. There was a daily change of bill, featuring such standard melodramatic fare as *East Lynne*, *Leah*, *The Forsaken*, *The Two Orphans*, and Bartley Campbell's two plays, *The Galley Slave* and *Divorced*.[3]

The repertoire companies were also known as tent-rep. During the heat of the pre–air-conditioned summer most theatres closed, forcing acting troupes to appear under tent. After 1900 these companies became especially common in the Midwest and South. Also, after 1910, when motion pictures began crowding stage performers out of the nation's theatres, the budget melodrama companies found tents the only alternative. Tent-rep was rural entertainment. The most popular dramas extolled the homely virtues of rural life and expressed suspicion of the city. The red-haired, freckle-faced rustic "Toby" became the stock hero, giving these companies the title of "Toby shows." During the winter months managers secured actors for the upcoming season in Chicago and Kansas City or through trade journal ads. Tent-rep provided work for many actors; in the summer of 1914 it was estimated that eight hundred actors found employment within a three hundred mile radius of Kansas City.[4]

Repertoire troupes varied in size, the average having ten

players, which made doubling and even tripling of roles common. The spectacle *Quo Vadis* was once presented with a cast of seven! Additionally, vaudeville was presented between acts, so players had to work up a specialty number. As in earlier days, there were companies composed of entire families, such as the Spooner Company, headed by Mrs. Mary Gibbs Spooner with her son and two daughters. Many repertoire performers had had no theatrical experience. Stagestruck youngsters would join a troupe as it passed through town, filling a position that needed little preparation. Some, like Neil Schaffner, kept responding to ads in the *Clipper*, a theatrical trade paper, until they landed a job.[5]

Condescendingly called "prairie actors" by their eastern brethren, repertoire actors occupied a modest place in the theatrical world. Though their careers were played out in the shadows of the prestigious New York touring companies, they no doubt had their own following who anticipated their return to town each year. The popular prices of these shows, in fact, hurt the more expensive one-night road shows, so that theatre managers at times restricted their number in order to protect the first-class attractions.[6] But repertoire's days were numbered by the motion picture, which first drove them out of the theatres and into tents and finally killed them altogether.

* * *

More significant were the stock companies, which formed the normal producing unit through the greater part of the nineteenth century. Of course there was variety within this broad category. The lower end shaded off into the repertoire companies just discussed. The better stock companies had permanent theatrical homes located in cities large enough to support a theatre throughout the season. Stock companies were, to attempt a definition, autonomous local operations headed by a manager who owned or leased the theatre, hired the actors, picked the plays and offered a rudimentary form of direction to the cast. Seasons normally ran for forty weeks in the mid-nineteenth century. Six performances a week was standard, increasing to eight a week by 1870. Companies performed a staggering number of plays. The Boston Museum (museum was a common euphemism for theatre) produced one hundred and forty in the 1851–52 season. Obviously, long runs were rare; a successful play would get ten to twenty performances and those not consecutively. This repertory system bowed to the long run in the 1870s and 1880s with popular plays remaining on the bill as long as they drew. The Boston Museum produced only forty plays in 1881–82, and just fifteen in its last year, 1892–93. New York companies offered even fewer in the 1890s, five to ten a season.[7]

Permanent stock companies gave actors a chance to lead comparatively settled lives. A few actors achieved local prominence, such as William Warren, who was with the Boston Museum for thirty-five years and became a fixture in Boston society. A position in a solid company provided a measure of financial security; once in, a competent player could be fairly sure of being rehired. When Lawrence Barrett wrote Edwin Booth begging for help to get him out of stock and into starring roles, Booth replied: "Don't turn up your nose at stock. . . . Starring about the country is sad work—a home is better."[8] Yet actors kept on the move; long tenures such as Warren and Mrs. Vincent enjoyed at the Boston Museum were the exception. Edward Mammen has tabulated the duration of the nearly six hundred actors who appeared on the Boston Museum's stage in its fifty years. Over half left after a single season, another fifth left after two years. Most of the rest remained from three to five years. The proportion of turnover was almost constant for each decade from 1843 to 1893. In an average season twelve members were newcomers and five had been a member for only a year.[9] A study of the Empire Theatre Stock Company in New York during a later period reveals a similar pattern. In its eleven-year history from 1893 to 1903, 128 players performed, 56 acting in only one role, and only 8 actors staying as long as five seasons. Over 60 percent played one season or less.[10] If turnover was high at two of the most respected stock companies, it undoubtedly was even higher in others. In some cases actors moved on because pay was low or because of a personality conflict with other actors or the manager. But the most important reason for going elsewhere was ambition. Few actors wanted to spend their entire careers in supporting roles. A move, even to a company no more prominent, held the promise of better roles and greater appreciation by new audiences. The next move might herald stardom.

Stock companies varied in size. In the mid–nineteenth century the Boston Museum had sixteen to twenty actors, eight to twelve actresses, and eight to twelve ballet girls. It was bigger than many companies, but the ratio of men to women was typical, indicative of the greater number of males required by most plays. Such dramatic staples as *Othello* required ten men and three women, *She Stoops To Conquer*, twelve men and five women. Later in the century as drawing-room comedies became popular the number of women's parts reached par with men's. Augustin Daly's company in 1879–80 had even more actresses than actors, twenty-six to eighteen.

Lines of business (a theatricalism meaning the type of role one played) were followed fairly rigidly in most companies until the 1860s. Actors and actresses were hired to play stereotyped roles as either leading man or lady, heavy, low comedy, soubrette, old man and woman, walking gentleman, or utility. Some companies would have two actors in certain lines, a first and second comedian, walking gentleman, and so on. Just as the first chair in an orchestra plays the solos, the first actor got more—and better— roles. At the Boston Museum in 1850–51 the first low comedian had seventy-five roles to the second low comedian's forty. Salary was scaled accordingly.[11] In the 1870s casting became more flexible. Both Augustin Daly and A. M. Palmer are credited with breaking down the lines of business (although the terms continued in use through the rest of the century). At Palmer's Union Square Theatre Company in New York the prime concern became filling the role with the actor best suited to it, and actors were expected to play any part assigned them.[12]

The advent of the touring combination companies in the 1870s spelled the decline of the established stock companies.[13] Road shows and their star headliners occupied the stages, displacing local companies. Figures tell the sad story. Fifty permanent stock companies still operated in 1871, but by 1878 they were reduced to seven or eight. Such venerable institutions as Mrs. Drew's Arch Street Theatre in Philadelphia became combination houses. The remnant companies, Palmer's Madison Square Theatre for example, attempted to adapt by accepting the long run and sending idle players out on tour. But they staved off the inevitable only a little longer. Lester Wallack's company disbanded in 1887; the Boston Museum company broke up in 1893; Palmer's company bowed out in 1893, while Daly's company lasted until his death in 1899.[14]

One important stock company was born in the otherwise fatal 1890s: Charles Frohman's Empire Theatre Stock Company. Although Frohman wanted a company that would emulate Daly's famous troupe, in effect his organization served primarily as a training ground for his combination companies. A veritable Who's Who of early twentieth-century American theatre belonged to it at one time: Viola Allen, Henry Miller, William Faversham, Margaret Anglin, Ida Conquest, May Robson, and Robert Edeson. After ten years of stock, the Empire Theatre, too, displayed star billing in 1903.[15]

Although first-class stock companies—such houses as Wallack's, Daly's, Palmer's, which presented top quality production of both standard drama and new plays—disappeared, another form of stock, the so-called popular-priced stock companies, appeared in the 1890s as alternatives to the more expensive New York touring combinations. In the 1897–98 season twenty-one popular-priced stock companies performed; in 1898–99 there were forty-two. By 1910 roughly eighty stock companies dotted the urban landscape; some cities had several. In the summer many more stock companies formed, often playing in open-air theatres, imaginatively called air domes. During the summer of 1911, 149 companies operated, employing some 1,800 actors. Summer stock often featured stars, who appeared for two to four weeks in a city. James K. Hackett, Richard Bennett, Margaret Illington, Arnold Daly, and Amelia Bingham were among the celebrities who commanded up to a thousand dollars a week for their services.[16]

The characteristic feature of stock companies during the regular season, however, was their ability to survive without stars. These companies operated on prodigious schedules. Many companies put on two shows a day, six days a week in the East, where Sunday closing still prevailed, but often seven days a week in the West. Rehearsals ran from 9:30 A.M. to noon; then came a matinee at 2:00 P.M. and an evening performance at 8:00. Boston's Castle Square Theatre ran continuously winter and summer for six years beginning in 1897, twelve shows a week, with only two days closing at President McKinley's death. Unlike the older stock companies, which had a standard repertory of classic drama supplemented by one or two new plays a year, popular-priced stock presented comtemporary plays almost exclusively, meaning that each year stock players had to memorize many new scripts. The Castle Square Theatre, for example, in the 312 weeks of its first six years produced 212 different plays.[17]

The stock company system, then, though considerably reduced in importance, continued well into the twentieth century as a kind of minor league of the theatre. It developed many of the actors who went on to stardom. One could learn the craft in stock, but the only place to become a star was New York.

* 2 *

By 1880 Broadway had become a synonym for theatre. Its popular plays became America's popular plays. Theatre was not New York's only export, for in the late nineteenth century New York asserted itself as America's cultural arbiter by becoming the packager and dispenser of the arts for the nation. The popular tunes of the day spread across America from the music publishing industry centered in Manhattan, and the literary establishment transferred its headquarters there, symbolized by William Dean Howells's exodus from Boston to New York in 1888. Increasingly, book and magazine publishers settled in Manhattan. The new magazines, *McClure's*, *Munsey's*, *Cosmopolitan*, and others, broadcasted the tastes and fashions of New York to a national readership that was ready to shed republican simplicity for urban sophistication.

The centralization of the theatre in New York anticipated this pattern. New York had assumed theatrical leadership even before the combination system replaced stock. By 1850 it had more legitimate theatres and more stars than its two closest rivals, Boston and Philadelphia. In the early 1870s there were twenty-eight theatres in Manhattan, fourteen of them along Broadway. Contemporary observers explained this concentration of theatres as a consequence of the boardinghouse life led by many New Yorkers. A weakened family life led Gothamites to substitute stage entertainment for domestic pleasures.[18]

But New York's theatrical predominance rested on more than its own theatres; it also headquartered the combination companies that toured the nation. Combinations, to suggest a short definition, were theatrical companies that performed a single play for the season on a prearranged tour. Combinations required a center where actors and managers could meet and negotiate. A few companies organized in Chicago or San Francisco, but New York, where individual stars had traditionally booked their tours, logically evolved into the dramatic hub. Plays were produced and staged in New York. A successful run there ensured even greater profits when the show was taken on the road because the country looked to New York for standards of taste.[19] The career of Clara Morris exemplified this power. Hooted by audiences in Cincinnati and Cleveland early in her career, she met a different reception in New York: critics and audiences loved her. Favorable reviews of Morris's performances were reprinted in newspapers throughout the nation, and New York's opinion became that of America's. "I had suddenly been lifted high into popularity by the whim of the first city in the land," she wrote.[20]

The precise origins of the combination company are clouded. Dion Boucicault claimed to have originated it in England in 1860 when he sent out a production of *Colleen Bawn* to the provinces. Joseph Jefferson and Charles Wyndham put together what may have been the pioneer American company in 1868. In any event, the growth of the combination companies was largely a function of the American railroad. In 1840 fewer than 3,000 miles of railroad existed, and direct travel from New York to Boston was impossible. By 1860 this had increased to over 30,000 miles of track and to nearly 129,000 miles in 1885. This enabled whole companies complete with their scenery to travel rapidly and in comparative comfort to cities throughout America.

Touring combinations burgeoned in the last two decades of the nineteenth century. In the 1881–82 season 138 combinations took to the road: 94 dramatic companies, 18 musical and operatic, 9 variety shows, 9 musical parties, 3 pantomine troupes, 3 individual musicians, and 2 Uncle Tom companies. The number climbed to 234 combinations in 1894–95 and peaked in December of 1904, when 420 companies were touring.[21] Especially popular plays were performed by a number of companies simultaneously. *Hazel Kirke* was toured by three separate companies of the Madison Square Theatre in 1880, where it was becoming the longest-running play in Broadway history up to that time. Three years later fourteen companies played it (usually in pirated editions) across the country.[22]

The rise of the combination companies was also tied to the star system, which had gained momentum since 1810 when the English luminary George Frederick Cooke made his American tour. By the 1830s stock companies hosted a procession of touring stars. Their impact upon stock companies, according to William Wood, was ruinous. The stars brought along their own plays, which the supporting actors had not seen. Since the performance would be the evening after the star arrived, rehearsals were hurried. Actors might have to learn from three hundred to five hundred lines in a day. Modern theories demanding reflection upon one's role were necessarily unknown to them. They did well to understand the plot. The star system, according to Wood, also devastated morale:

> The companies here found, night after night, some new person they had never before heard of, announced in big letters—all their own plans deranged, themselves forced into extraordinary and severe study, and their whole time absorbed, and their powers overworked—merely that they might act as subsidiaries, or, perhaps as foils to some foreign adventurer, who possessed no merit half so great as their own; while he took away in one night twice as much as they could earn in their whole weekly wages.

Naturally the stock players would not tolerate this situation indefinitely, and many abandoned their companies in quest of their own stardom.[23]

The star system evolved into the combination companies during the 1870s, which by 1880 were well entrenched. Its financial advantages few denied. The last year that Mrs. Drew's Arch Street Theatre operated on the repertory principle, it lost $9,000.

Using traveling attractions the next year it netted $12,000.[24] Moreover, the major dramatic weekly of the era, the *New York Mirror*, applauded the combination system in 1881 for its ability to launch actors on a starring career.[25] Yet the theatre was basically a conservative institution, and such a fundamental structural change raised questions. The devastation of the stock company was thought inimical to high artistic standards, especially since it eliminated the primary means of training actors. By 1884 the *Mirror*, reconsidering its earlier endorsement, thought that the combination system had been overdone and called for a return to stock. "Most of the evils and abuses from which actors now suffer can be traced to nomadism," it editorialized in 1891, "Esprit de corps, artistic progress, pecuniary advantage—these things are difficult under the tramp system."[26] But the combination system had come to stay, and players quickly resigned themselves to it.

* * *

Though the combination system may have been faulted by theatre purists, it supplied what Americans wanted. The public came to the theatre less to see great drama than to see great performances. Actress Olive Logan observed in 1870 that "with all their ardent love for theatrical amusements, I have no hesitation in saying that the Americans care much more for the actors than for the merits of the play itself. This predilection is constantly accompanied by a regard less to a perfect ensemble than to the excellence of the 'star' of the evening."[27] Clara Morris, herself a star, noted that natural movement and development of character were often sacrificed to the star's role.[28]

Of course preoccupation with the star was not confined to America or to nineteenth-century audiences. English audiences had flocked to see the first men and women of the stage from Betterton to Garrick, Mrs. Siddons, and Kean. Yet the expansion of theatricals throughout the 1880s offered unequaled opportunities for new stars to appear. Improved transportation enabled actors to reach a vast audience and nourish a wider reputation. And with a national network of newspapers and magazines a star's accomplishments could be trumpeted in a city before he or she ever set foot there. Americans enjoyed a range of stars: such comedians as Lotta Crabtree, Joseph Jefferson, John Drew, May Irwin, and Ada Rehan; musical comedy performers, DeWolf Hopper, Lillian Russell, Elsie Janis, Anna Held, George M. Cohan, and Francis Wilson; emotional actresses, typified by Clara Morris and Mrs. Lester Carter; matinee idols, James K. Hackett, Kyrle Bellew, John Barrymore, and Richard Bennett; tragedians, such as Edwin Booth, Lawrence

Barrett, Mary Anderson, Richard Mansfield, Edward H. Sothern, and Julia Marlowe; and a kind of star difficult to categorize, such as Maude Adams or Minnie Maddern Fiske, whose idiosyncratic charms captivated audiences.

The tangible benefits of stardom were many. Theodore Dreiser's *Sister Carrie* (a novel unequaled in the literary canon for theatrical description of the era) offers a vivid commentary on the fruits of theatrical success. Carrie Meeber's overnight triumph brought a huge raise, which relieved her previously stringent budget. And it also meant that the management now made requests of her rather than giving orders and that other members of the cast now deferred to her. She enjoyed the luxury of a private dressing room. Letters of adulation and proposals of marriage poured in from an adoring public, and writers interviewed her for gossipy newspaper columns. Above all, she realized that the applause was now for her—the sweetest reward of all.[29]

Starring actors carefully protected their prerogatives. In the third act of *A Wife's Stratagem*, star Margaret Anglin had almost no lines. She protested that it would never do to have the curtain go down on the scene with her a near nonentity, for the public expected to see the star when they went to the theatre. The act was modified.[30] In 1893 Augustin Daly negotiated with Richard Mansfield to appear at his theatre. Mansfield replied to the offer, "One thing is very distinct in my mind and that is the impossibility of making an appearance here otherwise than as a star of the first magnitude."[31] But no one received a star billing at Daly's, and Mansfield, whose career was beginning to blossom, felt that an appearance might be against his interests:

> I would very gladly give up a large share of my profits to be with such a master as you and to be guided and directed by you. But I cannot sink my identity and I cannot give up the little I have accomplished in the past years of incessant labor. My name must be upon my banner as the actor. . . . I am exceedingly ambitious & I confess it—I desire to produce great plays and to play them greatly.[32]

Mansfield did have a legendary ego. But his jealously guarded stardom resembled that of many players.

Below the stars existed a vast range of featured actors, the yeomen of the stage. The various types, leading men and ladies, heavies, comedians, character actors, old men, and grand dames, filled the important roles of combination companies. Tables 1 and 2 estimate the number and percentages of actors and actresses in the various lines of business in 1888.

Ranking next to the stars were the leads. The principal lead played opposite the star; a female star had a male lead and a male star had his leading actress. Many plays required what were called juvenile leads, but it was juvenile construed broadly. Juveniles could be anyone from teenagers to thirtyish adults. With their romantic intrigue and impetuous behavior they added a comic subplot to the play. Leading roles required good looks and cultured manner. Stars frequently rose from the ranks of leading men and ladies—Marguerite Clark, Marie Burroughs, Blanche Walsh, Rob-

Table 1   Actors by Line of Business in 1888

Line	No.	%
Stars	68	4.7
Leading men	138	9.5
Heavy leads	7	.5
Leading heavies	47	3.3
Heavies	100	6.9
Character actors	222	15.4
Leading old men	8	.6
Old men	108	7.5
Character old men	17	1.2
Eccentric old men	2	.1
Leading juveniles	48	3.3
Juveniles	162	11.2
Singing juveniles	1	.1
Leading comedians	19	1.3
Comedians	251	17.4
Singing comedians	40	2.8
Light comedians	34	2.4
Low comedians	11	.8
Eccentric comedians	47	3.3
Character comedians	7	.5
Walking gentlemen	22	1.5
Singing walking gentlemen	1	.07
Responsible	16	1.1
Utility	60	4.1
Total	1,436	99.6

Source: Harrison Grey Fiske, ed., *The New York Mirror Annual* (New York, 1888), pp. 161–86.

Table 2   Actresses by Line of Business in 1888

Line	No.	%
Stars	73	7.7
Leading ladies	151	16.0
Heavy leads	2	.2
Leading heavies	17	1.8
Heavies	16	1.7
Characters	47	5.0
Leading old women	4	.4
Old women	82	8.7
Character old women	7	.7
Eccentric old women	4	.4
Singing old women	2	.2
Leading juveniles	47	5.0
Juveniles	128	13.5
Singing juveniles	3	.3
Leading comedians	7	.7
Comediennes	18	1.9
Eccentric comediennes	12	1.3
Light comediennes	3	.3
Singing comediennes	2	.2
Ingenues	24	2.5
Leading soubrettes	4	.4
Singing soubrettes	65	6.9
Soubrettes	138	14.6
Boy's parts	6	.6
Singing chambermaid	1	.1
Chambermaid	1	.1
Walking ladies	24	2.5
Responsible utility	10	1.0
Utility	22	2.3
Children's parts	25	2.6
Total	945	99.6

Source: Harrison Grey Fiske, ed., *The New York Mirror Annual* (New York, 1888), pp. 161–86.

ert Edeson, John Drew, and Otis Skinner, to name a few. There were also leading players who never attained the rank of star but who nevertheless enjoyed acclaim in their supporting roles. Holbrook Blinn, for example, earned respect as leading man for a number of stars, particularly Mrs. Fiske.

Character actors specialized in playing particular types, such as professional men, ethnic types, or heavies. Thomas Wise was an eminent character actor, confined to these roles because of his obesity. Felix Morris was another, whose "Scotch Professor" became a classic of character acting. When actors specialized in humorous peculiarities, often with affected dialect, they were known as eccentric comedians; Daniel Sully's Irish and J. K. ("Fritz") Emmett's German portrayals were among the most popular eccentric roles. The heavies played either a serious lead or the villain. Naturally, the older actors and actresses played the parts of old men and women. Some younger players such as May Robson, however, also specialized in elderly roles.

Utility actors ranked below the featured performers. As stage novices they apprenticed by taking whatever bit parts were called for and sometimes helping out backstage. From utility they progressed to walking gentlemen and ladies, serving to fill out the scene by their presence and occasionally having a few lines to speak.

On the fringe of the dramatic world existed the supernumeraries and chorus girls. The supers composed the crowds in scenes calling for a mass of nonspeaking parts. In New York they were supplied by a super broker, who normally had a crowd at his office looking for an easy way to earn fifty cents a night. Supers were treated like props, ordered about the stage without being given a hint of what the play was about. A super captain was responsible for their work, and in some theatres he also recruited the plebes. There were two classes of supers: stage aspirants who took a menial role as an entree to the profession, and, more commonly, those simply curious about the theatre or in need of quick money. The ineptitude of supernumeraries was proverbial. On one occasion a line of supers portrayed grenadiers who were to fire their muskets. At the officer's command all the firing pins snapped but no volley was heard. Every super had feared the gun's kickback and unloaded his weapon, assuming that the others would cover his silence![33]

Sharing the mudsill with supernumeraries were members of the chorus. Increased demand for chorus girls accompanied the rising popularity of operettas and musicals in the late nineteeth and early twentieth centuries. A chorine needed good looks, a fair

voice, knowledge of a few dance steps, and perhaps most important, a fashionable dress for the job interview. Some took chorus
positions out of financial necessity and were satisfied to pocket the
twenty dollars every week. Others aspired to greater things, hoping to be picked out of the chorus line and thrust into stardom. A
few notables did indeed graduate from the chorus: Marie Dressler,
Lillian Russell, Elsie Ferguson, and Fanny Brice. Others who did
not sometimes had the consolation of marrying wealth. The six
Floradora girls became the toast of New York in 1900 when they
tripped on stage, parasol in hand, and gave their coy response to
"Tell me, Pretty Maiden." The original sextette all married millionaires, a few with English titles attached. The image of the chorus girl on the prowl for wealth became a stereotype, labeled in the
title of Avery Hopwood's *The Gold Diggers*.[34]

The lower ranks of players were constantly reminded of their
position. As a utility player at the Philadelphia Museum Stock
Company in the late 1870s the young Otis Skinner had a firsthand
view of the caste system. He felt unwelcome in the presence of the
"Olympians," and if the leading players noticed him at all it was
with condescension.[35] The members of Marie Wainwright's company were not allowed to speak to her unless first addressed by the
temperamental star.[36] Likewise, when touring as a Charles Frohman star, Billie Burke insisted that respect for rank be maintained.
Before one tour she complained to William Seymour, Frohman's
stage director, about certain arrangements. In her company were a
Mr. and Mrs. Holding—Mr. Holding a leading player, Mrs. Holding only a supernumerary. They wished to share a dressing room,
but Burke objected to this, afraid it might cause friction in the company. "Anyone who is playing a subordinate part or walking on,"
she wrote, "should be prepared to keep that position, at any rate
inside the theatre; this I do not believe Mrs.Holding is prepared to
do." Burke consequently asked Seymour to fire her.[37] A successful
tour required backstage harmony, and that could be assured only if
each member accepted the boundary of his or her position.

*   3   *

Through the 1880s and '90s Union Square was the center of
the New York theatrical district, not only because of the theatres
bordering it, but also because it hosted an array of businesses supporting the theatre. Dramatic agencies, costumers, wigmakers,
two telegraph offices, several printshops, theatre bookshops, Samuel French's play-publishing house, and offices of the *Dramatic News*
and the *Sporting and Dramatic Times* all were nearby. Within a few

blocks hundreds of actors and actresses lived in apartments or boardinghouses. In Union Square combinations were organized and booked.[38] Comedian Nat Goodwin gave a colorful if idealized description of the Union Square milieu:

> We were masters of our own enterprises. Like the brokers on the curb we arranged our bookings on the street. Hither and thither we flew, now procuring a week in Pittsburgh or a night in Dayton, crossing and recrossing from the Morton House to Union Square, corralling a manager for a two weeks' tour in the sunny South or four in the unattractive Middle West, ever and anon stopping on our way to engage the services of some particular actor we desired for the play. We made railroad rates with hustling agents, always on the lookout to do business with professionals. . . . We made contracts with printers and appointments with authors simultaneously! Thus the day was occupied from ten until three when all work was suspended.[39]

When a manager cast a play he normally went to a Union Square dramatic agency to find his actors. Agencies were a post–Civil War phenomenon, a function of the combination system. Agents acted as theatrical brokers, bringing together players and managers. Among the best-known agents in the 1880s and '90s were T. Alston Brown (who also authored an authoritative history of the New York dramatic stage), J. J. Spies, and Colonel James Milliken. Small agencies continually appeared and faded, working out of small offices until they found the market too competitive to survive.[40]

Actors registered at all the major agencies. They filled out questionnaires concerning their qualifications, which were then kept on file. They described their wardrobe, parts they had played, their speed at learning parts, their ability to sing or dance, their physical characteristics, and the company they were with last. The agency categorized the applications and suggested qualified players for the various roles managers needed filled. When the agency found them a job, actors paid back one-third to one-half of the first week's salary. Failure to pay meant blacklisting, though as added insurance some agencies got their money directly from the company's treasurer.[41]

Managers gave agents explicit instructions about the kind of actor they needed, especially so when they were already on tour and needed an immediate replacement. Manager James Silver wrote anxiously to Colonel Milliken: "Can you send me a soubrette for a small part—must do a GOOD CATCHY SPECIALTY; Irish dialect part but dialect can be dispensed with; one night stands, small towns; am making money and paying salaries; WILL NOT ADVANCE

more than RR. fare unless I know the party and will not pay but
$20; board will average $7, no more." [42] Of course, agents could
never be sure that their top recommendation would please the
manager. E. A. Warren, manager of *Nobody's Claim*, complained to
Milliken:

> I am sorry to say that the man you recommended to play a small
> part did not turn out all right, for when he came to read the part I
> found out that he had never spoken a line before in his life and did
> not know anything about stage business; therefore I could not keep
> him. I told him to sit down for a while and the last I saw of him he
> was in a bar getting happy. Trusting that the next time it will turn
> out all right when you get anyone for me. [43]

Making the rounds of the agencies became a daily ritual for
unemployed actors. Before her days as a star Dreiser's Carrie scur-
ried from one agency to another seeking entree to the stage. These
were small, dreary offices, run by agents who offered such a new-
comer no encouragement. [44] Inevitably, the agencies became the
focus of players' hostility, who saw the brokers as controlling their
destiny. And abuses occurred. Established actors received preferential treatment; minor players suffered petty indignities by rude
agents. Some actors bribed agents to get the first chance at a job,
and wealthy amateurs paid well for a few nights' engagements. [45]
Conversely, one of Dreiser's fictional agents tried to shake down
Carrie for fifty dollars without even an assurance of a job. *New York
Dramatic Mirror* editor Harrison Grey Fiske demanded agency reform. According to Fiske, agents "exercised a system of petty tyranny, unjust discrimination, deception, barefaced extortion, without interference. The victims have groaned and suffered but they
have seen no avenue of escape from their wretched bondage." [46]
Even with hyperbole, the problem was serious enough to cause
both the Actors' Fund and Actors' Society of America to set up
their own actor-run agencies. Although the reform agencies failed
to dislodge the commercial establishments, agitation prompted the
New York state legislature to enact a law in 1910 requiring agencies
to be licensed and stipulating how much they could charge. [47]

Some combinations were directed by actor-managers, who attempted the twin tasks of organizing their own company and tour,
plus directing and starring in the production. The leading actor-
managers included Edwin Booth, Lester Wallack, Richard Mansfield, Edward H. Sothern–Julia Marlowe, Henry Miller, and Walter Hampden, though at one time or another most stars produced
their own play and took it on the road. Yet the planning and attention to detail involved imposed burdensome responsibilities. The-

atre had become a complex business, and players' proverbial lack of business sense proved too often true. Realizing their limitations, stars generally relied on business managers to coordinate their tours.[48]

The future of stage producing lay not with actor-managers but with powerful and independent producers. A select few of these men, such as Augustin Daly and David Belasco, were theatrical geniuses. As the preeminent American regisseurs, they oversaw every detail of their productions, Daly in his stock company, and Belasco in his combinations built around his stable of stars. Though most of the producers were less involved in the artistic details of their plays, such men as Charles and Daniel Frohman, Henry Savage, Charles Dillingham, J. M. Hill, and Henry Abbey wielded great power within the theatre.

The undisputed king of theatrical producing was Charles Frohman. He learned the business in the 1880s as manager of one of the Madison Square Theatre's road companies of *Hazel Kirke* and as a booking agent. After entering the producing ranks with Bronson Howard's great hit *Shenandoah* in 1889, Frohman established himself in the next twenty-five years as the most powerful figure on Broadway (he went down with the *Lusitania* in 1915). At one time he operated five theatres in New York City, and one in London, and through his membership in the Theatrical Syndicate controlled the bookings in several hundred theatres.[49] Frohman heartily believed in the star system and gained fame as the great star maker. Maude Adams, Ethel Barrymore, May Robson, Robert Edeson, Margaret Anglin, Henry Miller, and William Faversham were only a few of the actors whose careers blossomed with Frohman. Many other established stars put themselves under his capable management, and at one time Frohman had twenty-eight stars in his fold. He gave his stars a large measure of autonomy in arranging their careers. May Robson, for example, once declined his suggestion that she go on tour, claiming that her salary made touring less profitable than "jobbing" in New York. Frohman's stars could also choose their supporting casts.[50]

Despite Frohman's reputation for fairness, the entree of the large-scale theatrical producer altered traditional relationships between actor and manager. In the era of stock most managers were also actors, and fraternal ties united the two groups. In times of hardship all suffered together. But the modern producer was wealthy, and unlike the common player, largely immune to the vicissitudes of theatrical life.[51] And not all producers were as deferential as Charles Frohman to their stars. When musical comedian Francis Wilson prepared to star in Al Hayman's production of

Laughter of Fools, he insisted on the right to play it a few weeks out of New York to see if the part was strong enough for him. This Hayman denied. Wilson objected that "it would be little less than professional suicide not to insist upon the privilege, and I do not understand with all your expressed confidence in the play why you did not see fit to grant that privilege." [52] Although Wilson's involvement in the fledgling Actors' Equity may have had something to do with Hayman's treatment of him, it nevertheless indicated the power relationship of even an established star vis-à-vis the major producers.

Another sign of change in the theatre was the new importance of contracts. Whereas many veteran stock performers worked without a written contract, trusting in the manager's fairness, relations between actors and managers in the combination system became primarily contractual. In summer managers and actors shared Union Square benches to negotiate contracts for the upcoming season. If the middle of August passed without a prospect, actors began to get nervous. Knowing this, managers sometimes waited until early September to sign their cast, hoping to panic players into accepting a lower salary. [53] Conversely, it was not unknown for actors to sign several contracts during the summer, then to fulfill the most lucrative. Francis Wilson signed a contract with Edward Aronson in 1887 only to turn around and make another contract to appear at Wallack's Theatre. He justified his action with the pointed comment: every man for himself. [54]

The contract, in fact, caused more turmoil than anything else in the theatrical world, often binding together actors and managers in an unholy alliance and leading to the flood of litigation which the theatrical trade papers chronicled weekly. The stars, in a position of strength, had little trouble with contracts—Charles Frohman often dispensed with written contracts when dealing with his stars. For the lower order of players it was another matter. The provisions of most contracts put them under the manager's thumb. The inequities started with the rehearsals, during which time the players received not a cent. If the play failed or the actor proved unsuitable for the role, he would be "at liberty," as the theatrical euphemism went, having to seek another position—a difficult task since most of the combinations for the season were already cast. Another injustice was the two-week clause, whereby either party could terminate the contract with two weeks' notice. It sounded fair enough, but in practice it went against the player. The actor who invoked it and left the company, unless he or she was an important figure, risked blacklisting among the managerial fraternity. Managers did not hesitate to make use of it, though. The clause originated as a device to get rid of incompetent players, but was used arbitrarily. Often players were dropped for the sake of economy. Margaret Mather terminated supporting actress Maida Craigen's contract under terms of the two-week clause after one performance, reportedly because she would not accept a salary reduction from $100 to $75 a week. Finally, contracts generally stipulated that players would receive only half salary during the week preceding Christmas, Easter, and a presidential election, supposedly because of bad business at those times.[55]

Contracts sometimes demanded certain conduct from the players. Charles Parsloe's contracts included clauses stipulating that the actor would not be boisterous in restaurants, depots, hotels, or other public places, and that all members of the company show proper respect toward one another and make an effort to cultivate friendship and harmony.[56] Managers had grounds for terminating a player's contract if he quarreled, was rude to the manager, the rest of the company, or the audience, or practiced open immorality while on tour.[57]

Frequently theatrical business was carried on in an atmosphere of distrust and suspicion. Neither party regarded the contract as inviolate; managers often invoked the two-week clause and actors frequently asked for a release to take a better offer, or just left. Both actors and managers constantly threatened lawsuits. Usually a compromise was reached before the parties got to court; the lawsuits that did make it through legal channels most often were decided for the defendant, a commentary on the tangled nature of the contracts.[58] In 1891 a group of managers founded an Arbitration League to resolve disputes between actors and themselves. This move followed a number of court decisions that had gone against managers. Under the plan, when actors signed a contract they would also agree to arbitration if a dispute arose. Predictably, players were suspicious of the League's impartiality, and their resistance doomed the plan.[59] Players' casual attitude toward contracts contributed to the legal hassles. They would sign the contract without scrutinizing it, only later discovering an unhappy clause. When Wilton Lackaye signed to play under Augustin Daly in 1889, he thought they had agreed that he would play only leading roles. When he was cast in the supporting role of Oliver in *As You Like It*, he understandably became upset. It was even more upsetting to Lackaye when he discovered that his contract contained no promise for leading parts. He left.[60]

An actor who jumped his contract sometimes found himself forbidden by court order from joining another company. In 1891 the New York Supreme Court relieved actors from this contractual bondage by ruling that managers could not prevent players from joining another company after breaking the contract as long as the desertions did not do irreparable damage to their show. Injunctions would henceforth be granted only when the actor had qualifications that were "special, unique, or extraordinary."[61] The decision liberated the common player, but constrained the star, whose talents were by definition extraordinary. A few years later the New York court further ruled that actors could not be arbitrarily fired under the two-week clause. The test case involved actor James R. Smith, who sued Stuart Robson for abruptly dismissing him without cause. In the future, the court decided, the manager, if challenged, would have to demonstrate the actor's incompetence to a jury.[62]

Above all else, contracts concerned money. Actors' devotion to their art seldom detracted from an ever-present financial concern. The average player fought a continual battle to earn an adequate income. This was partly because work was seasonal. During the hot summer months patrons refused to come into theatres, so most shut down. Forty weeks constituted the standard season, but actors might feel fortunate to get in a solid thirty.[63] Actors had to have saved enough money from the previous season to see them through or else they had to look for a temporary job. This situation improved somewhat with the popularization of summer stock after 1900, which gave more jobs to players. But acting was also risky because unemployment remained high even during the season. Unlike the relative security provided by the old stock company system, an actor in a touring company might find himself out of work after only a few weeks if the play flopped.[64] Moreover, even though touring companies proliferated in the last two decades of the century the number of recruits increased even more rapidly so that job competition was cutthroat. The United States Census reported that in 1900 27.8 percent of the actors and 39.1 percent of the actresses were unemployed—this, despite the prosperity of the 1899–1900 season, with more companies on the road than ever before. The rate of unemployment among actors was in fact among the highest of any professional occupation.[65] Unemployment was such a problem that when the income tax appeared in 1913, Actors' Equity petitioned the Treasury Department to exempt actors from withholding tax, claiming that their irregular income made it unfair to withhold part of their salary.[66]

The continual flood of stage aspirants aggravated unemployment. Many people willingly suffered deprivation for the chance to act. The large (though not necessarily talented) pool from which managers could draw to fill out their companies put them in a commanding position, as an unruly thespian could always be replaced. Unemployed players in New York formed a sizable minority of the profession. "I have just come in," wrote Marcus Moriarty, an unemployed journeyman actor, "having been 'prowling' up and down Broadway since 7 o'clock hoping to hear of something. . . . I went to the professional matinee at the 14th Street Theatre, and witnessed 'Blue Jeans.' The house was 'packed' with professionals, which causes one to consider the number of actors and actresses in New York—half of them at least, idle." [67] In all probability players brought some unemployment upon themselves. The most strong-willed refused to sign a contract that did not pay what they thought themselves worth, and managers responded by hiring cheaper if inferior performers. Rather few actors could say along with comedian Owen Fawcett, who in 1903 looked back on a fifty-year career in supporting roles, that they had never been out of an engagement. [68]

As in other ways, stock and combination companies differed regarding pay. In stock companies the pay was relatively low but at least regular. Actors in New York stock companies generally received more than those in the other cities. Around 1860 Gotham's leading stock performers commanded $50 to $100 a week. Supporting players could expect $15 to $40 a week. Because women's parts were fewer and shorter at this time, they averaged only one-half to two-thirds of what men got in corresponding lines of business. General utility, supers, and ballet girls received $3 to $10 a week. The salary scale at the Boston Museum was slightly less in this era, leads receiving $30 to $50 a week and the rest of the company $4 to $20. Beginners were paid $2 a week in 1863, which was less than what apprentices earned in most occupations. Salaries remained stable in the 1870s, which combined with the generally deflationary trend of the last few decades of the nineteenth century helped the players' situation a bit. Beginners and utility players, though, still existed on the subsistence level. Some stock actors supplemented their pay with an outside job, such as J. A. Smith, a comedian with the Boston Museum, who worked as a tailor. [69]

In addition to their salaries stock actors were allowed a yearly benefit night when they would take a percentage of the receipts. The actor had the privilege of choosing the role he would play and the responsibility of drumming up business. The performances were gala occasions when loyal patrons would turn out to cheer their favorite thespian. Important actors had several benefits a season, whereas less important members often had to share a benefit evening. As the star system expanded, so did the number of benefit performances, to the point where they became a nuisance. Stars demanded many benefits, and they held back their best performances until that night. Audiences, knowing this, would wait to come until benefit night, deserting the theatre the nights before and after. This interference with the course of business upset managers. They first limited benefits to leading players, then followed the example of Lester Wallack of abolishing them altogether.[70] A few actors continued taking them in the early 1880s, but players began to look upon the practice as inconsistent with professional dignity. Later benefits became occasions for helping stage notables who had fallen on hard times or for worthy causes outside the theatrical orbit.

If the combination system brought more insecurity, it at least had the redeeming feature of offering generally higher salaries. Combination company salaries remained fairly constant from 1880 to 1900, increasing some after the turn of the century in line with the inflationary trend. Salary depended largely upon the player's New York reputation. In the first-class companies the more popular leading men and ladies commanded anywhere from $75 to $250 a week. The best comedians or character actors could get $100, and juveniles, ingenues, old men, or other important supporting players received $30 to $75. Utility players and the chorus earned $12 to $18 a week. Generally, wages on Broadway were higher than on the road, and the combinations put together in New York paid better than those originating in Chicago, where salaries rarely topped $100 a week. In the second-class companies $50 was big money and most players worked for $30 to $35.[71]

In 1894 F. F. Mackay estimated that the average player's salary was $35 a week, which for a typical season of twenty-five weeks meant an annual salary of $875. Accepting for the moment Mackay's rough estimation, one can compare the actor's income with that of other occupational groups. The annual earning of all manufacturing employees averaged $386 in 1894, less than half the player's income. Clerical workers averaged $728, postal employees $919, and ministers $824.[72] These figures would seem to place actors in the modest middle class. Leading actors and actresses with higher salaries would obviously be able to live in comfort. It must be kept in mind, however, that actors experienced extended periods of unemployment.

The troubling question of pay dominated relations between actors and managers. Well aware of the prevailing wage scale, actors demanded an equal salary for themselves. In 1882 many players held out for more money after the Mallory Brothers, owners of the Madison Square Theatre, began paying exorbitant salaries to their actors.[73] An insight into the bargaining that went on was provided by a letter to Augustin Daly from one of his young debutantes, who pled her case for a raise beyond the $20 a week she earned:

> I hate to talk about money, detestable stuff! but I must. I have managed to scramble through this season with the aid of what I saved from last; that fund is now pretty much exhausted & I am living entirely on my salary. I will give you a fair estimate of my living expenses:
>
> | | |
> |---|---|
> | Board & Room .... | $10.00 |
> | Laundress .... | $1.50 |
> | Car fare .... | $ .90 |
> | Lunch during rehearsal .... | $ 2.00 |
> | Escort home at night .... | $ 1.50 |
> | Toilet articles .... | $ 1.00 |
> | | Total $16.90 |
>
> Allow a fair margin for proper clothing, dentistry, travelling expenses and board during summer's rest and you will have my lowest terms, of which I am gladly willing to give you the benefit.[74]

The consequences of the letter remain a mystery.

Stars had no cause to worry about such mundane expenses, for their income was potentially enormous. Most of the famous players took a percentage, usually half, of the profits. Richard Mansfield, who was his own manager, was one of the richest. In the last few years of his life he probably earned at least $150,000 annually. A single visit to San Francisco netted him $42,400. Lotta Crabtree left an estate of nearly $4,000,000, much of it earned from shrewd investments. David Warfield was said to have earned over $300,000 one season from playing *The Music Master*. Maude Adams, Edward H. Sothern, John Drew, Ethel Barrymore, William Gillette, and Mrs. Fiske all took home over $50,000 tax-free dollars during the height of their popularity.[75] One has to be careful about accepting huge salary figures at face value however, for actors' self-promotion sometimes carried over into their financial claims. Starring could be risky, too, particularly if the star's income was based solely on a percentage of the profits. A production that failed to draw a respectable audience hurt not only the star's pride but also his pocketbook.

Most likely there existed two categories of actors: stars, leading actors, and those established comedians, character actors, and others preeminent in their line of business, who could count on steady employment and who earned enough to be either rich or comfortably off; and a larger group, consisting first of the journeymen players, who were capable enough but lacked the distinguishing talent that insured a ready job, and second, those actors even more on the margins of the profession who never rose above utility roles. Economic survival was a constant challenge for this group, and only the inescapable lure of the theatre kept them loyal to Thespis.

American actors of the 1880–1920 era, then, labored in a theatre as extensive and diverse as our country has ever seen. The theatre, more than any of the other arts, had always been a commercial venture that required attention to business detail. But beginning in the 1890s with the formation of the Theatrical Syndicate, a trend toward centralized business control of the theatre became apparent. This development prodded actors into protective organization—and ultimately unionization.

Two 🌸
The Show People

*W*ho were the people who spent their lives before the footlights? Where had they come from? How did they get their start in the theatre? And once established, what kinds of careers did they make for themselves? These questions are rarely addressed by theatre historians, and for good reason. Actors and critics seldom reflected on such matters, and when they did they spoke in the broadest generalities. Even now, conclusions must be tentative since detailed information is incomplete. But the attempt is imperative, for a social and occupational profile of actors provides the knowledge on which further generalizations about their profession can be based.

Although this study focuses on the white, English-speaking stage, the final section of this chapter examines two sub-groups of the American theatre: actors of the Yiddish and black theatres. They remind us that America's theatrical heritage is a rich and varied one, and, less pleasantly, that the stage was not exempt from the prejudices of the society at large.

* 1 *

A social analysis of the acting profession can begin in the musty pages of the census record (though for reasons mentioned before its figures necessarily remain an approximation).[1] The 1900 census, for example, offers a glimpse into the national and ethnic origins of actors (see Tables 3 and 4). These figures reveal the overwhelming predominance of native-born whites in the acting profession. Even the blacks, Indians, and Orientals counted were probably not to be found on the legitimate stage; rather, they would perform in minstrel troupes, Wild West shows, or entertainments for their own ethnic group. The racial composition of the stage closely resembled that of the other professions. In 1900, 81.8

percent of all male professionals were native-born whites compared to 79 percent of male actors, an insignificant difference. Yet compared to the other major occupational groupings (agriculture, domestic and personal, trade and transportation, manufacturing and mechanical, for example), the acting profession had a much higher percentage of native-born whites.[2] And most of the nonnative-born performers were either transplanted or visiting Englishmen, types easily accepted by American audiences.

This Anglo-American stage dominance carried an unspoken significance. Although the ethnic makeup of the acting profession remained fundamentally unchanged through the nineteenth century, the ethnic composition of American society changed considerably around the turn of the century, with the tremendous influx of immigrants. Consequently, the early twentieth century was a time of ethnic self-examination in America. The tide of immigrants from eastern and southern Europe raised fears among native

Table 3   National and Racial Composition of Male Actors in 1910

Ethnic group	No.	%
Native white		
Native parentage	8,208	50.3
Foreign or mixed parentage	4,502	27.6
Foreign-born white	2,735	16.8
Negro	750	4.6
Indian, Chinese, Japanese, and all other	110	.7
Total	16,305	100.0

Source: Bureau of the Census, *Special Reports: Occupations at the Twelfth Census* (Washington: GPO, 1904), p. cxlv.

Table 4   National and Racial Composition of Actresses in 1910

Ethnic group	No.	%
Native white		
Native parentage	6,518	54.4
Foreign or mixed parentage	3,236	27.0
Foreign-born white	1,678	14.4
Negro	529	4.4
Indian, Chinese, Japanese, and all other	31	.3
Total	11,992	100.5

Source: Bureau of the Census, *Special Reports: Occupations at the Twelfth Census* (Washington: GPO, 1904), p. cxlv.

Americans that this country's racial stock was threatened, and they sought reassurance that the Nordic race was still in command. The theatre gave this support (though probably not by conscious design) by offering a procession of actors and actresses who were models of Anglo-Saxon gentility and femininity. By contrast, ethnic roles remained safely subordinate, being predominately low comedy.

The age distribution of actors and actresses reveals other social characteristics of the profession (see Table 5). The age distribution of actors holds no surprises, being similar to what one finds in other occupations. For actresses, however, the figures tell a different story. Nearly half of all working actresses were under age twenty-five, twice the percentage of youthful actors. The high percentage reflects the many chorus girls and utility actresses who went on the stage and then retired when married. On the other hand, comparatively few actresses remained in the theatre beyond age thirty-five, and more men appear to have taken up a lifetime career in the theatre than did women. On the surface these figures would seem to suggest that, like most women of the day, actresses were not strongly committed to an independent career. Yet the figures take on a different significance when compared to those of other women's occupations.

At the turn of the century most working women filled semiskilled or unskilled positions. They took domestic, clerical, or factory jobs at young ages and normally left their work upon marriage. Women aged sixteen to twenty-four comprised 44.2 percent of the female work force. In the twenty-five to thirty-four age bracket the percentage of laboring women fell to 24.2, reflecting the early retirement. In comparison, 36.7 percent of all actresses fell in this age category, the highest percentage among women's occupations and an indication that actresses were more career-minded than most women in other occupations. The occupations with the next highest percentages in this age group, as one might

Table 5   Percentage of Actors According to Age in 1900

	Actors			
Ages	10–24	25–44	45–64	65–over
%	24.2	58.7	15.4	1.7

	Actresses					
Ages	16–24	25–34	35–44	45–54	55–64	65–over
%	48.8	36.7	10.1	2.9	.7	.4

Source: Twelfth Census, p. ccxviii; Bureau of the Census, *Special Reports: Statistics of Women at Work*, 1900 (Washington: GPO, 1907), p. 158.

expect, were those requiring extended training: teachers and college professors, musicians and teachers of music, and literary and scientific persons. The percentage of actresses over age thirty-five, however, drops off rapidly, even when compared to other women's occupations. This statistic testifies to the importance of youthful looks and vitality. All actresses agreed that the theatre made extraordinary demands upon them. Only the sturdiest could endure repeated seasons of touring. Helena Modjeska, Fanny Janauschek, Mrs. Drew, the octogenarian Mrs. Gilbert, and a few others were exceptional in their longevity; most actresses had ended their careers by their middle or late thirties.

The census, furthermore, confirmed a favorite claim of promoters of the theatre: that the stage offered women more opportunities than did other professions. In 1900 the traditional professions contained a comparative handful of women, and discrimination against them was nearly universal. The theatre, by contrast, had no long-standing barriers against females, and successful actresses stood on equal footing with the men. In simple figures the number of actresses was not great: 1,820 in 1880, 6,374 in 1900, and 13,237 in 1970. But the more than six thousand actresses in 1900 comprised 43 percent of the acting profession, a far higher percentage than in the other leading professions.[3] Understandably then, the *Dramatic Mirror* took pride in its declaration in 1891 that the stage offered women an opportunity to work and recognition that they could find in few other places.[4]

*   *   *

A more complete social profile of actors requires moving beyond the census. This task presents its own difficulties, as the biographies of most players are as evanescent as the characters they portrayed onstage. Details about the lives of the common players are not sufficient for confident generalization. Consequently, one must rely on biographical information about leading actors. This method is not entirely satisfactory, as the stars' backgrounds may not have typified all professionals. There is, however, no overriding reason to think that their social and geographic origins or levels of education should differ greatly from the average player (with the exception that the most successful players may have come from theatrical homes more often than did the journeymen players).

Of the 196 actors sampled, 142 were born in the United States and 54 were born abroad. The American-born actors hailed from 29 different states, the greatest number from New York (34), Pennsylvania (17), Massachusetts (15), and California (11). As might be expected, New York City produced the most players (19), but right behind it came Philadelphia, a city with a great theatrical tradition, the birthplace of 15 stars, including the Drew-Barrymore family, Joseph Jefferson, Rose Eytinge, and Francis Wilson. Leading players came from all parts of the country, however, an indication that Broadway and the New York road shows drew upon a nationwide talent pool. The 54 foreign-born actors accounted for over a quarter of the sample, a significant percentage which would seem to contradict the earlier assertion of Anglo-Saxon dominance. But a closer look reveals that 24 of the 54 players had English origins, 10 had Canadian, 5 Irish, 3 Scottish, and 2 Australian. The one Indian-born player was the progenitor of the legendary Barrymore family, the Oxford-educated and quintessentially English Maurice Barrymore. Only 9 of the 54 came from non-English-speaking lands.

The social origins of America's leading actors may be seen in Table 6. The most evident feature of Table 6 is the great number of actors whose fathers ranked high on the occupational scale. This appears particularly striking when compared to the occupational distribution for all American males in 1910 (see Table 7). A study of theatrical also-rans might reveal more modest origins. Moreover, some from theatrical families might be considered marginally middle class. Yet even taking that into account this sampling indicates

Table 6   Occupations of 143 Players' Fathers

Occupation	No.	%
Professional, technical, kindred workers	72	50.3
Managers, officials, and proprietors	43	30.1
Farmers	5	3.5
Clerical and sales and service occupations	4	2.8
Skilled workers	15	10.5
Semiskilled and unskilled workers	4	2.8
Total	143	100.0

Source: Biographical information from *Dictionary of American Biography, National Cyclopedia of American Biography*, and *Notable American Women 1607–1950*. Where possible, gaps in information about an actor have been filled in from other sources. The sample included 115 actors and 83 actresses, 198 in all. But since details are lacking concerning many players' family background and education, the sample for the various categories is usually a smaller number than that. The only criterion for inclusion was that some portion of the player's career fell between the years 1880 and 1920.

that actors generally came from solidly middle-class backgrounds. Michael Baker's study of the Victorian actor in England came to similar conclusions. Where in the earlier nineteenth century actors had often come from humble backgrounds, players who started their careers between 1860 and 1890 were of middle-class origins with a few from the upper class. Baker suggests that the changing pattern of recruitment contributed to an elevation of the actor's social status; one could infer that a similar trend in America had a similar effect on the player's status.[5]

One other result is significant. Of the 72 fathers who were professionals, over half (37) were actors themselves. Eighteen of the actors had one parent who acted professionally and 19 were born into families where both parents acted. Thus, 25 percent of the 143 players had been born in the theatre. That these actors represented the best of the profession may account for the high percentage. Yet Ronald Taft's study of journeymen Australian actors found a nearly identical percentage of actors who had one or more parent on the stage: over one-quarter.[6] One may reasonably assume that players' children had doors open to them that outsiders did not, and in many cases may have been blessed with talent.

The great acting families held an esteemed position in the theatrical world. The Booths, Jeffersons, Drew-Barrymores, Wallacks, Hacketts, Hollands, and Sotherns were the first families of the theatre, all of whom had members who graced the English or American stage through at least two generations and sometimes three.[7] Familial loyalties to the stage grew out of the intensive the-

Table 7   Male Occupational Distribution in 1910

Occupation	%
Professional persons	3.1
Proprietors, managers, and officials:	
Farmers	19.9
Others	7.9
Clerks, salespeople, and kindred	9.2
Skilled workers and foremen	14.5
Semiskilled workers	11.2
Unskilled workers:	
Farm laborers	14.0
Others	20.2
Total	100.0

Source: J. Kahl, *The American Class Structure* (New York: Holt, Rinehart and Winston, 1964), p. 265.

atrical subculture. Even though actors' children witnessed the drudgery of rehearsals, the endless one-night stands, and a life that sometimes seemed to consist of trains and hotels, they also saw one or both parents applauded and envied by audiences, and they breathed the heady atmosphere of the theatre. It was a life difficult to resist.

Many actors discouraged their children from a dramatic career, aware of their vocation's failings. Junius Brutus Booth wanted his son Edwin to be a cabinetmaker. But at thirteen Edwin had to accompany his widowed and inebriate father on his tours, leading to Edwin's remarkable career.[8] Edwin A. Sothern wanted his son, Edward Hugh, to become a painter, and even sent him to Europe to study art. Against his father's wishes Edward H. returned to America and went on stage, eventually teaming with Julia Marlowe to form America's greatest Shakespearean team.[9] Likewise, some progeny who later left their mark in the theatre turned to their parents' vocation only after abandoning their first career choice. James K. Hackett, whose father had been a famous American Falstaff, was a fixture on New York's active amateur stage while he attended college. He decided, however, to take up law and entered law school. Yet he could not escape the stage's siren song and joined Palmer's Stock Company in 1892.[10] Ethel Barrymore wandered into acting unintentionally. She was a talented pianist and wished to be a musician. But her family fell into difficult times and she had to go to work at age fourteen. Despite her impeccable theatrical pedigree and subdued good looks she had trouble landing a job, and for four months she trudged from agency to agency without result. Finally her uncle, John Drew, talked Charles Frohman into giving her an understudy role and a great career had its start.[11]

Biographical references to an actor's education are often vague, making generalization even more difficult than in the case of social origins. Table 8 gives an approximation based on available information. Clearly there is diversity in levels of education, yet overall, successful actors had more education than the average American. In 1900 only 6.3 percent of Americans earned high school diplomas and only 2.3 percent were enrolled in college.[12] Actors had more education possibly because of their middle-class origins, as their families valued schooling for their children. The percentage of players who attended or graduated from college is surprisingly high, especially for an occupation that demanded no formal training or degree. The figures refute the charge of many contemporaries that actors were uneducated simpletons. This accusation had prompted theatre publicists to stress players' learning

Table 8   Education Level of 141 Players

Level	No.	%
Little or no formal schooling	17	13.0
Grade school (either public or parochial)	44	33.6
High school	30	22.9
Some college	24	18.3
College degree	9	6.9
Art or music school	7	5.3
Total	131	100.0

Source: Biographical information from *Dictionary of American Biography, National Cyclopedia of American Biography*, and *Notable American Women 1607–1950*.

and love of books. Margherita Hamm, in her study of actors at home, observed that

> the theatrical profession is one which calls for mental rather than physical exercise, and involves study, knowledge, and training. These become matters of habit so that an actor in vacation time is usually prone to adopt modes of recreation which involve intellectual effort. . . . Many devote themselves to reading on a large scale; several cultivate the muse or pursue courses of severe study.[13]

Hamm described in detail the reading habits of various stars, such as Julia Marlowe, who carried a library of two hundred books on her tours. Another author noted that musical comedy star Francis Wilson had a library of over ten thousand books, which included many first editions and one of the finest Napoleonic collections in America.[14] "It is pretty safe to assume," R. O. Loud wrote in 1913, "that any dramatic artist of the front rank in America is well read, and makes a constant companion of books."[15] In addition, by the turn of the century defenders of the stage repeatedly asserted that more and more college men and women were going on stage.[16] This was true. Yet a college education did not guarantee success; neither was it a prerequisite for dramatic fame. Two of America's greatest actors, it must be recalled, received virtually no formal education: Edwin Booth and Joseph Jefferson.

*   2   *

A life in the theatre was the dream of countless young Americans of the nineteenth and twentieth centuries. If many felt called, few were chosen, for the odds against success were great. We cannot know how many theatrical hopefuls failed for every one that succeeded, but certainly the ratio was high. And even working players constantly worried about a steady job. These reasons and others contributed to the theatrical literature that warned youths to suppress their histrionic passions and choose more sensible vocations. Philip Hubert, in his book *The Stage as a Career*, concluded "that in nine cases out of ten the same intelligence, energy and taste will be productive of more happiness if utilized in other fields."[17] Arthur Hornblow, editor of *The Theatre*, also counseled against a stage career, believing that any other occupation would bring more happiness.[18] Even actors dashed cold water upon the hopes of aspiring thespians by reciting the gloomy tale of their lives: the uncertainty of employment, the hardships of travel and lack of home life, the danger to morals. Clara Morris warned in 1900 that the field had become overcrowded due to the acting schools, which put out more trainees than the profession could absorb. She knew of only three certain avenues to the stage: a fortune, influence, or superlative beauty.[19]

Advice against an acting career was particularly strong for females. Clara Morris, who wrote prolifically after her retirement, authored a theatrical novel entitled *A Pasteboard Crown*, which narrated the efforts of a young woman to become an actress. In the story the heroine chanced to meet one of Broadway's reigning queens and asked her help in launching a career. The actress (a character modeled after Morris herself) replied that it was easy to get a job if one had been through divorce court or had been part of a scandal, but for an innocent and principled girl it was almost impossible. Nevertheless, she introduced the young woman to a Broadway star, who agreed to aid her ambitions, though not without warning her that stardom might turn out to be a "pasteboard crown." Inevitably, she fell in love with the married matinee idol and surrendered her virtue. She found stardom, but at the cost of her self-respect. The novel warned young women that theatrical fame could be hollow.[20]

Other prominent actors urged females to avoid the stage. A New York socialite (probably Mrs. Cora Urquhart Brown Potter) with visions of stardom met Lester Wallack at a dinner party in the early 1880s and gave a reading for him. Wallack complimented her talent, but added: "I detest acting and always have. Never allow yourself to be persuaded to adopt the life. A man may be able to stand it, but absolutely the stage is no place for a woman, and more particularly when the woman happens to be a lady."[21] Stage beauty Maxine Elliott concurred, elaborating, "If you saw a dozen people struggling in the water, and realized that only one or two could possibly escape drowning, your instinct would be just as ours is— to warn others against jumping in. That is why we shout 'don't!

don't!' in the hope that it may save somebody from drowning." [22]
According to actress Elsie Ferguson the stage presented more
temptations than other occupations because "right and wrong
merge easily; and unless one is an expert in moral latitude, it is not
always easy to discern the dividing line." [23] Similarly, Philip Hubert
explained:

> No matter how refined and quiet a girl may be when she enters
> this feverish life, the stage will leave its mark upon her in five cases
> out of six. Insensibly she will contract some of the free and easy
> manners of the life. The constant playing with the emotions, the
> mockery of love which goes on, all ends by dulling even the most
> sensitive nature. [24]

The frequency of these warnings poses an interesting question: if actors wanted to improve their profession's public image (as
they did), why their strong statements about its dangers? Why discourage those wanting to act?

The warnings in part were an honest acknowledgment of
the shortcomings of the actors' profession and of the beginner's
slim chances. Almost never did an actor whitewash the theatre's
pitfalls when advising prospective thespians. There was no need
to recruit new actors with primrose promises—indeed the very
opposite was the problem. Yet the cautions signified more. The
public's estimation of actors' work and life-style affected the players' self-image. It was a truisim that temptation stalked young
actresses, so players dutifully repeated the warning. Likewise, actors were stereotyped as impractical and unable to conduct their
business affairs sensibly, an accusation some actors glibly conceded. These admissions indicated that to a degree actors still
wore a badge of inferiority. Their desire for social respectability
encouraged a public obeisance to the values of middle-class decorum and achievement. When they compared their profession to
the Victorian ideal, they could see its faults all too clearly. This recognition, whether at a conscious or subconscious level, inevitably
compromised players' self-respect. Ultimately, any attempt to re-
mold public attitudes would have to be accompanied by a similar
upgrading of their self-esteem.

The warnings of course rarely discouraged those few who
were single-minded in their determination to go on stage. Individuals possessing and possessed by the notion of a theatrical career,
come what may, have always been viewed with particular interest.
Acting seems a category of obsession all its own. The nature of the
people caught up in this, consequently, has been an enduring topic
of speculation. What kind of person wishes to devote himself to

living the life of another? What prompts the urge for continued display? Are actors truly a different people? This is a debate that will have no end, fueled by the persistent fascination actors hold for the public. The testimony of modern social science suggests that the popular view of the player's uniqueness may not be wrong. A number of psychological studies attribute distinctive personalities to actors. One researcher has found that they commonly have an immature emotional pattern, which leads them to seek constant attention and approval from others. The stage appeals precisely because it offers unmatched possibilities for display.[25] Another study of American acting school students concluded that they were extroverts.[26] Many of the students admitted to being "queer ducks." Drama had appealed to them at a young age, younger, on the average, than had other professions to nondrama students. Many had never wanted to do anything but act and had not even bothered to look into other careers. They realized their talent early in life and dedicated themselves to its development. This utter confidence in their ability helps explain the persistence of would-be actors in the face of great odds.

Ronald Taft, in his study of professional actors in Australia, came to similar conclusions.[27] Two-thirds of his subjects discovered their talent and interest in theatricality by age ten. Relatively few simply drifted into the profession. Parental opposition to a stage career, Taft found, was still strong in the 1950s, even among parents who were themselves theatrical. Taft characterized the acting personality as one marked by anxiety and tension. He found actors, moreover, to be obsessed with themselves to a pathological degree, and only by expressing themselves in a way that disregarded social conformity could they maintain a psychological equilibrium. Acting provided a greater opportunity for nonconforming behavior than did any other occupation.

We can reasonably assume that these personality traits described a fair number of nineteenth- and early twentieth-century actors. Comic opera star DeWolf Hopper agreed that actors "cross the footlights out of an egoistic desire to strut before an admiring world." They would like to make a fortune, he conceded, but would willingly starve if given adequate publicity.[28] Although not true in every case, most players set their eye on the stage during their early youth. Mildred Holland, who first received acclaim in the 1899 production of *Two Little Vagrants*, confessed, "I cannot remember the time I did not long to become a great actress. From a tiny child that one thought and idea has dominated me. I would think and dream of it and the determination to go on stage grew with me."[29] Holland's testimony lends credence to the reflections of Dreiser's Carrie regarding the multiple attractions of the stage: "How often had she looked at the well-dressed actresses on the stage and wondered how she would look, how delighted she would feel if only she were in their place. The glamour, the tense situation, the fine clothes, the applause, these had lured her until she felt that she, too, could act—that she, too, could compel acknowledgement of power." [30]

Young girls were especially vulnerable to the glamour of show business. So many ran away from home to go on stage that in 1912 representatives of the police and theatrical agencies met to draw up a plan to prevent flights from home. Thirty agencies adopted a resolution discouraging the hiring of young girls without acting experience. [31] This affliction struck more mature types as well. A fortyish Harvard-educated, established attorney from a large Southern city became convinced that greater things lay ahead for him onstage, so he left his practice and went to New York where he secured a job as callboy at a Broadway theatre. In his enthusiasm he was the first to arrive and last to leave the theatre each evening. [32] Unfortunately, his enthusiasm alone could not carry him to stardom.

Further investigation into the sample biographies of leading players shows that most of them started young (see Tables 9 and 10). Eighteen was the most common age for men to debut, but quite a few did not begin until their twenties. For actresses, on the other hand, the age of initiation was generally younger, sixteen being the modal average. The higher age for men may reflect their

Table 9   Age of 94 Male Actors at the Beginning of Their Stage Careers

Age	No.	Age	No.	Age	No.
4	1	14	1	24	5
5	1	15	3	25	5
6		16	5	26	2
7	1	17	11	27	
8		18	19	28	1
9	1	19	5	29	
10		20	8	30	1
11	1	21	7	31	
12	2	22	7	32	1
13		23	6		

Source: Biographical information from *Dictionary of American Biography, National Cyclopedia of American Biography,* and *Notable American Women 1607–1950.*

greater probability of having attended college. A large number, 23 actors (26.4 percent) and 31 actresses (42.5 percent), had acted as children, either professionally or in amateur productions. In most cases child actors came from theatrical homes, but it was not unknown for parents to put their young prodigies on stage to help support the family. Agnes Booth, who debuted at age twelve, and Eva Tanguay (later of vaudeville fame), who donned the britches of Little Lord Fauntleroy at age eight, are two examples of the latter. Edward Mammen's study of the Boston Museum Stock Company from the 1850s through the 1890s uncovered a similar pattern of recruitment; most novice players joined the company between the ages of seventeen and twenty; a few started younger, others in their twenties.[33]

How did the prospective actor break into the profession? Answers abounded in popular magazines and books, usually preceded by the litany about the stage's dangers. The consensus among actors was that beginners should start with a stock company, where they would be exposed to many roles. They must not be impatient for stardom, but should advance up the ladder deliberately, giving themselves time to master the craft. They must avoid type casting, which could handicap a career. Certain actors, for example, played the butler in production after production; others acted nothing but dowagers. The greatest thing urged upon the tyros was serious application to the high art which they had chosen. John McCullough, himself an example of achievement through disciplined effort, exhorted aspirants to forego "the fri-

Table 10 ◆ Age of 73 Actresses at the Beginning of Their Stage Careers

Age	No.	Age	No.	Age	No.
3	2	13	6	23	0
4	0	14	7	24	1
5	2	15	2	25	3
6	1	16	14	26	1
7	1	17	5	27	0
8	4	18	7	28	1
9	0	19	2	29	0
10	0	20	5	30	0
11	0	21	6	31	0
12	2	22	1	32	

Source: Biographical information from *Dictionary of American Biography, National Cyclopedia of American Biography,* and *Notable American Women 1607–1950.*

volities and dissipations of life" and resign themselves to unremit-
ting labor and self-denial.[34] Likewise, Mrs. Fiske admonished: "Be
reflective, then, and stay away from the theatre as much as you
can. Stay out of the theatrical world, out of its petty interests, its
inbreeding tendencies, its stifling atmosphere, its corroding influences. Once become 'theatricalized,' and you are lost, my friend,
you are lost."[35]

Friendly connections in the theatre expedited job hunting. Of
the thirty-nine beginners at the Boston Museum, ten had friends
or relatives who were in the company or known to the management.[36] Stage hopefuls sometimes managed to find a sympathetic
ear among influential players. Mrs. Fiske wrote several letters of
introduction for aspiring actresses to William Seymour, Charles
Frohman's stage manager. If they had no connections, beginners
had to sell themselves to a manager or agent through letter or personal interview. David Belasco spent many nights backstage in his
theatre listening to recitations. His indulgence of the would-be
Roscians stemmed from John McCullough's kindness years earlier
in California in listening to him recite and then offering him a job.[37]

A show of bravado often accompanied job applications, typified by a letter to a theatrical agent, Colonel James Milliken:

> I want an engagement commencing in September next. I am a
> young amature emotional actor well up in elocution and voice ex-
> pression in which I have made a study of for the past years. Also a
> dancer in many stiles for I have been dancing and impersonations
> especially that of a miser. I want thirty dollars a week and would
> not go for less for I know I am worthy of it. I am so far away that I
> cannot show my self to professional eyes and the managers of com-
> panys passing through will not pay any attention nor allow me to
> show them. Please give me your advice and I am very much
> oblige.[38]

Another wrote Augustin Daly for a position, frankly admitting that
she would not have thought of taking up a theatrical career if she
had not a "transcendent genius."[39]

But managers could usually see through such bluff. They
knew what they wanted in a player and chose accordingly. Besides
rating ability and experience, managers looked for a resonant,
well-modulated voice, attractive physical features, and a good
wardrobe. A stress on appearance was natural, since that is where
an actor's art begins. Serious physical deformities eliminated most
from consideration, though a few, like Henry Irving, who had a peculiar crablike walk, managed to overcome their deficiencies.[40] In
the eyes of many observers theatrical managers overvalued appearance. When putting together a touring combination managers

frequently hired an attractive novice over a veteran, and many players got their start simply by exhibiting good looks and stylish clothes.[41] This practice is partially explained by an economic motive, as managers could hire a beginner more cheaply than an experienced actor. But the tendency to exalt appearance over ability transcended the monetary. It also witnessed to the increasing importance of physical appearance in American society at large.

Although appreciation of the feminine form had been present since women first appeared on the seventeenth-century English stage, the early nineteenth-century American theatre placed little emphasis on beauty. Barbara Whitehead has pointed out that the young republic's leading actresses were not only plain, they were massive—Mrs. Whitlock, Mrs. Melmoth, and Mrs. Merry being of mammoth dimensions, and Mrs. Battersby said to be "so large that she looked like a mountain of flesh on a molehill." Femininity nearly disappeared in the person of America's greatest actress, Charlotte Cushman. Her homely face and muscular figure fitted her for the more than thirty male roles she played, most notably that of Romeo. Cushman accentuated her masculine image off the boards by mannish dress, sometimes wearing a man's coat, hat, and Wellington boots. The male disguise Cushman appropriated so profitably was a common dramatic convention in the early decades of the nineteenth century. Whitehead ties the penchant for donning breeches to the republic's self-image as a youthful, manly nation. Femininity was thought to mark a mature nation on its way to decadence. The muscularity of Charlotte Cushman, like that of Edwin Forrest, proclaimed America's continuing heroic virtue. Since Cushman's asexuality eliminated the corrupting power of desire, audiences could view her passionate performances while keeping themselves untainted by effeminacy or desire.[42]

As the nineteenth century progressed American audiences overcame their fear of passion. The melodramatic formula offered a way to display refined femininity while keeping it unspotted. Consequently, requirements for acting success changed. Actresses had to exhibit qualities of face and form. Mid-century actresses Lola Montez, Adah Isaacs Menken, and Clara Fisher whetted the public appetite for beauty, and the popularity of burlesque indicated that the female legs had become objects of public admiration.

Abetting the muse of beauty was the photograph.[43] The 1870s marked the advent of theatrical portraits, with shop windows, hotels, and restaurants displaying pictures of stars, along with cheaper reproductions on cards in cigarette packages. The camera's two-dimensional portrayal excluded consideration of voice or characterization; it caught only the physical form. The public came to view these pictures as displaying the essential quality of actresses, their beauty. *Cosmopolitan* announced in 1893: "This is preeminently the period and ours is the country of the Stage Beauty. . . . So great is the might of a fair face that the happy owner conquers managers, triumphs over critics and wins the golden favor of the public, even though her histrionic abilities are of the slenderest."[44] The acknowledged beauty queen of the stage, until marriage brought an early retirement in 1890, was Mary Anderson. The soft, regular features of her face suggested to some the reincarnation of a Greek goddess, and she possessed an air of purity and refinement, an incorruptible innocence that caused the public to take her into their hearts as "Our Mary."[45] No other beauty was as loved as Mary Anderson, but Rose Coghlan, Lillian Russell, Blanche Bates, Ada Rehan, Maxine Elliott, Effie Shannon, and others similarly turned their looks into acting careers.

The stage beauty became the model for other American women. A cult of beauty swept America in the late nineteenth century, leading women to endure strange nostrums and unpleasant treatments in order to capture the promised prize of loveliness. Beauty parlors became as common as barber shops. Victorian prejudice against makeup gave way to a plethora of cosmetological aids in the 1890s as makeup moved out of the theatrical dressing room into respectability. The English theatrical beauty Lily Langtry aided the process. Her flawless complexion graced ads for Pears soap, a leading cosmetic at the time. Popular magazines carried article after article on beauty tips, some authored by such actresses as Billie Burke and Elsie Janis, and regularly featured portraits of beautiful women.[46]

Photographs invariably showed actresses in exquisite gowns, and audiences expected nothing less when they saw them in person. To uphold their position as fashion leaders actresses patronized the leading hairdressers, wigmakers, and milliners. Sarah Bernhardt's sumptuous attire on her American tour of 1880 prompted American actresses to extravagant imitations. Fanny Davenport's five outfits for *An American Girl* that same year cost about one thousand dollars, and the play was advertised as "The Most Superbly Costumed Play Ever Presented in America." Her outfits were so numerous, according to stage chronicler George C. D. Odell, "as almost to confuse the audience, and some were perhaps too rich for certain scenes in which they came trailing clouds of silken glory."[47] Actresses' wardrobes constituted their major investment, for it was not enough that they appear richly dressed; they had to actually wear gowns sewn by fashion designers. Four- or five-hundred-dollar gowns were not unusual for stars at the turn of the century.[48]

Good looks aided actors nearly as much as it did actresses. The romances and drawing-room plays that filled the era's theatres called for heroes of suitable proportion and flair. Such actors became matinee idols, attracting women and girls to generally mediocre plays on the basis of sex appeal. James K. Hackett, William Faversham, Dustin Farnum, James O'Neill, Otis Skinner, and John Mason had well-developed physiques to fill out their costumes. A few, such as Maurice Barrymore, William Faversham, and James K. Hackett were sports and physical fitness enthusiasts. All agreed with Henry Miller's dictum that the two essentials for an actor were to "keep his hair on and his belly off."[49]

* 3 *

More than any other aspect of players' lives, their career patterns defy easy description. There was no prescribed course for stage success, and examples abound of every type of career imaginable. The older stock companies had provided a fairly orderly system of career advancement. One began as a super, advanced to utility, then responsible utility, and from there to walking gentleman or lady. After that one made the jump to juvenile, comedy, character, or whatever line one would specialize in. With luck one became a lead, or perhaps even a star. Advancement progressed at varying rates, but at the end of four years of acting the majority of the Boston Museum's trainees had reached the type of role each would follow.[50] The combination system upset this ordered notion of a career. For an attractive and talented player the hundreds of combinations forming each year offered possibilities for quick advancement. Players catching a manager's eye might avoid apprenticeship as a utility and move directly into leading roles.

The profession, then, became more fluid, but this fluidity was offset by the decreased security of the combination system so that competition for jobs was intense. Considering the chronic unemployment, one must assume that many players moved in and out of acting. If a position could not be found for the season a player had no choice but to take other work. For those on the margins of the profession, an acting career probably meant sporadic acting jobs interspersed by long periods of labor in whatever other skill they had.[51]

It would be misleading, then, to try and set up an ideal type of a career pattern. More to the point would be an indication of the rich variety of careers players experienced. The series of thumbnail sketches which follows, not just of stars, but of featured players as well, is intended to give a sense of the wide range of careers and accomplishments of players.

Felix Morris was born in 1845 in England, the son of a sea captain. He trained for medicine in London, but was carried away in an amateur theatrical craze during his school days. He decided to abandon medicine for the stage and came to America in search of his theatrical fortune. He managed to secure a job at the box office of an Albany theatre, using his spare time to study the standard plays. In his first opportunity to perform a small part Morris failed miserably and lost his job. Following a stint of work in an iron foundry and a drugstore, he got a position as head supernumerary at a rival Albany theatre and finally began to work his way up. Morris's forte lay in low comedy. He supported Lotta Crabtree, John Raymond, Helena Modjeska, Mary Anderson, and other luminaries. He toured the country with New York companies and traveled to Canada, the West Indies, and London before his retirement in 1896. Although never a star, Morris earned the reputation of an accomplished character actor.[52]

Frank Bacon came from California. Leaving school at age fourteen in 1878, he went through a succession of jobs before joining a popular-priced San Jose stock company in 1890. He learned his craft by acting over six hundred roles. Later, Bacon formed his own company in Oregon, then joined the well-known Alcazar Stock Company in San Francisco. After the great earthquake of 1906 he went to New York, where he obtained supporting positions in several first-class combinations. With Winchell Smith, Bacon wrote *Lightnin'*, a play in which he took the starring role of a folksy innkeeper. Bacon was well-suited for the role and the show became a hit. It opened in Washington in 1917, moved to New York the same year, and continued playing until Bacon's death in 1921. Frank Bacon offers an example of an actor who enjoyed modest success but little notice during most of his career. Then at age fifty-four he found himself catapulted into stardom. Not often, but occasionally, the theatre's greatest rewards came late in life.[53]

Alberta Gallatin (nee Alberta Jenkins) was born to a prominent Virginia family in 1860. After showing a proficiency in all the arts while still young, she joined a St. Louis dramatic club at age seventeen, then three years later went to New York where she studied elocution with Alfred Ayres. Gallatin's professional debut came at age twenty-five in *Satan's Daughter*. She made a starring tour two years later, then joined Daniel Frohman's Lyceum Theatre as a general understudy. Alberta Gallatin's major success came in Shakespearean roles, playing opposite the leading men of the day, including Thomas Keene and Otis Skinner. She later branched out into vaudeville and silent movies before her retirement at age sixty. One of the most versatile women of the theatre, she wrote the scripts to some of her plays, composed essays on poetry, and invented stage mechanisms.[54]

A contemporary of Alberta Gallatin, Jessie Shirley, experienced a very different career. Born in Illinois in 1866 and raised in Iowa, she toured the western United States as a child elocutionist at twelve years of age. Her theatrical career began in 1892 with repertoire companies in the Midwest and California. With her husband she organized the Jessie Shirley Repertoire Company in 1898 and toured the Pacific coast. From 1905 to 1909 her company played stock engagements in Spokane, achieving the longest continuous run of stock ever played by the same company of actors. With a career largely limited to the theatres of the Pacific Northwest, Jessie Shirley exemplified the hundreds of competent players who never made it to New York or played first-class touring companies, but whose talents won the loyalty of a localized public.[55]

Few performers had as varied a career as Robert Hardaway. Born in Georgia in 1883, the son of an architect and engineer, Hardaway began in show business with juggling and comedy acts at Kansas City theatres' amateur nights. He later signed on with a touring "Uncle Tom" show, then at age eighteen joined an Omaha stock company. In 1901 he traveled to New York and for the next fifteen years Hardaway appeared in contemporary plays, Shakespeare, and vaudeville. He later became a leading man in a number of stock companies across the country and in Canada. Hardaway also formed his own company of players which toured the Midwest and West. All told, he played over 640 roles during his fifty-year career. But he did more than stage work. He appeared in the early motion pictures that were made in Long Island, and in the 1930s went into radio writing, acting, and producing. His voice was heard in the radio series "Little Orphan Annie" and "Captain Midnight." In 1939–40 he wrote and acted in some sketches for the first Zenith experimental television shows. Throughout his career Hardaway had volunteered entertainment for the Elks, Masons, little theatres, and schools, as well as United States Army and Navy hospitals during the wars. Hardaway, again, was an actor who never received star billing on Broadway, but he was a leader in utilizing new technologies in the drama.[56]

Henrietta Crosman, born in 1861, was the daughter of a retired United States Army officer. Her early success in amateur theatricals prompted her impoverished family to encourage a career on the stage. Her great uncle introduced her to a manager, and in 1883 she debuted at New York's Windsor Theatre in Bartley Campbell's melodrama, *The White Slave*. Crosman's early career involved work in both stock and combination companies, including a stint with Augusin Daly and Charles and Daniel Frohman. The turning point in Crosman's career came when she and her husband bought the rights to *Mistress Nell*, a romantic comedy based on the life of Nell Gwyn. With this performancce she entered the ranks of a star. For the next decade she starred on the legitimate stage, occasionally playing the more profitable vaudeville tours when finances dictated. Her strength lay in light comedies and farce, though she matured into weightier roles, doing some Shakespeare and Shaw. Stage appearances became less frequent, by choice, in the 1920s. During these years she acted in a number of movies, both silent and talking.[57]

Another player who reached the plateau of stardom was Wilton Lackaye (born William Andrew, in 1862 in Virginia). After graduating from Georgetown University, he spent six years preparing for the priesthood. While on his way to Rome for final study he stopped in New York and went to see the Madison Square Theatre's current hit, *Esmerelda*. The play convinced him that his future lay in the theatre. Lackaye returned to Washington, D.C., and joined an amateur theatrical society. Lawrence Barrett, while on tour, spotted him and gave him a place in his company. Lackaye debuted professionally in 1883 in New York City, then gained experience by playing summer stock in Dayton. Within a few years his competent performances in supporting roles made him greatly in demand and he appeared with many companies. Lackaye could do comedy and tragedy, melodrama and romance. He excelled in character parts, being particularly good as a villain, but he could also be a leading man. The turning point in Lackaye's career came with his performance of the malevolent hypnotist, Svengali, in the 1895 thriller *Trilby*. The play became the talk of America and thrust Lackaye into stardom. He later featured in such well-known plays as Israel Zangwill's *Children of the Ghetto* and *Quo Vadis*. Lackaye possessed a caustic wit and was a center of attention at the Lambs Club, as well as being a popular after-dinner speaker. Active in theatrical organizations, he helped organize the Catholic Actors' Guild and Actors' Equity.[58]

These biographical sketches only hint at the variety of careers. So much of an actor's life depended upon getting the right breaks, getting cast for a part that both suited his particular abilities and caught the public fancy. Of course actors helped make their breaks by diligent study that prepared them to grab the golden ring when it came within reach. Helen Ware, for example, just two years after graduating from the American Academy of Dramatic Arts, secured a job as Blanche Bates's understudy in *Under Two Flags*. She took her understudy role very seriously, and when Bates fell ill after opening night, Ware stepped in and triumphed.[59]

A few players started at the top and stayed there. Mary Anderson played nothing but starring roles, her auspicious debut coming at age sixteen as Juliet. Julia Marlowe, after an intensive period of private instruction, also played leads exclusively. But stardom had its own dangers. Many players set out on starring tours prematurely and, when they failed, fell back to supporting roles for several years or even for the rest of their careers. And once-popular stars such as Olga Nethersole, Robert Edeson, and Amelia Bingham saw their public appeal disappear for no obvious reason.[60] A danger of the opposite kind arose when stage characters became so loved that the public demanded them over and over. Frank Mayo recreated the life of Davy Crockett for more than two thousand performances, from 1872 until two days before his death in 1896. Effie Ellsler triumphed in the title role of *Hazel Kirke*, but the part trapped her and probably stunted her development as an actress. Denman Thompson's celebration of rural New England values in *The Old Homestead* was said to have earned him three million dollars. But he had to live the part of Joshua Whitcomb from 1887 until his death in 1911. The public could imagine him as no one else.

The most famous example of character entrapment was James O'Neill's portrayal of Edmund Dantes in *The Count of Monte Cristo*. O'Neill took up the part in 1883 and immediately scored a popular success, as the public flocked to see the count. O'Neill had been considered a promising tragedian and he had ambitions for more fulfilling roles; but in no other part could he make the money that he could in Dumas's costume drama. He grew to loathe the play and despise himself for selling out his genius. O'Neill's personal tragedy was recorded by his son in *Long Day's Journey into Night*:

> That God-damned play I bought for a song and made such a great success in—a great money success—it ruined me with its promise of an easy fortune. I didn't want to do anything else, and by the time I woke up to the fact that I'd become a slave to the damned thing and did try other plays, it was too late. They had identified me with that one part, and didn't want me in anything else. They

were right too. I'd lost the great talent I once had through the years
of easy repetition, never learning a new part, never really working
hard.[61]

A prospective player, then, had no certainty about his future,
knowing only that the odds were against him. There was no regular course of advancement as one could expect in other occupations; careers took sudden dips and turns. An actor might trudge
along in supporting roles for many years, then happen into a role
that would catapult him to fame. Conversely, a celebrated player
might suddenly find that his technique no longer satisfied the
fickle public. More than the play itself, the actor was the center of
attention, and a player's star rose or fell according to his ability to
be the focus of that attention.

* 4 *

The American stage was dominated by people of English ancestry. There were, to be sure, the Nazimovas and Salvinis and
Bernhardts to spice up theatrical fare. But their limited presence
hardly distracted from the thoroughly Anglo-Saxon base of the
theatre. Nevertheless, two special groups, the Jews of the Yiddish
theatre and American blacks, deserve notice. The Jewish and black
stages stood apart from the larger theatrical world, partly by
choice, but primarily because of the exclusive barriers of language
and race. Yet a finished portrait of the American theatre requires at
least some attention to its border detail; and in the case of the Yiddish and black theatres it is a detail of unusual richness.

The American Yiddish theatre was established in the 1880s.
Like the English-speaking stage, the Yiddish theatre centered in
New York City, with its three major theatres—the Thalia, the People's, and the Windsor—located on the Bowery, in the heart of the
Lower East Side's Jewish community. It quickly became the leading
source of entertainment for the immigrant ghetto dwellers, and its
stars were figures of importance in the community. The Yiddish
theatre, as Irving Howe describes it, was a theatre of festival, its
exuberance partaking of the spirit of a secular Sabbath. Yiddish
thespians outdid even their counterparts on the English stage with
their lavish, sweeping style and heightened emotions that moved
audiences from joy to pathos.[62]

The Yiddish theatre's organization resembled the English
stage's in its adoption of the star system. Jacob Adler, David Kess-
ler, Boris Tomashevsky, and Bertha Kalich dominated the theatre,
dictating both the plays to be performed and their acting styles.

Yiddish stars undoubtedly wielded even more authority than their American counterparts, for they had no dominating group of theatrical managers to contend with. While most performances took place in New York, the actors also toured other cities with large Jewish immigrant populations, notably Chicago and Philadelphia. The Yiddish theatre was a creation of a small community of artists; Hutchins Hapgood estimated in 1902 that there were but seventy to eighty professional actors and a dozen playwrights.[63]

The early Yiddish actors came from working-class backgrounds. They lacked artistic training and did not possess the sophistication and polish usually associated with players. Their only theatrical experience had been in amateur dramatic clubs, though a few of the leading players had performed in the European Yiddish theatre.[64] But as the theatre matured, higher standards were desired, and so, as happened elsewhere, an acting school was started: Tytachony, First Yiddish School of Acting. The school received letters from eleven applicants willing to pay the three-dollar deposit, eight men and three women. The applicants' occupations underscored the working-class origins of Yiddish players: they included a painter, an embroiderer, a sales lady, a paperhanger, a tailor, a cap maker, a stock clerk, and a garment worker. None had any acting experience.[65] The obscurity into which Tytachony has fallen suggests that the school led a short life.

Yiddish players enjoyed comfortable and fairly secure incomes. Originally they were paid by shares rather than a straight salary. Incomes for the various ranks of performers ranged from an average of $14 to $75 a week. Stars, along with their actress-wives (Jacob and Dinah Adler; Boris and Bessie Tomashevsky) could earn as much as $125 a week, modest in comparison with the earnings of a Richard Mansfield, but in the impoverished world of the Lower-East Side it enabled them to live regally. Stars also received the proceeds of annual benefits, occasions not only for financial reward, but for the artistic rewards of playing more challenging roles.[66]

Two of the most eminent Yiddish actors were Bertha Kalich and Jacob Adler. Born in 1855, Jacob Adler came from Odessa, Russia, where he acted with a troupe of Abraham Goldfaden, the leader of Europe's incipient Yiddish theatre. A Czarist ban on Yiddish theatricals prompted Adler to leave in 1882, and he drifted around England and America before settling in New York in 1890. Fame did not come instantly. But starring in the plays of the preeminent Yiddish playwright, Jacob Gordin, Adler became acclaimed as New York's greatest Yiddish player. Unlike many

American stars, Adler was never content doing inconsequential plays, even if they were lucrative. He wished to act in serious plays of merit. Adler's first significant role was as Shylock in Gordin's translation of *The Merchant of Venice*. Adler's fiery interpretation caught the attention of the English press and led to an offer to play Shylock on Broadway in 1903. This performance—with Adler speaking Yiddish, the rest of the cast English—was hailed by critics as comparable to Henry Irving's, and Adler's success focused new attention on the Yiddish theatre. Reviews of Yiddish productions began appearing in New York's press, and Broadway players frequented their theatres. Although Adler succeeded on Broadway, he returned to the Yiddish stage for the rest of his career. Adler reigned supreme in the Lower East Side, the bond between him and his audience surpassing anything known by Broadway stars.[67]

Bertha Kalich was born in Galicia in 1874, the daughter of a brush manufacturer. She received a strong musical education and debuted in the musical theatre at age thirteen. For the next seven years she sang leading roles in Yiddish theatres in Hungary and Rumania before accepting the offer of Joseph Edelstein in 1894 to come to America and become the leading lady at New York's Thalia Theatre. In America Kalich gradually moved from musical pieces to the more serious drama of Jacob Gordin, her repertoire ranging from Yiddish translations of *King Lear* to plays descriptive of contemporary life in the Jewish ghetto.

Kalich's immense popularity in the Jewish community also earned the notice of Broadway managers. She was receptive to an offer; she already had been eyeing a move to the English stage and had worked hard to overcome her Polish accent. Her debut on the English stage came in 1905 in the title role of Victorien Sardou's *Fedora*. This led to several more offers and her acceptance of a contract to play at Harrison Grey Fiske's Manhattan Theatre. Fiske was a leading crusader for a higher dramatic art, and Kalich, who denied having left the ghetto stage in the mere pursuit of wealth, shared Fiske's belief that drama should stand for a higher ideal. Under Fiske's management she premiered for English audiences in Belgian playwright Maurice Maeterlinck's *Monna Vanna*. Her acting won immediate praise. She went on to play in five other Fiske productions, then starred under other producers, and even made a few movies. Blindness forced her from the stage in 1931, ending a remarkable career that included 125 roles in seven languages. Called "the Jewish Bernhardt" and "the Yiddish Duse," she found acceptance on the English stage. Yet her Jewishness remained a fact to American audiences. One newspaper noted that "nowhere is she able to shake off her own strongly remarkable racial characteristics," and a Boston paper felt that "in nothing but an exotic part, where she is either a woman of foreign birth or a strange creature doing strange things can the American public accept her."[68] If actors were holding a "mirror to nature," American audiences preferred to see an image that was as much like themselves as possible. Foreign-appearing actors could be accepted only if their foreignness was plainly stated in the play.

If American audiences had some difficulty taking Jewish actors to their hearts, the problem was even worse with black actors. In fact, with the exception of the musical and comedy stages, no black actor achieved prominence on a Broadway stage before 1920. Moreover, few blacks were to be found in even minor roles. Mixed companies were rare. An occasional black player appeared in budget repertoire companies, especially "Tom shows" that wanted a realistic Uncle Tom or Topsy, though it was not until 1877 that a black Tom appeared with a white company. Their absence from the legitimate stage sharply contrasts with other entertainment forms, where blacks had been influential since the mid–nineteenth century.[69] In dance, Juba (William Henry Lane) has been called the father of American tap-dancing. American music was immeasurably enriched by both black composers, such as James Bland ("Carry me back to old Virginny") and later ragtime composers, and such performers as the "Black Patti," Sissieretta Jones, who had one of the great operatic voices of her age. American blacks found the main outlet for their theatrical talent, of course, in minstrel shows. By the 1870s black minstrel troupes traveled throughout all of America and in many parts of the world. Most of the 1,490 Negro "actors and showmen" enumerated by the census of 1890 belonged to a minstrel group. Black minstrelsy provided a showcase for the musical, dance, and comic talents of many performers. But the minstrel stereotype also kept black performers from being taken seriously in drama by caricaturing their physical characteristics and lampooning their intelligence.

The black musicals of the 1890s, beginning with the 1890 production of *The Creole Show*, continued the minstrel tradition. But a break with the minstrel formula came with the 1898 musical, *A Trip to Coontown*, written by Bob Cole. Its presentation in New York marked the first show with a story line that was written, produced, and stage managed by blacks. The "coon shows" that followed provided the format for some great performers during the next decade: Ernest Hogan, Ada Overton, Billy Walker, and Bert Williams.

The comedy team of Williams and Walker ranks as one of the greatest in entertainment annals. After a career of vaudeville in the West they hit New York in 1896, where they made the cakewalk the rage of high society. Moving from vaudeville to musicals, they made Negro theatrical history in 1902 when they produced *In Dahomey* at the New York Theatre in Times Square. The musical propelled them into the limelight of the theatrical establishment. The two complemented one another, Walker playing the cocky, elegant man-about-town, while Williams portrayed the clumsy, down-and-out darky—humor in the tradition of minstrel racial stereotypes. Walker's retirement due to illness in 1909 checked Bert Williams's career only temporarily. In 1910 he signed on with the Ziegfeld Follies and became a headliner. His comedy routines—set between the acts of an otherwise all-white cast—became classics, and Williams was hailed as a comic genius.

The paradox of Bert Williams's career was that even in success he exemplified the tragedy of the black performer. His potential as a comedian was always restricted to the black-faced parodies. He could never develop his ability as a storyteller, wrote Heywood Broun in Williams's obituary, because the public demanded racial humor.[70] American audiences were delighted with black performers as long as they relied on self-abasement as their comic persona. But any pretensions to serious drama were met with derision or hostility. Typical of the prevailing attitudes was a response to a letter written to *The Theatre* in 1886, inquiring if there were any successful colored actors on the American stage. The answer:

> There is not, nor is there likely to be. . . . The negro is naturally disqualified as an actor of the better order of character, and even in his native antics—the songs and dances peculiar to plantation life—he finds a superior on the stage is the imitation darkey of the white man. He is entirely unfitted to represent the finer thoughts, sentiments and emotions.[71]

A more hostile reaction came after blacks had begun to make their presence felt. A white critic complained in the 1890s about "the all pervading negro" in show business. Their presence was not the worst of it, according to the author. "If they were content to be 'darkies' with an exhibition of the rhythmic charm which made the 'darky' fascinating, one might endure them," he wrote, but they had the audacity "to do white sketch acts."[72] One has only to recall the deterioration of black civil rights in the United States in this era to understand the tenuous position of Negro entertainers. During the 1900 New York City race riot Ernest Hogan was beaten so badly that he had to leave his show, and the popular George Walker had to spend a night in a cellar to escape the crowd.[73]

In the face of ridicule only a few blacks attempted dramatic acting. As far back as the 1820s, the African Company, a semiprofessional group, put on performances of Shakespeare and other classic plays in New York. The audience was mostly black, and the disorder that whites caused led to the theatre's closing. But an amateur dramatic production in New York during these years inspired Ira Aldridge, who became the nineteenth century's greatest Negro actor. Born to a free black family in 1807, Aldridge was sent to school in Glasgow; he decided on a stage career and went to London. After initial difficulty in securing a job, he got the role of Othello at an East End theatre. From there his career advanced steadily. In England, but more so on the Continent, Aldridge was hailed as a first-rank tragedian, the "African Roscius." He specialized in Shakespearean roles, and as might be expected, Othello brought him his greatest acclaim, playing it to Edmund Kean's Iago. Aldridge's career lasted until the mid-1860s, yet in all that time he never came back to perform in America. America's greatest black actor never played to his countrymen, and for that reason his accomplishment must remain a footnote to American theatrical history.[74]

In the late nineteenth century a scattering of Negro stock companies formed, performing white plays for black audiences. In a sense these companies represented a form of black self-help, an embodiment of Booker T. Washington's contemporary teachings applied to the artistic realm. With the major Broadway and combination companies closed to them, blacks could look only to themselves. The first notable stock company was Worth's Museum in New York. For a time the company was headed by the versatile Bob Cole, whose sketches and stage direction made Worth's Museum All-Star Stock Company a popular institution among Gotham's blacks. The true development of a black theatre came with the cultural flourishing of Harlem in the early decades of the twentieth century. Two stock companies organized in the Lincoln and Lafayette theatres putting on the melodramas that had thrilled downtown white audiences. The Harlem theatres trained players who in the freer days of the 1920s moved onto the Broadway stage.[75]

Outside of New York stock companies sprang up in Philadelphia, Chicago, and Washington, D.C. Chicago's Pekin Theatre deserves special mention. Founded by Robert T. Motts, the company consisted of fifteen principals and a chorus of forty. The company was organized to serve a black audience, but the quality of its productions enticed so many whites that thirty boxes were set aside for them each night. Comedies and musical comedies made up the usual fare. Negro author J. Ed Green traded on black stereotypes for his humor, his plays ridiculing the Negro's childishness, love of games, vanity in dress, and adoration of tinsel and titles.

The Theatre reported that "the old Southern apothegm that negro blood alone spells comedy is being aptly and entertainingly proven by the daily performances."[76]

Negro stock companies generally performed plays that had little in common with life as blacks experienced it. For this reason a performance by the Coloured Players in Madison Square Garden's theatre in 1917 took on special significance. The three one-act dramas, written by Ridgely Torrence and directed by one of the day's leading theatrical innovators, Robert Edmund Jones, portrayed scenes of Negro life. The actors managed to shed conventions of white acting and give highly sensitive performances. The ultimate aim of the group was to create a folk drama of Negro life. For the first time critics took a black play seriously, and their praise was nearly unanimous. George Jean Nathan placed two of the actors, Opal Cooper and Inez Clough, among his top ten performers of the year. The event was seen by the *Dramatic Mirror* as a major advance in the "attainment of true democracy among the white and colored people of this country in the appreciation and interpretation of each other's lives."[77]

Despite the enthusiastic reception accorded the performance, the fact remained that it had more to do with the art theatre movement than it did with Broadway's commercial theatre. The production was financed by drama lover Mrs. Emily Hapgood and was never expected to return its investment. Perhaps a more important augury of racial liberalization in the theatre came on November 3, 1920, when black actor Charles Gilpin took the title role in Eugene O'Neill's *Emperor Jones* at the Provincetown Playhouse. Overnight Gilpin became famous. His strong performance in a demanding part convinced knowledgeable observers that blacks could carry a dramatic role as well as anyone. Gilpin's achievement surpassed that of any previous black on the legitimate stage in America. The battle was not over, for Gilpin's award from the Drama League as one of the ten people having done the most for the theatre during the year precipitated a crisis over his attendance at the awards dinner.[78] But with hindsight one can see that by 1920 the corner had been turned regarding blacks in the theatre. The next decade would produce Paul Robeson, Rose McClendon, Abbie Mitchell, and Richard B. Harrison, all highly acclaimed for their contributions to New York's live stage.

Three 🌺

The Player's Life

*B*y its very nature the actor's work is thought to set him apart from other people. To some the unreality of actors' stage lives suggests an artifice to their private lives, characterized by sham and pretense in personal relationships. Others imagine that actors' lives offstage are extensions of the adventure and romance they experience onstage. Both pictures are caricatures, of course. Nevertheless, they contain an element of truth, for actors lead special lives. This was even more true of the nineteenth-century player, whose contacts with nonactors were limited by prejudice and the demands of work. Drama critic Henry Clapp described players as distinct from the rest of society, being "immersed in the unreal realities of the mimic life," and "driven both by natural impulse and by professional competition to whet their talent to the sharpest edge." "The guild of actors," he continued, "is the most charming, naif, clever, contrasted, conventional, disorderly, sensitive, insensible, obstinate, generous, egotistic body in the world, and—'unique.'" [1]

Clapp's testimony must be judged to some degree as an example of the exaggerated rhetoric so often employed in discussing actors. Yet he caught the sense of distinctiveness about the profession which defined both the actors' image of themselves and the public's attitude toward them.

This distinctiveness was rooted in the professional culture of actors. The players' culture encompassed their way of life in the theatre and at home, on Broadway and on tour, their language, their values, and their beliefs. It was a culture created to meet the common situations and problems that actors encountered. Admittedly, there was great variety within the ranks of legitimate performers, from the highly paid stars to humble tent-rep actors. Styles of life differed widely: Julia Marlowe and Edward H. Sothern could enjoy a luxurious New York apartment, while the profession's troupers endured second-class hotel or boardinghouse accommodations. The social circles actors moved in also varied. Few besides Joseph Jefferson enjoyed a cameraderie with a United States president.

Yet the defining characteristics of cultural unity are not levels of income or social accessibility. The essence of a culture has to do with the understandings of a group, the outlooks and values that are shared. From this perspective all levels of actors partook of a single acting culture. They belonged to a community by virtue of their common identity as actors. Actor Lew Benedict, reflecting on his years in the profession, wrote: "We were as it were related to one another and if we were only in the profeshion [sic] WE all knew one another. We were brothers and sisters."[2] The kinship was also displayed in the nostalgic reminiscences of the "palmy days" that filled the trade papers and published memoirs. Players were consumed by their craft and by the great figures in it. This strong sense of memory bespoke an intensive professional culture.

The network of obligations and expectations that bound actors together did not remove all disagreements and uncertainties. Cultural values are mutable, and there was a continuous discussion within the profession about certain points of behavior. The major debate centered on the desirability of their social distinctiveness. Players recognized their insularity and to some extent gloried in it. But at the same time they longed for the social respectability that a more conventional life would bring. The conflict between Bohemian pleasures and middle-class respectability posed a serious issue for the thinking members of the profession who wished to upgrade their vocation's image.

*   1   *

A consideration of the players' culture rightly begins in the theatrical mecca of New York. Gotham held a magnetic appeal for actors, not only for its career opportunities but also for its excitement. Whenever a touring actor's route came near New York, he slipped into the city to greet friends and see a play.[3] The theatre district, centering on Union Square in the 1880s, continued its northward move up Broadway as it had throughout the century until it came to rest at Times Square by about the turn of the century.[4] This stretch of Broadway, the Rialto, was the players' turf. A sunny afternoon in the mid-1880s would find them in couples or groups strolling up and down the avenue between Twenty-third and Fortieth streets. Gregarious by nature, actors needed little excuse for socializing. Friends would stop and chat, new acquaintances would be made. The Hoffman House Bar and Broadway Saloon offered congenial settings for swapping stories of recent times. The social arena of the Rialto reinforced players' professional identity. Recognition by peers, or more significantly by superiors, reaffirmed one's place in the community. Theatrical apprentices would gauge their career progress by the attention paid them. A nod from John Gilbert or John Drew meant one had been noticed and accepted into the fraternity.

As important as recognition by other actors was recognition by the public. Actors sought this by dressing and behaving in a manner that marked them immediately as such. Players meeting on a street, in a hotel, or in other public places frequently engaged in loud "shop talk," letting all nearby know that they were actors. On meeting an actress in the street an actor might hold her hand as they talked, letting onlookers appreciate the familiarity between them.[5] Players might also be identified by their outré dress. Actresses were known "by their saffron hair, painted eyes and eyebrows, flaring hats, gorgeous-hued gowns and other tokens of loudness," said the *Dramatic Mirror* in 1888, "and also because nearly everybody they pass turns, contemplates the general get-up and smiles." Male actors were distinguished by silk sashes about the waist, gaily ribboned straw hats, and russet shoes.[6] The repertory actors had their own dress: an ascot or windsor tie, stetson hat, and in winter paddock overcoats with velvet or fur collars. Managers and leading men wore diamond rings and stickpins and carried gold-headed canes.[7]

Admittedly, much of this display occurred among the second-rank performers. Many stars shunned any manner or dress that drew attention to themselves. But this proclivity for exhibitionism indicated that not all acting was confined to the stage. The urge to display carried over into everyday life. Such behavior can be explained partly by the extroverted acting personality.[8] But more than personal idiosyncrasy was at work here. Erving Goffman's dramaturgical approach to social behavior may aid an understanding of actors' conduct.[9]

Goffman theorizes that people present themselves to others through performances, much as an actor portrays a role to an audience. The image expressed comes not only from what he says about himself, but more importantly from the expressive signals he gives off, perhaps unconsciously. A person's routine becomes his "front," defining the person for those who observe him and signifying that he has certain social characteristics. By claiming to be a person of a particular kind he "exerts a moral demand on others, obliging them to value and treat him in the manner that persons of his kind have a right to expect." Conversely, by such behavior he gives up all claims to be things he does not appear to be and thus foregoes the treatment such individuals could expect.[10]

The gaudy dress and loud talk of players constituted an off-stage performance. Their behavior announced their presence, allowing the public to respond to them according to its custom. Habits of dress and conduct were both a legacy and enduring symbol of actors' low status. Conscious of their position as outsiders, actors cultivated a distinctive behavior. The public expected actors to be indiscreetly familiar with each other, to use slang, and to dress outrageously. At an opening of a play, for example, three actresses sat up in the boxes, laughing, talking, and attracting attention from the audience. Their carryings-on brought annoyed glances, but when they were recognized as actresses, the audience seemed to shrug it off, apparently regarding this conduct as normal for players. "The public impression," the *Dramatic Mirror* concluded, "seems to be that everybody connected with the stage has an itch for notoriety."[11] By behaving in the expected manner, actors, if not earning society's respect, at least had the security of a well-defined social role.[12]

But as the players' self-image changed, the kinds of signals they wanted to communicate changed. Professional status required a new front. Instead of talking and dressing in their peculiar manner, actors would have to conform to social norms, meaning a more conservative sartorial touch and subdued manner while in public. Theatre manager Augustin Daly tried to suppress all Bohemian tendencies among members of his company. He imposed strict rules on their public behavior, forbidding certain fashions and curbing the habit of ostentatious parade up and down Broadway.[13] Theatrical observers commented on and encouraged the change. The *Dramatic Mirror* wrote in 1882 that the "obnoxious habit" of talking shop in public was disappearing, at least among the full-fledged professionals. Actors need not be ashamed of their calling, the *Mirror* continued, but there was no reason to arouse "vulgar curiosity" among outsiders by loud talk about their work.[14] An anonymous actor wrote an article for the same journal in 1888 complaining about the public behavior of a few players that brought opprobrium on all: "There are people, especially, I grieve to say, women who, by their loud and 'shoppy' talk and monstrous apparel, make a carful of people immediately aware they are in the presence of a 'troupe,' and look upon them as vulgarians to be summed up, with a neighborly nudge, by the sobriquet, 'show folk.'"[15] The writer went on to excoriate the behavior of some players in hotels, who were complaining of their room assignments, demanding immediate room service, making scenes in dining rooms, and even stealing towels and linen. Concern about eccentric behavior would continue into the twentieth century. "It is unfortunate that the very small people of the stage," complained Philip Hubert in 1900, "with their affectations, vulgarities, and absurdities, the men in their 'loud' clothes, the women decked out in cheap finery and forgetful of the fact that rouge belongs only to the stage, should so largely represent the dramatic profession as seen off the boards. The actors worthy of the name are often most modest people, rather averse to advertising their profession." [16]

Actress Jessie Busley tried to convince other players as well as the public that actresses should not be considered any different from other women. Actresses, she felt, were generally classified into two categories: those wildly anxious to attract attention, and those extremely reclusive. She refuted these stereotypes, asserting that actresses took a commonsense attitude toward their work. Busley concluded:

> There should be, I think, a sort of line, a kind of barrier, between the actor and the public, but it certainly should not go to the extent of putting the player, of either sex, in a class alone, covering them with the cloak of romance. . . . We who in the course of our business are forced to cover our faces with messy, smeary grease paint, we get up in the morning, eat three meals a day, work, play and go to bed again, just like the rest of you. [17]

Her remarks revealed the profession's ambivalent desires: wanting to be thought normal people who go through the normal human activities, yet also believing there ought to be a separation between themselves and the public. Acceptance should not destroy distinctiveness.

The players' new front would not be established easily, for it involved a redefinition of themselves and of the image they wished to portray. Accordingly, change did not proceed uniformly among actors. Generally, it was the more successful players, those who worked on Broadway and in the first-class road shows who were most interested in gaining complete social acceptance. On the other hand, those in the lower ranks of the profession, who played the cheaper companies and who viewed themselves as modern-day strollers outside the boundaries of social respectability, continued to dress and behave in a more flamboyant manner. This qualification should not be carried too far, however, for the eccentricities of manner and dress among Broadway stars were too firmly established in the public mind for the Bohemian image to disappear.

As distinctive as their dress was the actors' way of speaking.

They coined an enormous slang vocabulary. To outsiders such expressions as "a frappe house" (an unresponsive audience), "fifty and cakes" (fifty dollars a week and expenses), "foundries" (acting schools), "trying it on the dog" (a one-night stand where a play is previewed), "Frohman" (a manager of a country opera house), or "a frost" (a play that failed) had no meaning. But by understanding and using theatre slang a player showed that he belonged to the culture.[18] Actors were also given to exaggeration. And though defenders of the stage denied it, profanity was common backstage, even among actresses. The *Actors' Society Monthly Bulletin* (*ASMB*), an early professional journal, published "A Plea for the Prude" in 1902, asking, "Why should we as a profession be so extremely plain spoken? Why not 'assume a virtue' if we 'have it not' and be clean in speech at least. The women are much more to blame in this matter than the men." The journal then related an instance of an actress vulgarizing a remark by an actor and concluded: "If the evil were confined to what we are pleased to call the lower branches of the profession it would be different, but we as a class seem to pride ourselves on an emancipation from conventionality that in our speech becomes positively ill bred and common."[19] As with the issue of dress, the players' trade journal viewed coarse speech as contrary to pretensions of higher status.

Not only offstage but even before an audience actors occasionally displayed a lack of discipline. They might play games with each other or with the audience during a performance. On the 1904 tour of *The Sorceress* Mrs. Patrick Campbell, the play's star, clowned around on stage making audible remarks to her friends in the boxes. The antics of even the strong-willed Mrs. Campbell stopped when producer Charles Frohman got wind of them.[20] Louis James —an habitual practical joker—while playing Othello once took some of his dark makeup and marked a moustache on the face of a sleeping Desdemona. Her back was to the audience so it did not see her. But the other actors did as they came on stage and their fits of laughter destroyed Shakespeare's dramatic intent.[21] Professional jealousies were another problem, sometimes leading to attempts to upstage one another (in the literal sense a player moved upstage from the audience while being addressed by another actor, forcing him to turn his back on the audience while speaking; this, not surprisingly, was a serious breach of etiquette).[22] Less vindictive was the practice of adding extemporaneous quips to get laughs. Musical-comedy star Francis Wilson gagged incessantly, freely departing from the scripts of his plays.[23] However, the frequent off-color asides heard on the stage of Jacksonian America were largely absent from the post-1880 theatre, as actors respected their audiences' middle-class canons of propriety.

These incidents were trivial and generally harmless. But horseplay on stage weakened actors' artistic pretensions. It suggested a failure to take their work seriously, a charge that for some actors may have been true. Yet the problems of a performing art must be taken into account. Where painters and writers had to worry only about the quality of their finished product, actors displayed their art eight times a week. With the strains of travel, the possibility of personality conflict within the cast, and the uncertain variable of the audience, polished performances could not happen on every occasion.

But the theatre's reformers would hear no excuses. The *Dramatic Mirror* scolded the Duff Company in 1887 for having "grinned, giggled, grimaced, and gagged to their hearts' content," seemingly more interested in entertaining one another than the audience. The paper reminded the profession that "a player has no more right to trifle with his audience than the clergyman with his congregation, or the lawyer with his court and jury."[24] The *Mirror* also reprimanded Rose Eytinge for unprofessionalism. She had lectured a Bowery audience for a fictitious grievance, then on another occasion had quit during the middle of a performance because of the behavior of a single drunk.[25] Stage and later screen performer George Arliss emphasized the player's obligation in his 1912 address to the graduates of the American Academy of Dramatic Arts: "You are bound to remember . . . that you have lured each member of that audience into the theatre, nailed him to his seat, taken two dollars away from him, and dared him to move. Now if you don't let that poor creature see and hear all that is going on, I consider it nothing short of Broadway robbery."[26]

Despite their many lapses, professional responsibility was the theme imbedded in much of acting's folklore. Stories abounded concerning an actor's carrying on the show in the face of personal hardship. The story was told of Mrs. Gilbert, long of Daly's Stock Company, who acted into her early eighties despite nagging health. On one occasion she fainted during an entrance, and her fall cut her lip severely. Nevertheless, with the aid of two stage hands she got up and walked on stage, half-dazed but immediately assuming the light-hearted air of her role. She had to keep her shawl pressed to her lip to absorb the blood, but she finished the scene.[27] Another tale told of an actress in Philadelphia who received news of her son's death just before curtain time. She went ahead with her part, maintaining firm control of herself until the third act, when she

spoke the line, "Farewell, farewell—I shall never see thee more."
Here, the words brought a realization of her son's death and she
fainted.[28] These stories, which could be repeated in great number,
formed the body of sentimental legend (part of any group's mythic
history) that served as a didactic example of the trouper spirit.

While New York may have been the player's dream, life on
the road was usually the reality. For most actors an acting career
meant an endless procession of towns, hotels, and theatres. Where
the stock-company performer enjoyed the luxury of a settled life,
the combination-company and repertoire-company actors knew the
pleasures of home only in the summer and not even then if they
worked summer stock. Road tours generally began in the fall and
ran until spring if all went well, or if not, until the show folded. In
an eight or nine month span an actor could travel a vast area. The
famous Edwin Booth–Lawrence Barrett tour of 1887–88 played 258
performances in 72 towns. Companies that played strictly one-
night stands covered even more territory. Bert Wheeler recalled
that in 1910–11 he acted in a touring show called *Mutt and Jeff* that
played forty-seven weeks of continuous one-nighters.[29]

What made these prodigious schedules possible were the
railroads. Actors accepted cinders and timetables as part of their
routine. Most railroads offered special theatrical rates to traveling
companies, two cents a mile reduction plus a free baggage car for
baggage and scenery if twenty-five tickets were sold. While most
companies traveled in coaches alongside other passengers, a few
large companies required their own train cars. The Jennings Dramatic Company used two coaches, two Pullmans, and a combination baggage car when it toured Texas in 1917.[30] The common players further endured the straight-backed seats of the coaches on
most trips, only occasionally enjoying Pullmans. The biggest stars
such as Sarah Bernhardt and Richard Mansfield owned their own
plush cars. These were lavish vehicles. Helena Modjeska's wine-
colored palace car was richly decorated with interior woodwork,
hangings, frescoes, and landscape oils. Maude Adams, ever the
perfectionist, had her car fitted with scenery that slid on grooves,
so that her company could practice while traveling.[31] The grueling
schedule of one-nighters meant that players practically lived on the
trains. Early in the morning following a performance, the troupers
roused themselves out of bed, checked out of the hotel, and
dragged their trunks to the station. They proceeded by train to
their next date, which might be a few hours or a full day's journey
away. Sometimes, after the evening performance the troupe would
pack up and get on a sleeper to leave that night.

The personality of the manager or star largely determined

whether or not the tour would be a pleasant one for the company. Joseph Jefferson was popular with his touring cast. His popularity began with his eating the same food as the rest of the company, prepared by the show's cook. (By contrast, Dion Boucicault had special meals made up for him and his family while traveling.) Jefferson also took his actors on fishing excursions when they were in Minnesota and Wisconsin, chartering a locomotive for the occasion. Julius Kahn, a member of his company, noted that the cast played with "a better grace" after such outings. On arriving in town Jefferson always made sure that an omnibus picked up the players and their luggage to take them to a hotel. He thought it demeaning for a company to struggle down the street with their baggage. And after the show at night, if the company had to leave town immediately, Jefferson provided sandwiches, salad, and beer. A tour with Joseph Jefferson offered comforts actors could seldom expect, but it paid off with high morale and sharp performances.

Less pleasant to travel with was manager Charles Parsloe, with whom Julius Kahn also toured in the 1880s. On a junket of one-nighters through New England Parsloe would rouse his company between 5:30 and 6:00 every morning to catch the train, even though a later train would have gotten them to the next town on time. The troupe arrived at the hotel so early in the day that they often had to wait in the parlor for the previous night's guest to vacate. Parsloe also forced his company to get themselves and their luggage from the depot to the hotel as best they could.[32]

Whatever the disadvantages of train travel, it was certainly an advance over the previous modes of transportation. An illustrated cover of the *Dramatic Mirror* in 1886 made this point, albeit in exaggerated form. The cover had two pictures, entitled "The Actor's Christmas—Past and Present." One pictured actors struggling out of a snowbound stagecoach and wading through high snowbanks to shelter. The other showed an actor and actress relaxing in a train car, the actress playing the piano while a Negro porter brought the actor a drink. With each illustration came a verse seconding the message of progress. Under the picture of Christmas past ran the doggerel:

> Sturdily plodding through rain and wind
> Blinded with snowdrift, stung with sleet.
> The poorhouse before and the sheriff
>   behind
> With fainting stomach, on aching feet
> All our havings and holdings on weary
>   backs,
> With never a crust and never a dime

And our ramshackle shandydan stuck in its
      tracks.
How roughly we fared in the sad old time!

The other verse celebrated the amenities of the railroad:

Speeding along without trouble or care.
Merry with wine cup and brave with bread.
While sunbeams glint through the
      sparkling air;
Fair weather within and clean azure
      overhead;
While our days flow onward to blissful ease
With smiles of beauty and music chime,
While no sounds but soothe us, no sights
      but please
How gayly we fare in the glad new time![33]

Idealizations aside, long tours were physically demanding. Irregular hours of sleep, uncertain quality of food, and exposure to
the elements between the depot and hotel took their toll. Yet even
more taxing than these annoyances was the continually hard pace
of life on the road. There was no letup. When a player got ill he
pushed on. It required stamina, a quality actors always recommended to aspiring performers. The unpredictability and even the
dangers of the road made it attractive to some actors, however.
Julie Opp Faversham claimed she never tired of touring. "Once
you are launched," she wrote, "the 'road' . . . possesses a lure distinct, perennial and gripping."[34]

Still, the hardships of travel were frequently given as reasons
for women to avoid the stage.[35] Perils to health and—more to the
point—moral pitfalls awaited a young unmarried girl in unfamiliar
towns day after day. New York, of course, had more than its share
of "mashers" and "stagedoor Johnnies." But young women were
particularly vulnerable on the road, staying in strange hotels and
encountering men of uncertain scruples. They generally had to
fend for themselves, though it was not uncommon for the mother
of a young actress to accompany her on tour.

Touring actresses found a friend in the Charlotte Cushman
Club, established in Philadelphia in 1908. It catered to low-salaried
actresses, offering a room to those who otherwise would have trouble finding suitable lodging. It provided regular meals, including a
special midnight supper for after the show, laundry room, and music room. The club sought to be as much like a home as possible,
surrounding the girls with "loving, proper influences." Founded
by persons not connected with the theatre, the hope was that

branches would spring up in other cities. That never happened. With the exception of a few actresses such as Mary Shaw, the acting profession was apathetic in its support, and philanthropic women hesitated to give to something that might encourage more girls to go on stage. The Philadelphia chapter, however, thrived and moved to larger quarters in 1919.[36]

The physical and emotional demands of acting turned some players to drugs and alcohol. Probably no image of the actor in the nineteenth century was as pervasive as that of the tippling performer struggling with his lines. It was a stereotype with a solid basis in fact. Accounts of players showing up stone drunk for performances fill theatrical annals, and managers usually had an actor or two in every company who had to be kept away from bars. Part of the reason for excessive drinking was loneliness. Even with the companionship of one's company, the rootlessness of touring brought feelings of isolation. Actors also used alcohol as a stimulus during performances. Overworked players such as John McCullough and Lawrence Barrett found it necessary to drink to get through the show. Edwin Booth drank a lager beer during a performance, "just to keep my 'mad' up," as he put it. The nervous energy expended in acting allowed actors to drink amounts which in normal circumstances would have floored them.[37] There also appears to have been a fair degree of drug use in the profession. Again, players found drugs a useful antidote for the loneliness of travel and the chronic ailments that they might suffer. An advertisement in the professional trade paper, offering an easy home cure for those addicted to opium, morphine, or laudanum, suggests that drugs were a problem.[38]

Another health problem plagued players: syphilis, especially its later stage of mental debility known as paresis. The *Dramatic Mirror* commented several times in the late 1880s that many prominent players had succumbed in their prime to this disease.[39] The dramatist Bartley Campbell, one-time variety show partner of Edward Harrigan, Tony Hart, and most eminently, John McCullough all suffered the gradual madness accompanying paresis. McCullough's last days were pathetic. A large, robust man renowned for his roles as Virginius and Spartacus, McCullough's health began deteriorating in 1883 when he was fifty-one. Paresis leads to a progressive inability to concentrate on a task and a loss of memory. Within a year McCullough had fallen to this state. His career came to an end at Chicago's McVicker's Theatre, September 29, 1884. He was portraying Spartacus in *The Gladiator*, a vigorous part that demanded more than McCullough could then give. He was confused, stretches of silence punctuated his speeches caused by memory lapses, and his supporting cast repeatedly had to prompt him. The audience misunderstood his condition. Believing him drunk they hissed and shouted insults. After stumbling through the performance, and hurt by the audience's treatment, McCullough addressed them: "If you had suffered as I have tonight, you would not have done this." McCullough left the stage and shortly thereafter was committed to a New York asylum, where he died the next year.[40] The carefree Maurice Barrymore also paid dearly for his libertinism. Around 1900 he began showing the debilitating symptoms, a failing memory and lapses of incoherence. Barrymore finally had to be committed in 1901 to the Long Island Home for the Insane, where he remained until his death in 1905.

Acting itself posed occasional hazards to players, especially as stage spectacles necessitated increasingly realistic effects. In *The Girl I Left Behind Me* at New York's Academy of Music, a cavalry scene called for a score of horsemen to ride onto the stage as the rescue party. The actors on stage had to hustle out of the horses' way each time. But on one occasion an actress got trapped and would have been trampled, save for another member of the cast, Frank Mordaunt, who gallantly rescued her, and in so doing was himself seriously injured by the onrushing horses.[41] In *Joan of the Shoals* golden-haired Henrietta Crosman had to simulate climbing up a cliff to replace a beacon light. Directly behind the light was a large electric fan that gave the effect of heavy winds. As Crosman leaned close to the fan her dress caught in the flanges and began ripping to shreds. It momentarily appeared that she might be drawn into the fan. Her screams brought patrons on the front rows to their feet before Harry Woodruff, her leading man, rescued her. As in the case with most stage accidents, the scene continued as if nothing had happened.[42]

Given the hazards of work and travel actors did their best to hedge their bets. They were an extremely superstitious group of people, and to get along with the other members of a company one had to observe the accustomed superstitions. A fictional short story told of a soubrette who made herself unpopular with her company by unwittingly defying the superstitions. She wore peacock feathers in her hat, whistled in the dressing room, walked under ladders, and did not carry an amulet, all of which were thought to bring bad luck. So despite her compelling charms, members of the company avoided her.[43] Among the many theatrical superstitions was the belief that a play rehearsed on Sunday would result in salaries not being paid on time, failure of the play, or a death in the company, and that bringing a Bible on stage was bad luck. The supersititous bent among players was further evidenced by a regular column on astrology in the *ASMB* beginning in 1904. The capricious, uncertain lives actors led probably explains this predilection. Unable to predict or guarantee success, they turned to the realm of the magical, hoping at least ward to off bad luck and achieve a degree of security.

* 2 *

Even if actors avoided the bad luck of unemployment, alcoholism, or accident, there was one other source of potential trouble: marriage. The player's life precluded a stable, family-oriented existence. A marriage had to endure long separations during tours, unless of course both husband and wife belonged to the same company, which was commonly the case. But some managers avoided hiring husband and wife teams, because if they had trouble with one, both would leave. A group of attractive, emotionally charged, and sometimes lonely actors and actresses traveling together created a situation to test the constancy of marriage vows. When Helena Modjeska toured the country she made obvious and repeated overtures to her leading man, Maurice Barrymore, despite the presence of Barrymore's wife, Georgianna Drew Barrymore.[44] Tours made and unmade marriages. James K. Hackett and Mary Mannering met while playing in the same company. They fell in love and married. Both became stars in due course and headed up different companies (under the theatrical axiom that the public loses interest in leading men and ladies who are married in real life).[45] Hackett and Mannering went their own way on tour, and before many years passed went their separate marital ways as well.

The difficulties inherent in theatrical marriages gave rise to conflicting views about the desirability of matrimony for players, especially for women, who would have the dual responsiblity of a career and homemaking. An anonymous starlet confessed to the emotional conflicts she experienced as actress and mother and advised beginners, "Either give up the stage, or give up marrying, there is no combining the two."[46] On the other hand, Clara Morris, one of the theatre's champions of domesticity, asserted that a career and marriage were compatible and even desirable. With an eloquence worthy of her status as America's greatest emotional actress she wrote:

> So young actress and singer, what are you to do? You were women before you were professionals and received certain God-implanted

instincts that set you to dreaming sacredly sweet dreams you could not put into words. Instincts that set the quick blush in your cheek and the prickle and thrill in your lips, that make your eyes fill and your heart thump at the aimless clutch of a baby hand or the burning glance of one man's steady eyes.[47]

Most actresses sooner or later heeded Clara Morris's advice. The 1900 census listed 52.4 percent of actresses and showwomen as single, 38.4 percent married, 6.4 percent widowed, and 2.8 percent divorced. Although over half of the profession's women were unmarried, when compared with the percentage of unmarried women in other occupations the figure is low.[48] The reason so many actresses were unmarried was that it was largely a profession of young women in their teens or barely past. The 38.4 percent of actresses who were married gave the profession the third highest percentage of married female workers. Unlike most occupations in which single women worked until marriage retired them to the home in their early twenties, many actresses kept their jobs after finding a husband. Of course some husbands insisted that their new wives leave the Bohemian environs of the theatre. But in all likelihood it was the lesser lights of the stage and the chorus women who considered acting only a temporary career and quit the theatre at marriage. With a few notable exceptions, such as Mary Anderson, star actresses pursued their career after marriage.

One can also infer from the census record that there were relatively few single women over age twenty-five in the profession and probably many married ones under that age.[49] Yet the successful actresses tended to marry later than most women. Of a sample of fifty-one actresses, thirty married at age twenty-five or after, this at a time when the median age of women at their first marriage was 21.9.[50] A few famous actresses never married. Maude Adams's mystique stemmed partly from a solitary life untouched by a hint of romance. Likewise Lotta Crabtree never wedded, perhaps the legacy of an overprotective mother.

The gentlemen of the stage had a different marital pattern. The 1900 census reported 50.9 percent of actors and professional showmen as single, 45.0 percent married, 3.3 percent widowed, and .8 percent divorced. On the surface actors' marital statistics do not appear radically different from actresses'. But there was a great difference in the comparative ages of the two groups. Whereas only 52.2 percent of actresses were twenty-five or older, 75.8 percent of actors were in that age group. The greater age of actors indicates that many were either marrying late or remaining bachelors.[51] Late marriage or permanent bachelorhood is understandable in an occupation antithetical to rootedness. The insecurities of an acting career may have inhibited actors from taking on the responsibilities of a family. Of course it is possible that the broad census category—which included professional athletes, circus performers, dancers, and balloonists—may have colored the statistics, for these were the kind of men who would lead a roving life. Though nearly all the star actors married, the impression persists that among the middle and lower ranks of the legitimate theatre many bachelors worked. Ronald Taft's recent study of Australian actors found that most players (including actresses) had never been married. Moreover, he estimated that 50 percent of the males were predominantly homosexual.[52] This topic is ignored in the nineteenth- and early twentieth-century theatrical literature, and until further evidence is found speculation would be groundless. But one might surmise that acting served as an outlet for certain homosexual traits in the nineteenth century as well as later, and that this could help account, though in a small way, for the many single actors.

A theatrical axiom said that actors or actresses should not marry outside the profession. The *Dramatic Mirror* arrogantly commented in 1883, "As well mate an eagle with a barnyard fowl as an artist with a mere worker."[53] There were good reasons for this advice. An actor-actress couple would have a better chance of working together and thus of being near one another than would a couple in which just one belonged to the theatre. The closed society in which players worked encouraged endogamous marriage. A survey of fifty-eight leading actresses showed that thirty-seven of them married someone connected with the theatre—actor, producer, or business manager.

Although players normally sought publicity assiduously, their marriage ceremonies were uncharacteristically subdued, and elopement was not uncommon. Frank Bennett and May Bowers, both in Augustin Daly's company, were secretly married in 1880 at The Little Church around the Corner. At the wedding reception given later by Daly it came out that another Daly couple had been secretly wed.[54] Clara Morris gave a good explanation for this tendency. Girls in private life wanted their marriages to be social extravaganzas, she said; it was their day to play the leading role. Actresses, on the other hand, were on exhibition every day. Thus they wanted to make their marriages as private as possible.[55]

If players tried to keep their marriages quiet, there was no way for them to avoid the publicity accompanying a divorce. Stage marriages often became objects of ridicule for the public, who cynically observed that it was only a matter of time before affections would be alienated. A headline in an 1895 issue of the *Custer County Chief*, a Nebraska newspaper, typified the kind of press actors received: "Divorces almost of Yearly Occurrence—Majority of the Actresses Have Tried the Wedded Stage from Two to Six Times."[56] A few players contributed to this image through their carefree marital life. Most notorious was comedian Nat Goodwin, who frolicked through five marriages. Challenging Goodwin for the dubious distinction of most-betrothed player was musical comedian DeWolf Hopper, who also married five times. At every change in partner these men had an appropriate quip for the public to relish. Actresses Lillian Russell and Agnes Booth also did their part to uphold the image of the fleeting theatrical marriage.

Theatre publicists combated this image by pointing out the idyllic love affairs among players.[57] But their mission was difficult because actors indisputably had a high divorce rate. In 1900 male actors and professional showmen had the third highest percentage of divorce in the census's occupational categories.[58] Actresses had the fourth highest rate among working women.[59] The incidence of marital separation appears even more striking when one examines the lives of the stars, those upon whom public attention focused. Out of a sample of ninety-eight male actors who had been married, thirty-two had been divorced at least once (32.7 percent); of seventy-one actresses who had been married, thirty-two had also divorced (45.7 percent).

A divorce could have serious consequences for a player's career. Matinee idol Robert Mantell had alimony problems after divorcing his first wife. The settlement of one hundred dollars a week proved too much after several shows failed, and he fell behind in the payments. A judge ordered Mantell's arrest, so he fled New York. For ten years, from 1894 to 1903, he was exiled to the provinces, at times reduced to being virtually a barnstormer. His career seemed over. Only by putting together a popular vaudeville act did Mantell get back on his feet. By 1901 he managed to settle his alimony debt for ten thousand dollars and could return to New York. But it took three more years before he reestablished himself as a star on Broadway.[60]

The flippant manner in which many players approached marriage (DeWolf Hopper: "Marriage for me has become an incident, not a conquest") and the frequency of their divorces hindered their bid for public respect. "No profession that is stigmatized by such an appalling number of divorces," wrote an anonymous author in 1906, "can be recommended as a suitable calling for your son or daughter, your brother or sister, or yourself."[61] The *New York Times* reprimanded those actors whose many divorces cast disrepute on the whole profession. Players could "remove all the old reproach from their calling," the newspaper editorialized in 1913, if they only recognized their social responsibilities.[62]

The problem of divorce was a particularly lively one in the Progressive era. Marriages were breaking up at increasingly higher rates, and modernists and conservatives battled over the desirability of easy divorce. There were organized attempts to standardize state divorce legislation, or even to create a federal statute, and committees and leagues on divorce and family life were organized. Although no major change in the legal status of divorce occurred during the Progressive era, public attitudes slowly swung toward acceptance of the legitimacy, if not the desirability, of divorce.[63] Actors were caught in the middle of the crossfire. Condemned by moralists for their loose lifestyle, they simultaneously were on the forefront of an emerging morality. But players had gone further than most people could easily accept. That Americans began to accept some marriages as irredeemable did not mean that they condoned hopping from one partner to another on little more than a whim. Few actors did this, of course. But the stereotype thrived and marked players as people who lived by a looser set of rules.

Marriages were problematic in part because a secure home life was elusive for most players. Hotels never became a satisfying substitute, despite actors' efforts to decorate them with photos, rugs, or vases. More congenial were the theatrical boardinghouses that survived in the larger cities through the early twentieth century. They offered reasonable prices and the companionship of fellow players. Vaudevillians and circus performers could also be found in theatrical boardinghouses, but their inferior artistic status was reinforced by an imposed social distance from the resident thespians.[64] Increasingly, though, in the early twentieth century, actors became home owners, so that even if they traveled extensively they had a place of their own to return to. Some actors found this trend disturbing, fearing that by living alongside ordinary people actors would become assimilated into society. Assimilation, they felt, would deprive the profession of the public's interest, which sprang in large part from the actor's exclusiveness.[65]

Accompanying this trend toward home ownership was a large popular literature describing actors at home. The writing about actors' homes stressed luxury and domesticity.[66] Margherita Hamm wrote:

> Taken as a class they [actors] certainly are as domestic as people engaged in mercantile pursuits, and are more so than members of the other professions. This, of course, refers to their tendencies rather than to their actual living. The exigencies of their calling

keep them on the road or away from their homes a large part of
every year; but when they are at liberty, two-thirds of them retire
to private life, and generally lead as quiet and regular a home-life
as can be imagined.[67]

The invocation of domesticity served to reassure the public that actors and actresses led lives not so different from everybody else's.
Good Housekeeping ran a series of articles by star actresses in 1912,
which "exhibits in a remarkable way the home hunger of the modern star."[68] In the first article Margaret Anglin, perhaps not quite in
the spirit of the series, recommended techniques for managing servants, candidly admitting that a lady of the theatre had no time for
housework.[69] By contrast, Mary Mannering, who married a Detroit
industrialist, described her efforts to design attractive bungalows
for her husband's workers. She personally supervised the land-
scaping and interior design of the dwellings, a feat which must
have convinced any reader of the proper domestic inclination of
the actress.[70]

Julie Opp, actress and wife of stage star William Faversham,
while agreeing that the public generally questioned actresses' domestic credentials, strongly denied the accusation, insisting that
most actresses were starved for home life: "I do not look upon my-
self as the exception, so I feel that I can say, without being egotistical, that the actress, successful or otherwise, has more genuine
happiness in the little homelife she has than in her artistic triumphs. . . . She is peacefully happy only when she gets back to her
home and is her own, real self."[71]

These sentiments reveal that the domestic strain in American
culture, which had defined women's social role since early in the
nineteenth century, still carried great weight into the twentieth.
Even actresses, who in many ways pioneered women's freedom for
an independent career, had to pay lip service to the domestic ideal.
"A woman really ought to have a home and be in it most of the
time," Julie Opp soberly noted.[72] Actress Ada Lewis gave a similar
testimony to the personal fulfillment of domesticity: "I cannot
imagine a situation in life more beautiful than that of a woman with
a lovely family of children. No matter how high she might climb in
art, nothing that she could ever attain could reach the sublimity of
her position as a mother."[73] The public was assured that regardless
of the success an actress enjoyed in the theatre, her first duty and
greatest satisfaction came at home. Although the primary domestic
burden fell upon actresses, actors were not overlooked. Valerie
Hope wrote that many of the matinee idols, despite hordes of adoring females, were thoroughly attached to their families. John
Drew's popularity never diminished "his fondness for the calm and

comfort of domesticity." Likewise, Francis Wilson was commended for his dedication to hearth and home.[74]

* 3 *

If theatre publicists liked to stress actors' and actresses' domestic content, they gave even more attention to their social instincts. Players loved to gather together, drinking, singing, telling stories, reflecting on careers. Their penchant for entertaining carried over to their private lives. To relieve the tension following a performance actors would meet at a favorite night spot, perhaps Rector's on Broadway, for a late supper. On tour social life centered around the hotel. Accommodations varied, of course. The stars stayed in the city's finest hostelry; while lesser members put up in a modest hotel or boardinghouse. But socializing remained within the group. Actors ate together, played cards together, and walked to the theatre in groups. They constantly visited each other's rooms, munching on snacks and reading their lines to one another.[75]

Given their social nature, actors quite predictably established a host of theatrical clubs. These clubs provide some important insights into the acting community and bear examination.

The Actor's Order of Friendship might be considered the first theatrical club in America, though its major function was as a fraternal society. The AOOF was founded in Philadelphia in 1849, but in 1888 the Edwin Forrest Lodge was established in New York and it quickly became the dominant branch, with 187 members in 1890 to Philadelphia's 30. The New York lodge headquartered in a house on 47th Street, where members relaxed in a restful atmosphere and enjoyed the fine library (a gift of Joseph Jefferson). But the benevolent functions of the AOOF always remained uppermost. Dues-paying members were eligible for benefits if incapacitated, and upon the death of a brother, one hundred dollars was sent to his widow or next of kin and funeral arrangements were made. Prominent members included Milton Nobles, John Drew, Louis Aldrich, F. F. Mackay, and George Fawcett.[76]

Another theatrical society, theatrical at least in its early years, was the Benevolent and Protective Order of Elks. It originated in the bar of New York's Star Hotel, where a coterie of entertainers who tagged themselves "the jolly corks" met weekly. They decided to add a more serious fraternal policy to their merrymaking, and in 1868 the BPOE was born. Lodges spread rapidly to other cities, in part because its predominantly actor membership traveled widely and encouraged new branches. Through the 1880s actors remained the backbone of the Elks. "Ours is essentially a theatrical order," declared the Grand Exalted Ruler in 1887. The Elk's charity fund depended largely on the benefit performances of such actors as Frederick Warde and Daniel Sully. But as the Elks flourished the theatrical flavor of the order rapidly declined, and by the turn of the century there was nothing distinctively theatrical about it.[77]

A more important theatrical organization was the Lambs Club. It was conceived at a dinner given for Henry Montague, Lester Wallack's leading man, at Delmonico's in 1875. The festive occasion was so enjoyable that those present decided to make the suppers a monthly affair. They rented a room next to Wallack's Theater, accepted Montague's whimsical suggestion for a name, and the club was born. In its early years the Lambs was primarily a social watering place for visiting English players (Wallack's company was nearly all English). But native players soon found it to their liking, and as the club grew over the next few decades it moved several times to larger quarters. It finally rested in 1905 on West 44th Street just around the corner from Broadway, occupying a stately clubhouse designed by Stanford White. By 1915 membership had climbed to over a thousand, two-thirds of whom were performers. The head of the Lambs was designated the shepherd; Henry Montague was the first, followed by Lester Wallack.[78]

The Lambs Club provided a retreat for male actors (women were never admitted to the clubhouse), a place where the vicissitudes of career were swept away in drink and comradeship. During the day members could stop by the club for lunch, to meet friends or use the library (though Lambs were not known as great readers). The 44th Street clubhouse was so near most of the theatres that if a player appeared only in the first and last act of a play it was not unknown for him to slip out of the theatre after the first act and go to the Lambs until time for his final appearance. The liveliest hours began about 11:30 at night, after the evening's performances, when players stopped by for a few hours' relaxation at the bar or pool tables. Liquor flowed freely in the club, contributing to the uninhibited atmosphere. On at least one occasion several members were arrested for disturbing the peace. Attention often centered on the club's resident wits: Wilton Lackaye, DeWolf Hopper, Steele MacKaye, and especially Maurice Barrymore.[79] Unpretentiousness characterized the Lambs. "The democracy of the place is complete and unfeigned," testified DeWolf Hopper. Actors were not the most self-effacing of people, but according to Hopper they managed to put aside their airs while in the club. The Lambs' motto revealed an egalitarian spirit: "You may be all the world to your public, but you're only an actor to us."[80]

The Gambols—periodic performances written and performed by members given in the club's private theatre—highlighted the club's activities. Once a year a public Gambol was produced, an event of such popularity that its proceeds contributed significantly to the club's solvency. The Gambols were original productions of new plays, ranging from farce and burlesque to tragedy. Several noteworthy plays received first hearings in the Gambols, among them Edwin Milton Royle's *Squaw Man* and Augustus Thomas's *Witching Hour*.[81]

Another theatrical club, though not primarily one for actors, was the Friars. It originated in 1904 among theatrical press agents in an attempt to weed out the spurious agents who got undeserved passes to theatres.[82] Three years later the club incorporated as the National Association of the Friars, aiming to promote social contacts among press agents, managers, and other theatrical men. But conviviality once again carried the day. The Friars built a handsome clubhouse on West 48th Street and began attracting actors to its lively lodging. The most popular friar was George M. Cohan, an ever present figure in the clubhouse and later the club's abbott.

Men did not have a monopoly on theatrical clubs. Actresses founded two of their own. Not much is known about the first, the Twelfth Night Club, organized in 1891 in New York under the leadership of Alice Fisher, Lelena Fisher, Maida Craigen, and Effie Shannon. The club endorsed programs of mutual aid for younger actresses, and provided them an opportunity for socializing with one another on a regular basis. During the theatrical season it also held monthly receptions with male stars as its guests of honor.[83] More active than the Twelfth Night Club was the Professional Woman's League, which enrolled 350 women within four months of its founding by Mrs. A. M. Palmer in 1892. The Professional Woman's League had its social function, but its primary purpose was to meet actresses' professional needs. It offered legal advice to those having contractual problems with managers. Actresses short of money could secure loans. Sewing classes were offered to help ease the financial burden of costuming. Additionally, its quarters at 1999 Broadway maintained a wardrobe, a kind of clothing library from which an actress could rent a dress for her upcoming role. And, initially at least, classes in French and German were offered, along with music, stage dancing, drawing, and painting lessons.[84]

In sum, these clubs served a variety of functions, social purposes being uppermost. But all the clubs assumed that actors must look to other actors for companionship and aid. They exhibited a pervasive traditionalism. Actors' reliance on each other for all their needs indicated that they expected little change in their relationship to society. The clubs were firmly rooted in the notion that an unbridgeable gulf separated players from the rest of society. It is in this assumption that the final actors' club to be examined parted company with its predecessors. Edwin Booth founded The Players in 1888 in a conscious attempt to break down the boundaries between actors and society and to elevate the actors' status through association with artists, men of letters, and leaders of the business community.

Edwin Booth, arguably America's greatest tragedian, has suffered the historical fate of being known to the general public largely as the elder brother of John Wilkes Booth. His contemporaries, however, knew better. To them he was America's answer to England's Henry Irving, proof that a worthy successor to the great Shakespeareans could be found in America. Booth was born to the stage, the son of Junius Brutus Booth, who in his day rivaled Edmund Kean for leadership of the English stage. From his birth in Bel Air, Maryland, in 1833 Booth knew only the theatre, touring with his father and playing supporting roles. Following his father's death in 1852, Booth kicked about the American West and Australia for a few years, then in 1857 he headed to New York with his reputation on the rise. For the next thirty years he would remain a leading star of the stage.[85]

Offstage Booth was a retiring person who preferred being alone with a book or with a few close friends to being the center of an adoring circle. He experienced more than his share of personal tragedies: the death of his beloved first wife, the murderous plot of his brother, fire and bankruptcy that plagued him financially, and a second wife whose progressive insanity fed hostility toward her husband. Not coincidentally, Booth suffered from recurrent melancholy. Interestingly, he was a poor public speaker, reduced to banalities when speaking extemporaneously, and thus he dismissed requests for public reading or lecturing.[86] But if Booth lacked power off the stage, onstage he exuded grandeur and authority. Not physically impressive in the manner of a Forrest, his power came through his intensity and intellectuality. Mary Anderson left a vivid description of Booth: "Small, lithe of figure, his dark, lustrous eyes flashing with nervous vitality and intellect, his pale face calm and supremely melancholy in expression."[87] The classical tragedies offered Booth his greatest roles: Richelieu, Shylock, Othello, Macbeth, Brutus, Richard III, and especially his Hamlet, which Charles Shattuck has called "the most famous personation in the history of the American theatre."[88]

More than most actors Edwin Booth felt a responsibility toward his art, not just while performing, but in a social sense as well. For a number of years he pondered what he might do as a permanent legacy to the profession he loved so dearly. The answer slowly built in his mind, partly a result of visits to London's Garrick Club, the meeting place of actors and fashionable society, and partly from conversations with Lawrence Barrett, Augustin Daly, and A. M. Palmer, who convinced him that an American club like the Garrick offered the surest means for "the elevation of the stage."

Why a club? Because, as Max Weber first explained, men's clubs held a central place in America's social ecology of status and power. During Weber's 1904 visit to America he became intrigued by the country's ubiquitous voluntary associations, especially the many Protestant sects.[89] To gain admittance, Weber noted, one had to meet the sect's standards of belief and moral behavior; acceptance implied that the member had certain qualities, such as honesty and reliability, which fostered trust on the part of creditors and customers. As society secularized, Weber further observed, other voluntary associations, notably social clubs, took on similar functions. But they did more than certify traits of character. Clubs provided a means for ascribing social position in a nation that lacked aristocratic titles. Money, of course, brought a kind of distinction, yet that was not enough. One needed a badge, a certificate, to indicate qualities of gentility. Admittance to a gentleman's club granted standing to a man and his family. "At the present time," Weber wrote, "affiliation with a distinguished club is essential above all else."[90]

Weber's observation gains credence in light of the plethora of clubs organized in the nineteenth century. New York alone had nearly one hundred in 1873—by the count of Francis Fairfield—ranging from artistic to sporting to political to ethnic clubs. The most exclusive clubs at the end of the nineteenth century—New York's Union and Knickerbocker, Philadelphia's Philadelphia and Rittenhouse, and Boston's Somerset—counted only the business and professional elite among their members.[91] The sole actor in the Union Club was Lester Wallack, whose membership probably rested on the strength of his father's reputation and his own ownership of New York's most fashionable theatre of the 1870s. Wallack also had a singularly aristocratic demeanor. He was, as Fairfield described him, "a fine example of physical manhood, or rather, of physical aristocracy; in manners a polished gentleman, . . . A face and head of extremely patrician type, massive yet delicate, rest upon broad and massive shoulders, and complete a tout ensemble which, for elegance and grace, is not exceeded on the Avenue."[92]

Wallack notwithstanding, the elite men's clubs were out of the question for most actors, even the stars. William Florence, the prominent Irish comedian, was blackballed at the Union Club in 1887.[93] Although actors increasingly moved among the better social circles in the late nineteenth century, gentlemen's clubs remained just beyond their grasp. Their rejection may be attributed to the clubs' absolute insistence upon respectability and predictability, essential values to the business world. Actors embodied different values—nonconformity and spontaneity. Although society was beginning to appreciate these traits in actors, America's patrician clubs as yet did not.

Players found an only slightly more cordial reception at the literary and artistic clubs of New York, such as the Century. The Century, a club with origins dating to 1829 when such luminaries as Asher Durand, Thomas Cole, and William Cullen Bryant gathered to sketch and talk, had by 1880 grown to a membership of six hundred and had become a cultural institution of New York City.[94] Its carefully nurtured balance of artistic conviviality and cultured dignity would have been ideal for actors to widen their contacts with other artists and patrons of the arts. But only Booth, Wallack, and Lawrence Barrett belonged at the time of The Players' founding. The relative absence of theatrical members suggested that they were not the equals of painters, sculptors, or authors in the artistic world.

Booth and his close friends laid out plans for The Players during the summer of 1887 on the yacht of lawyer and educator E. C. Benedict at anchor in a Maine harbor. The group—including Booth's frequent stage partner, Lawrence Barrett, and authors Thomas Bailey Aldrich and Laurence Hutton, among others—received his idea of a club enthusiastically. With Aldrich's suggestion of a name in hand, actual organization took place the following January, when fifteen of Booth's friends, actors, managers, artists, and writers met for lunch at Delmonico's. The problem of a home was solved when baritone David Bispham located a stately four-story residence in Gramercy Park, one of New York City's most exclusive neighborhoods in the 1880s, the home of Cyrus Field, Robert Ingersoll, Mrs. Stuyvesant Fish, Bishop Potter, and Samuel J. Tilden. Architect and club member Stanford White attested to its structural soundness and offered to remodel it.[95]

On New Year's eve of 1888, Edwin Booth handed the clubhouse deed to Augustin Daly, vice president of The Players, and delivered his Founder's Night address, an occasion for reflection on the purposes of the club. At the heart of Booth's speech was a frank confession of his ambitions for his profession:

Especially for the worthy ones of my profession am I desirous that this association shall be the means of bringing them, regardless of their theatrical rank, in communion with those who, ignorant of their personal qualities hidden by the mask and motley of our calling, know them as actors only. Frequent intercourse with gentlemen of other arts and professions, who love the stage and appreciate the value of the drama as an aid to intellectual culture, must inspire the humblest player with a reverence for his vocation as one among the first of 'fine arts'—which too many regard as merely a means to the gratification of vanity and selfishness. Such is the object of this club.[96]

Two primary, and in some ways contradictory, aims for The Players are revealed in his address. First, it was to prove to society that actors possessed admirable personal qualities. Nontheatrical members would come to know actors as people and subsequently gain greater respect for them. The esteem already possessed by himself, Barrett, Jefferson, and a few others, Booth wished extended to the profession as a whole. And as Max Weber noted a few years later, this could best be accomplished through a club. Second, The Players was to "inspire the humblest player with a reverence for his vocation as one among the first of 'fine arts.'" It would remedy the inferiority actors felt vis-à-vis painters, sculptors, and authors. Moreover, not only would The Players convince actors of the worthiness of their art, it would also provide the learning and taste that would make them truly the equals of anyone. One senses here an apparent contradiction in Booth's thinking. He considered actors the equal of other artists and worthy of society's respect, yet felt they needed the refinement and education that he hoped The Players would provide. This dichotomy reflected not so much confusion on Booth's part as a genuine ambivalence in his attitude toward actors and the acting profession. In the abstract he had the greatest respect for his calling. But too many of his fellow players betrayed that respect. Booth once wrote: "Actors are a set of mere vain, selfish, brainless idiots—seeking only their own personal glorification which consists in paper-puffery and large type on the play-bill."[97] He hoped that The Players would "excite ambition & self-respect in those who waste the better part of their nature in happy-go-lucky, Bohemian habits."[98] In a similar vein, Booth wrote about The Players: "It will be a beacon, I hope, to incite emulation in the 'poor player'—to lift up himself to a higher social grade than the Bohemian level that so many worthy members of my profession now grovel on from sheer lack of incentive to 'go up higher.'"[99]

This ennoblement would result from association with the

cultivated members of the acting profession as well as with the educated nontheatrical members of the club. The Players' constitution specified three classes of members: those in the theatre; those in other artistic fields; and patrons of the arts. A third of the original 750-member limit were to be actors, but the presence of nontheatrical dignitaries was crucial to Booth's aim. The club was to be a place, in William Winter's words, where actors "might find books and pictures, precious relics of the great players of the past, intellectual communication with minds of their own order, and with men of education in other walks of life, refinement of thought and of manners, innocent pleasure, and sweet, gracious, ennobling associations." [100]

Three years after the club's founding nearly 175 out of the 660 members were connected with theatre, including the stage's most illustrious names. If a minority, actors were the most visible group at The Players, often taking advantage of its serene atmosphere after a hectic performance. But other artists frequented the clubhouse as well. These included authors Laurence Hutton, Thomas Bailey Aldrich, Mark Twain, E. C. Stedman, and Richard Watson Gilder, sculptor Augustus Saint-Gaudens, and painters J. Alden Weir and John Singer Sargent. Mark Twain, resplendent in his white suit, later became a fixture at the club's pool table. The third class of members, "patrons or connoisseurs of the arts," composed a diverse group, including theatre buff General William Tecumseh Sherman, political notables Abram Hewitt, Chauncey Depew, Elihu Root, and Grover Cleveland, and a generous number of bankers and lawyers, including J. P. Morgan. The dozen or so millionaires on the rolls may not have frequented the club, but they contributed to its financial health.[101] Having political and financial leaders in the club also added an element of respectability that even the most prominent painters and writers could not supply. Booth wanted to prove not only that players stood as equals with other artists, but also that the patrician element recognized actors' worthiness. The Reverend Dr. George Houghton of The Little Church around the Corner and two other clerical members symbolized the church's blessing upon the profession.

In order to prevent any unpleasant confrontations as had occurred at London's Garrick Club, critics and reporters were barred from the club. When playwright and former critic Channing Pollock came up for membership in 1908, the committee on admissions read an article he had published in the *Smart Set*. The article criticized member David Belasco, had unkind words to say about a daughter of club president John Drew, and made untoward comments concerning other members of the profession. Regardless of his theatrical credentials, Pollock clearly could not belong (and it was 1935 before he got in).[102]

The Player's clubhouse had four floors and a basement. The basement held the office, billiard room, and bar. On the first floor was the lounge, with its inviting overstuffed chairs and fireplace, and in the back a dining room with walls covered by theatrical portraits and programs dating to the era of Kean. The second floor housed the card room and library. The library, to which Booth and Barrett had given their personal collections, was said to contain one of the finest collections of stage literature in the country. The third and fourth floors included sleeping rooms available to members and Booth's own quarters.[103]

The club strove to maintain a subdued and dignified atmosphere. Unlike the Lambs, The Players never gave any public entertainment. When Henry James visited The Players in 1904, he found it to be an "oasis of quietness and atmosphere." Yet The Players also possessed a convivial spirit, usually centering around the pool and card tables and the bar. The dignity Booth sought for his club never interfered with the telling of a good story. Henry James told Witter Bynner that The Players was one of the two or three places he most enjoyed visiting while in the United States. James wrote after returning to England: "In the Players' Club, as in other New York clubs, . . . I was impressed with the sociability of club life here in America. . . . You are more gregarious, more sociable at your clubs, more en famille."[104] In addition to its social functions the club also served as a convenient, relaxed place to cast a play. Frank Conlan recalled receiving several job offers while at the club.[105]

The Players housed a large collection of theatrical relics, 161 items in 1901. The safe where they were kept contained both historical curiosities, such as a lock of Edmund Kean's hair and the crooked staff Charlotte Cushman leaned on as Meg Merrilies, and items of great value, such as first editions of Ben Jonson and early folios of Shakespeare. Personal items belonging to Garrick, Macready, McCullough, Forrest, Ristori, and other luminaries were preserved. The relics were locked up, but throughout the clubhouse hung portraits of eminent players by Washington Allston, J. Alden Weir, Gilbert Stuart, Sir Joshua Reynolds, Thomas Sully, and John Singer Sargent. Shakespearean mottoes adorned the woodwork.[106] The club's interior immersed the modern player in the history of his calling. By surrounding him with the pictures, possessions, and words of the theatre's giants, the club intended the actor to catch a vision of his profession's nobility and to be challenged to greater accomplishments.

Most important of all were the artifacts and memories of Edwin Booth. Booth lived out his last years at The Players, directing his energies toward the management of the club, attending all the meetings, and scrutinizing the names of proposed members. From 4:00 in the afternoon until dinner he would likely be found in the reading room looking at periodicals or chatting with friends. As he became more feeble he kept to his third-floor room. When the end came on the night of June 7, 1893, a thunderstorm rolled over the city, nature seeming to pay its own tribute to the great tragedian.[107]

After Booth's death the clubhouse became his shrine. His room and personal effects were left just as they were at his death, the book he last read remained on the table. The room's hallowed quality has continued to the present. A 1959 publication of The Players reads: "A moment's view of the Booth room in befitting silence is a benediction every member should experience."[108] The spirit of Booth pervaded the clubhouse. Over the fireplace and dominating the reading room hung Sargent's full-length portrait of Booth. In the central hall hung John Collins's painting of Booth dressed in the cardinal's scarlet robe that he wore as Richelieu. On Founder's Night, celebrated every year on December 31, members would gather to pay homage to Booth. A short address was followed by the passing of the loving cup, each member drinking to the memory of the founder. These occasions helped develop a kind of hagiography around Booth.

Booth's enshrinement pointed up the special place he occupied in the acting world, not simply as an accomplished actor, but more significantly as an embodiment of important ideals. He was, first of all, an actor unusually dedicated to his art. Booth spent his life performing the great classical roles, roles that those players making more money in Belasco melodramas secretly desired. Second, he comported himself like a gentleman in public. Booth's name was never linked with any theatrical high jinks. He shrank from the puffery and self-exaltation of many players and was a genuinely modest man. Third, Booth had an entree into the higher social circles, where he was accepted as an equal. He was also a man of learning, at home among books, one who enjoyed serious conversations with the best artistic minds of the day. In sum, Booth embodied the dignity and professionalism that actors coveted. He offered a model of character and achievement. The Players enshrined not only the man Edwin Booth, but also the aspirations of the acting profession manifested in him.

The insistent respectability of The Players was not unanimously applauded by actors. Initially the club was regarded as an exclusive, somewhat snobbish association. The *Dramatic Mirror*, which for nearly a decade had been proclaiming the common player's dignity, caustically remarked, "actors . . . don't need any gilded halls and hammered brass grill rooms to make 'em acquainted or better their condition." [109] Contributing to The Player's snobbish image was its selectivity in choosing members. Actors considered too Bohemian were blackballed. William Florence was almost bypassed because Booth feared "he had become too convivial for so sedate a coterie as the 'Players.'" [110] However, membership was not restricted to stars. Among the original members were Frank Sanger, John Malone, and Harry Edwards, competent performers, but not headliners.

Another complaint commonly lodged against The Players was that by admitting so many nonprofessionals it was no longer truly an actor's club. William Collier, a member of the Lambs, disapproved of The Players because "you meet so few actors there." [111] The acting community had always been essential to the player, sustaining him through a peripatetic life and serving as a buffer against a frequently hostile world. A threat to this community, even if accompanied by a promise of social acceptance, evoked hostility among some. For these actors the Lambs Club with its gay, free-spirited atmosphere offered the more congenial environment. It reaffirmed the traditional bonds of fellowship and support. Safe within the club's confines, an actor could hold at bay a suspicious and not always friendly world. Frank Marshall White contrasted The Players and the Lambs in 1909. Actors went to The Players, he said, "to meet the leading-men of the stage; ceremonious and conventional . . . to enjoy an intellectual evening." They visited the Lambs, on the other hand, "to be introduced into an environment of gayety, good fellowship, and good cheer." [112]

Notwithstanding the resentments against The Players, it is hard to find an example of an actor turning down a chance to join. By 1893 the club had reached its theatrical membership limit of two hundred and fifty, and to accommodate the waiting list the ceiling was raised to five hundred. A number of actors belonged to both the Lambs and The Players and shared time between them. Dual membership aptly symbolized the two strains within the acting culture: one toward social respectability and assimilation, the other clinging to the traditional acting community with its permissive pattern of behavior. For the most part this conflict was not a conscious one. Rather, actors sensed that their profession was changing, for better or worse, and they responded accordingly, some enthusiastically embracing the change, others resisting.

Among those who, like Booth, wanted to see their vocation follow the high road to respectability and social acceptance was a group that urged upon actors the newest path to occupational prestige: professionalism. Professionalization became a driving impulse within the acting world in the last two decades of the nineteenth century as actors looked outward for models of social advancement.

Four 🌺

An Honorable Profession

*A*t no point does the history of acting and the wider history of occupations intersect more clearly than in the last two decades of the nineteenth century. Players became a part of the most important occupational trend of American history, the diligent pursuit of professional standing, which to the present shows no sign of slowing. Both as a prescriptive statement and as an ideal, professionalism has become the model for nearly all occupations requiring specialized training.

Despite the pervasiveness of the concept (or perhaps because of it) professionalization has proven to be as slippery as any that social scientists have devised. Every attempt to define the essential characteristics of a profession runs into stubborn exceptions to the rule. Part of the problem arises from the history of the term. In its original meaning it referred to the "learned professions"—medicine, law, and the ministry—occupations requiring formal training and owning social prestige. As the nineteenth century progressed the term broadened to include other occupations based on technical or scientific principles, having a prescribed course of training and a restricted entry, engineers, architects, and various academic disciplines being prominent new examples.

The onward march of professionalization, perhaps above all else, denoted the specialization that was coming to mark all fields of knowledge. Professionalism served as a way to organize the explosion of knowledge and technique during the nineteenth century in the sciences and social sciences. Virtually every occupation, as old as farming or as new as chemical engineering, underwent ongoing revolutions in the state of their art. The last half of the nineteenth century witnessed an institutionalizing of these advances through the founding of universities, libraries, and research institutes, the compilation of indexes and reference tools, and the organization of learned and professional societies. The latter was particularly significant. A sure sign of emerging professional self-consciousness was the creation of a national organization that united practitioners from throughout the country and instilled a sense of occupational identity. The proliferation of these bodies through this era was phenomenal, in fields as diverse as the American Dermatological Society (1876), the American Forestry Association (1882), the Institute of Electrical Engineers (1884), and the American Mathematical Society (1888).

But professionalism was more than a means of structuring knowledge. It took on an ideological life of its own and became one of the guiding values of the modern age. The distinctively American style of professionalism diverged from its European pattern. Traditional American suspicions of self-proclaimed elites and demands for democratic access to professional inner sanctums broadened opportunity. Professions of all kinds became thoroughly middle class, and the middle class in turn became captives to the professional system. One historian has suggested that a culture of professionalism emerged, which shaped middle-class values and ambitions. Professionalism appealed through the promise of career advancement and social recognition. It exploited the valued resources of knowledge and technique for social and economic reward. If Americans lacked the rigid European sense of class distinction, through the professions they established their own social hierarchy based upon occupational skills. Professionalism provided a means for reconciling egalitarian values with a lust for social prestige.[1]

Professionalism—as a way of structuring knowledge, organizing the training and recruitment of skilled workers, regulating the quality of public services, and allocating the distribution of limited resources—is integral to American society. Though an organizational achievement of the first magnitude, critics have spotted flaws in the system, such as a frequent lack of healthy self-criticism and the subordination of public good to professional interest. But these reflections of the mid–twentieth century were unknown to actors of the 1890s. They saw on every hand examples of rising esteem and occupational self-control in those groups that achieved recognition as a profession. The lesson seemed clear, but implementation proved difficult, as the criteria of professionalism—formalized training, legal control of entry, standards of performance, for example—contradicted the nature of their art. In short, actors' successful appropriation of the designation "professional" would not be matched by equal success in making their occupation conform to its meaning.

* 1 *

The crusade for professional standing emanated from an occupation that had known hardship. Problems of social discrimination, frequent unemployment, infrequent pay, and destitution during illness and retirement abounded. "Indeed, none but an actor can conceive how much he may be made to suffer, and often most undeservedly," wrote William Wood, a premier theatrical manager in the first half of the nineteenth century, whose observation applies equally well to the later period. "He commences his career in doubt and terror; pursues it in constant anxiety; trembling at every step for the preservation of the little reputation which his toil and privations may have gained him, and which he feels may be destroyed by even the slightest and most unintentional offence; by public caprice; by successful or unworthy rivalry, the sufferings of impaired health, or of domestic affliction." [2]

The inability of actors to deal effectively with these problems may be explained in part by the theatre's decentralization. Through the first three quarters of the nineteenth century the American theatre had no dominating center, being composed of independent stock companies in major cities. Little opportunity existed to form national associations where actors could meet and talk over their mutual problems. Common experience was not enough to bind them together into a class. Players needed an institutional structure that would unite them.

The theatre's rather informal relationships also retarded organization. During the dominance of the actor-manager no rigid line separated actors from management, and differences about salary or work could be arbitrated informally. The easy camaraderie was not conducive to organization building. Moreover, actors were extremely mobile, moving often to different stock companies. This fluidity acted as a safety valve against discontent. If a manager proved tyrannical, young actors could, as Joseph Jefferson did, break away and start their own troupe. [3]

Finally, actors' failure to improve their social status and working conditions stemmed from low expectations. All who wore the sock and buskin realized that hardship was their lot, that impecuniousness was likely, and that they would not enjoy a settled life as respected members of a community. For the most part actors bore their grievances quietly, accepting adversity as little enough to pay for the joy of acting. "In what other profession or calling," pondered tragedian Frederick Warde, "would the people engaged in it go weeks without receiving their salary, or possibly only a portion of it, live at inferiour hotels, suffer hardships themselves and deprive their families of adequate support, in loyalty to a manager employer, who sometimes proves unworthy of their confidence and leaves them stranded in a strange city without funds?"[4] Indeed, few other lines of work command this kind of loyalty from their practitioners. And at times even actors must have asked themselves if it was worth the price.

As the nineteenth century progressed, changes in the theatre and in society caused players to reconsider this attitude of resignation that Warde observed. The evolving theatrical structure brought new relationships and problems, encouraging actors to seek the strength of collective action. Simultaneously, other emerging professions offered a model for actors in restructuring their occupation.

The first major change was the growth of the occupation. Theatre critic William Winter estimated that 150 professional actors (most of them British) were performing in America in 1800.[5] By 1850 the census reported 722 men who acted for a living. Ten years later the census, including actresses this time, counted 1,490 players; this count increased to 2,066 in 1870. Between 1870 and 1880 the number of actors and actresses more than doubled to 4,812 and doubled again to 9,728 by 1890.[6] These figures cannot be taken at face value, because the census included many others besides legitimate stage performers in the "actor" category.[7] The estimates of A. M. Palmer, a careful observer of the dramatic world, help refine the census record. Counting only those who presented what he called the higher form of drama, he found fewer than 800 in 1860, multiplying over fivefold to about 4,500 in 1888 and increasing to 7,000 by 1895.[8] The figures are rough, but they indicate the tremendous growth of the acting occupation, a growth congruent with new demands for commercial amusement in urbanizing America.

Not only were there more actors, but the theatre's centralization in New York brought them into more frequent contact with one another. Actors discussed the past season and upcoming plans in Union Square or at the theatrical agencies nearby. They compared the merits of their managers and the comforts or inconveniences of different theatres around the country. Although spending the greater share of the year touring, actors now renewed professional ties annually while in New York.

Actors were only the most visible sector of what was becoming an increasingly specialized industry. *Harry Miner's American Dramatic Directory*, published annually from 1884 through 1887, and Harrison Grey Fiske's *New York Mirror Annual and Directory for the Theatrical Season of 1884–'85* reflected the need for a guide to the expanding, diverse theatre. The two directories intended to expedite theatre business by printing the names of actors, agents, managers, authors, critics, and music directors. Specialization meant that the informal process of theatrical business was changing. Verbal agreements gave way to written contracts. The various theatrical trades became more insistent on their rights, and in the twenty years after 1880 actors, producers, stagehands, musical directors, and agents each formed associations.

The most direct encouragement for actors to unite came from the *New York Mirror*, a theatrical paper founded in 1879 by Ernest Harvier and Stephen Fiske. Theatrical newspapers proliferated in the nineteenth century, but none was so explicitly committed to upgrading the theatre as was the *Mirror* (in 1889 it became the *Dramatic Mirror*). It felt that the dramatic profession had been degraded by having its affairs treated alongside reports of prizefights, cocking mains, baseball games, quoit tournaments, and billiard matches in the other theatrical papers. The *Mirror* complained that the *New York Clipper's* brand of journalism dragged actors down to the level of the circus. It asked for actors' help in making it the official organ of the theatrical profession, "a paper to fitly represent their interests and one to which they might prudently and profitably give support."[9] The *Mirror* claimed to be read by the clergy and others who never before would look at a dramatic paper: "We have demonstrated that in theatricals as in everything else, respectability pays."[10]

Toward the end of its first year of publication the *Mirror* was taken over by a stagestruck eighteen year old, Harrison Grey Fiske. Descendent of an old and wealthy Massachusetts family (his father bought into the *Mirror* for him), Fiske brought uncompromising dramatic standards to the paper which he edited for more than thirty years. During these years Fiske was the conscience of the theatrical profession, nagging actors' collective faults and urging cooperative endeavor.

A final spur to professional self-consciousness came from changes across the footlights in the audience. Through the first half of the nineteenth century audiences exercised a kind of veto power over the stage. A substandard performance was met with hisses, catcalls, and boos. A violation of national honor was an especially serious sin. Joseph Jefferson recalled that as a boy in the early 1840s he was to sing the National Anthem in St. Louis. When he forgot the words the unforgiving audience hissed him off the stage.[11] A more familiar incident to students of American history was the rivalry of Edwin Forrest and William Charles Macready, which led to the Astor Place Riot of 1849. But audiences did not voice their opinion only when dissatisfied. If they enjoyed a particular act they would demand a repeat performance and often chose the between-act songs. On their favorite performers audiences bestowed frequent and enthusiastic applause. The exuberance of Jacksonian democracy carried into the theatres.

The active, participatory role of audiences in the first half of the nineteenth century quieted as the century wore on, replaced by a stricter sense of decorum. Several reasons account for the change.

First, as David Grimsted points out, after about 1850 one theatre could no longer appeal to all classes. Where earlier theatres had been attended by a mixed multitude of lower, middle, and upper classes viewing entertainments that ranged from opera and tragedy to melodrama, farce, and even spectacle, later American theatres specialized their offerings. Vaudeville, circus, burlesque, foreign language drama, minstrel shows, opera, and the legitimate drama each had its own stage and its own appeal to different classes of theatregoers.[12]

Documenting the social composition of legitimate theatre audiences poses a challenge because contemporary observers showed little curiosity about the matter and beyond a few general comments have not left the historian many clues. The best source comes from a study the Russell Sage Foundation made in 1910 of New York theatrical audiences as part of a wider investigation of commercial recreation.[13] The study surveyed New York's so-called standard theatres, the thirty first-class houses that showcased Broadway's stars. These charged fifty cents to two dollars for admission and attracted an estimated weekly attendance of 158,000. Of this group 51 percent were thought to be of the leisured class, 47 percent of the clerical or business class, and only 2 percent of the working class. These categories are vague and would be of no help whatsoever had not the study's author gone on to describe the first two classes in greater detail:

> There are the fashionable, the literary, and the professional sets. There is the body of middle-class persons of moderate means, who cannot go frequently to high-priced houses and rarely to the high-priced seats, but who take the theatre frankly and seriously as a means of enjoyment and education for themselves and their children. By contrast follows the "sporty" set, numerically not large, but important to theatrical managers because it spends money freely. . . . Finally, we may name the "out-of-towners", the host of bourgeois visitors to the metropolis. This class is of particular significance. A family in New York for only a short stay will attend the theatre three or four times as often as will the average resident.[14]

Broadway theatres and the first-class touring companies attracted the most prosperous audiences, but as the survey showed they were not restricted to the elite. The popular-priced stock companies that appeared in virtually every American city by the turn of the century drew upon a more modest middle-class clientele. With their budget prices and fare of wholesome entertainment, stock companies attracted family audiences. Both first-class and popular-priced theatres served an essentially middle-class audience, which brought with it to the playhouse attitudes of restraint and order.

Also contributing to a more quiescent audience was the increasing number of women attending the theatre. In the first half of the century women comprised far less than half the audience, and no self-respecting woman would have been found in the gallery, which was a haunt of prostitutes. Theatres began offering matinee performances in the 1850s, catering to the family trade, and for the first time women began attending the theatre in large numbers and sitting in all parts of the theatre. By the early twentieth century women had become a large and important part of the audience. The Russell Sage survey estimated that 45 percent of the audience at New York's better theatres were women. Their presence, true to Victorian dictates, served as a refining force in the theatre.

A third development that may have influenced audience behavior was a change in stage design. The typical stage from the eighteenth through the middle of the nineteenth century featured a large apron projecting well beyond the proscenium arch, which allowed actors to move into the midst of the audience. The great tragedians strutted about the apron declaiming their best speeches. But if the close contact magnified the players' power, it also rendered them more vulnerable to the audience. The stage apron engendered a familiarity that was occasionally turned against the player. As scenic realism progressed through the century the apron was reduced in size until it disappeared during the 1860s, replaced by the boxlike proscenium-frame stage. The actor receded from the audience behind the proscenium arch. A sense of intimacy was lost, but the player gained new authority over his audience. Actors appeared to be a part of the scenic environment surrounding them, in another world from that of the audience and beyond their control. Audiences became more passive in the last decades of the nineteenth century; no longer was there the continual distractions of whispering or eating, rarely was heard a hiss or boo. By the turn of the century only applause and laughter at the appropriate moments were acceptable activities.[15] The actor had become the professional dispenser of entertainment, delivering his service with the expectation that the audience would not interfere, except to express approval.

*   *   *

Strengthened in number, centralized in location, exhorted by their trade journal, and emboldened by their stage authority, actors readied themselves to scale the professional heights. It would not be a unified assault. Only a minority of actors would in fact take part. As in all social movements it would be an activist faction that organized reform, entreating and cajoling fellow players to support professional uplift. No evident similarities linked the leaders; featured players and stars, comedians and tragedians, theatre managers and actor-managers were involved. Their only common feature was a sensitivity to actors' problems and a shared vison of a professional future. To them it was not enough that the vernacular termed them professionals (everyone in nineteenth-century America understood that a person "in the profession" was an actor). This loose usage lacked the prestige accorded other professions, and only by restructuring their occupation according to the accepted definition of professionalism would actors share this esteem.

*   2   *

The campaign began with an effort to remove the profession's stigma of indifference toward the poverty that afflicted many of its members. This was accomplished through the establishment of a theatrical charity. At a time when many charity organizations were religiously affiliated, actors were often excluded from their beneficences. While many besides actors suffered poverty, the newspapers' penchant for reporting that retired players were living or dying in neglect contributed to acting's poor reputation. An example was Eliza Newton. Once a well-known actress at the Olympic Theatre in New York, she remained unburied for a week after her death because funds could not be collected for a decent funeral. During that week the daily newspapers published appeals to actors for funds and chastised the profession for its unconcern.[16] Incidents such as this added ammunition to the guns of antistage moralists.

Benefit performances had been the traditional way of aiding indigents. John Brougham, for example, an eminently popular tragedian from the 1840s through the 1870s fell into poverty in old age. A benefit in 1878 netted $10,000, which was invested in an annuity for him.[17] When Ben Porter was murdered on tour in Texas in 1879, benefits provided generously for his widow and children.[18]

And even after the Actors' Fund was functioning, the impecuniousness of a retired Lester Wallack, the final member of one of England and America's illustrious stage families, called forth the efforts of the theatre's grandest names—Edwin Booth, Lawrence Barrett, Joseph Jefferson, Frank Mayo, John Gilbert, Helena Modjeska, and Rose Coghlan—in an 1888 benefit performance of *Hamlet*.[19] But for the lesser lights and for those who did not die in a spectacular shooting, infirmity and age often brought neglect.

Supplementing the benefits were several theatrical benevolent associations. The first was the General Theatrical Fund, began in Philadelphia in 1829, and largely underwritten by the great Edwin Forrest. The fund stagnated as the years went by, and the need for a more active association resulted in the establishment of the American Dramatic Fund Association in New York in 1848. It resembled many other benevolent and life insurance societies of the day. Members subscribed annual dues to the fund, augmented by public benefit performances. Actors, singers, dancers, orchestra leaders, scene painters, and carpenters among others were eligible for membership.[20] Though the fund operated for forty years its limited resources could never make more than a dent in the huge need. The aforementioned Actors' Order of Friendship carried on a similar work. Founded in 1849, the society prospered and by 1882 it enjoyed an annual income of $2,500. Yet because membership was limited to two hundred, its potential for extensive aid also remained small.[21]

The need for a broader application to the problem of theatrical poverty was manifested in the case of Harry Bascomb. Bascomb, an unemployed veteran of the Boston Museum Stock Company, walked from New York to Boston the winter of 1882 seeking a job. On the way he spent a bitterly cold night in a barn. Awaking in the morning he discovered his feet had frozen, necessitating amputation. Because he was poor he had to be cared for at the charity ward of a hospital. Once again the newspapers took up the theme of actors neglecting one of their own.[22]

Although accused of ignoring suffering in their own ranks, actors had fostered goodwill through their benefits for various public needs. Actors took pride in their reputation for public service. But the *Mirror* repeatedly pointed out that players needed to do more for themselves. While Harry Bascomb lay in a charity ward, New York's Fifth Avenue Theatre gave a benefit for the local Throat Hospital. At least, the *Mirror* argued, provision should have been made for the establishment of an actor's bed. And two years earlier, when Dion Boucicault proposed that all theatres hold a St. Patrick's Day Irish relief benefit, the *Mirror* objected:

We would not do anything to check the torrent of benevolence . . . but we should like to check the general inclination to demand help from the theatres when ANYBODY needs relief. The theatres have their own good work to do and they have no chance to do it properly because of the incessant requirements of these outside charities. Since the newspapers have taken up the task of supplying Ireland with funds, let them carry it out and let all of us help them to the fullest extent of our means, reserving the theatrical channel for another occasion.[23]

Fiske went on to outline his plan for a "theatrical Sinking Fund." Every manager throughout the country could give one benefit a year at his theatre. The money would be entrusted to a responsible New York manager such as A. M. Palmer. By this plan a fund would be raised "that would do more to relieve, elevate and strengthen the profession than any other scheme which has ever been devised." The *Mirror* predicted that within five years every agreement and contract in the theatrical business would donate one day's rent or salary to the Sinking Fund.[24]

It took two years of campaigning before Fiske's idea reached fruition. A number of actors had promised to get the ball rolling by playing a benefit, but none would actually take the initiative. None, until the shapely Fanny Davenport wrote from St. Louis that she would love to "begin the good work," and J. K. ("Fritz") Emmett, the German dialect comedian, promised a benefit when he played in New Orleans. Meanwhile, the groundwork for the fund was laid at a meeting of Brooklyn and New York managers in the Morton House on March 2, 1882, who acknowledged that the numerous cases of destitution coming to public attention demanded a dramatic charity. They set April 3 as the benefit performance date for New York and Brooklyn theatres.

But one New York theatre jumped the gun and presented the first in an extremely colorful tradition of Actors' Fund benefits. Haverly's 14th Street Theatre hosted M. B. Curtis in a new play, *Sam'l of Posen*, a play notable for introducing the first sympathetic portrayal of a Jewish stage character. The audience of stage and society luminaries became a regular feature of Actors' Fund benefits. That same day, March 12, the theatre managers met again, officially adopting the name Actors' Fund of America (AF) and outlining its principles of operation.[25] A similar institution was established in England in 1882, the Actors' Benevolent Fund, where annually on "Actors' Saturday" players donated their services in a benefit.[26]

Managers and actor-managers formed the backbone of the

AF. The seventeen initial trustees included actors Lester Wallack (who became the first president), Edwin Booth, Joseph Jefferson, and managers Henry Abbey, Henry Miner, P. T. Barnum, and A. M. Palmer. Such an ambitious cooperative venture, uncharacteristic of a group noted for its hardheaded competitive ways, calls for explanation. There was, certainly, a genuine altruism tied to a growing concern for the professional esteem of the stage. But another motive was operative as well, the desire to rationalize relief. Rather than the irregular benefits that disrupted business, benefit performances would be given at specified times and a central agency would dispense aid based on proven need. Furthermore, administration of the Fund would be safely in the hands of the theatre's businessmen.

The April 3 benefit fulfilled all expectation. Matinee performances at sixteen theatres netted over $17,000. Another $10,000 came in through the munificence of James Gordon Bennett, editor of the *New York Herald*. Altogether by April 18, the AF added $34,596 to its coffers. The *Mirror* jubilently declared that "the astonishing success of the Actors' Fund had proved the existence of a striking ESPRIT DE CORPS among the profession."[27]

The AF differed from the other theatrical benevolent societies in that it offered aid to all theatrical workers, not just those who paid dues. Its umbrella covered vaudevillians and stagehands as well as dramatic performers. To help maintain the player's dignity matters of aid were kept confidential. In its first year the fund aided over 400 theatrical workers throughout the country in amounts ranging from seven to two hundred dollars. It buried 32 and helped 12 stranded actors back to New York. Over the first decade of operation the fund spent $163,899 for burials, relief, medicines, and hospital charges; it afforded direct relief to 3,071 and buried 572.[28]

The AF offered social amenities to the profession as well. A reading room at fund headquarters, established with the help of Brander Matthews, Columbia's professor of dramatic literature, was frequented. Less successful was an actors' employment agency. Planned to be self-supporting through fees from those it placed, it eventually had to close. Another AF extension, the Ladies Hospital Committee, arranged visits by leading ladies of the stage to invalid actresses, bringing them books and food.[29]

A final fund operation took longer to initiate: a home for aged players. The profession already had one such institution, the Edwin Forrest Home in Philadelphia. Forrest left the lion's share of his fortune to the home, accompanied by strict instructions as to its administration.[30] But it accommodated a mere handful of people. Not only was its scope limited but the *Mirror* claimed its directors were operating the home negligently. There were frequent reports of financial mismanagement. Complaints of indifference and arrogance toward players by the directors multiplied. Harry Bascomb was refused admittance to the Forrest Home, reportedly because of his drinking, and consequently had to enter an almshouse.[31]

The Actors' Fund's third president, A. M. Palmer, initiated the idea of an actors' home in 1897, and his successor, Louis Aldrich, took it up and saw it through to completion. Since the fund supported forty-eight actors in other institutions it seemed logical to create a home just for actors. The *New York Herald* spearheaded a fund-raising drive that netted $50,000 in less than three weeks. A Staten Island country estate was purchased, and in 1902 the Actors' Fund Home opened its doors. Over the years it housed such luminaries as Fanny Janauschek, Rose Eytinge, Fay Templeton, Effie Shannon, and Nance O'Neill, actresses capable of earning a star's salary but incapable of saving it.[32]

Despite these accomplishments, the AF experienced its share of troubles. Some actors chafed at the managers' control of the fund. Indeed, save for W. J. Florence, after 1885 none of the original stars remained as trustees, and from 1885 to 1900 only three performers sat on the board for any length of time: DeWolfe Hopper, F. F. Mackay, and Louis Aldrich, who served as president from 1897 to 1901.[33] While planning her May 10 benefit Fanny Davenport wrote to the *Mirror* from Pittsburgh: "All the profession should have a vote as to what shall be done. They were the cause of the effect, and a committee of those might be chosen by their votes to decide all important questions."[34] But the advisability of democratic control was called into question at the fund's annual meeting in 1884. All rules of procedure were violated, bylaws were ignored, and "business was impeded by one or two old-time windbags who, with absurd pomposity, talked nonsense by the yard."[35] No doubt the fund was safer in the hands of business-wise managers.

Players' resentment reflected the widening gap between themselves and management. Many players felt that managers belonged to a different guild, with interests adverse to theirs. Still, the differences did not keep actors from taking pride in the organization, and later conflicts during the founding of Actors' Equity made the fund appear a glorious experiment in actor and manager cooperation. At the organization's seventh anniversary celebration in 1888, a "general shaking of hands and exchanges of pleasant salutations between actors, actresses, managers and playwrights took place as gave the event the flavor of a mammoth family reunion." A. M. Palmer hoped the event signified that actors were learning "the power there is in professional unity."[36]

A more serious difficulty for the AF was establishing an adequate endowment, a problem not solved until 1922. Most actors neglected to pay either the annual dues of two dollars or the lifetime membership of fifty. Additionally, by 1889 the fund counted only 707 members out of a profession numbering at least ten times that. Of the 681 applications for relief granted in 1899, only 38 were from dues-paying members. This neglect should not be laid to apathy on the players' part, but rather to another human failing. Since the fund offered aid to all there was little incentive for joining. To make up for the lack, other means of fund raising were tried: a 10 percent levy on complimentary tickets issued to actors, which never succeeded; and allocation of half the annual fifty-dollar licensing fee for New York theatres, which provided steady income until 1900 when it was discontinued.[37] But the backbone of AF support came from benefit performances and fund fairs. The first two annual benefits in 1882 and 1883 presented special performances of current plays. Although they were popular, a better idea, some thought, was to put on extra-special programs. A new formula was tried, a kind of super vaudeville, where stars performed excerpts from the plays and musicals they had made famous. An example of the kind of talent the benefits attracted can be seen in the 1887 performance of the Grand Opera House. Audiences were treated to an act from Edward Harrigan's *Pete*, the Lew Dockstader Minstrels, Henry Irving in a scene from *Jingle*, an excerpt from *The Rivals* with Joseph Jefferson and John Drew, and to climax, DeWolf Hopper and the beautiful Mrs. James Brown Potter in a series of surprise "turns."[38]

More extravagant was the Actors' Fund Fair of 1892. On the floor of Madison Square Garden Stanford White designed a village, eclectic in the extreme, combining Grecian columns, a Romanesque castle, a Tudor manor house, a huge maypole, and other exotic offerings that delighted the public for six days. There were booths displaying merchandise tended by the leading ladies of the stage and sideshows exhibiting circus and vaudeville acts. A souvenir program filled with pictures of the theatre's stars proved to be one of the most popular items. Altogether the fair brought in $163,000, making it the most profitable benefit the fund held.[39] The AF's new wealth was depleted the next year when the depression of 1893 sent relief applications skyrocketing and actors flocked to New York in the vain hope of finding work. Although it could not help everyone, the AF silenced critics who accused the stage of indifference toward its members. Establishment of the Actors' Fund marked the beginning of a tangible effort at self-advancement. If it was not directly aimed at the broader issues of professionalization, the fund nonetheless signaled actors to be a group committed to self-help and professional pride.

* 3 *

More directly tied to the formulation of a true acting profession were attempts to formalize instruction. During the late nineteenth century preparation for skilled occupations came to mean institutionalized training. Schools of business, pharmacy, engineering, law, and medicine proliferated; technical and vocational schools of many types flourished; and in the arts, schools of music and art found a climate congenial to growth either as independent entities or as part of a university. In every case the schools followed a technical or scientific approach to their subject. They stressed technical proficiency and a theoretical understanding of their field, usually incorporating a standard set of exercises to develop skills.[40] The ideal of systematic professional training for all practitioners dominated virtually all learned occupations and drove out the remnants of an earlier craft system. This trend, as ineluctable as any in modern life, swept along actors with the others. But actors, strongly rooted in their traditions, were less easily convinced of its virtues.

The time-honored method of training young actors had been through the stock companies. This was apprenticeship in its purest form. Neophytes at the Boston Museum (the stock company about which we know the most) played an amazing number and variety of roles. By tasting a bit of everything from low comedy to romance to tragedy beginners would find the line of business that suited them. Instruction came informally from veteran performers or the stage manager as the situation warranted. Since the bill changed nightly there was little opportunity for deep reflection over a role's psychology. Learning one's lines and cues was challenge enough. The stock system of training worked adequately for the rather undemanding standards of the day. It was intrinsically conservative, as techniques passed on nearly unchanged from generation to generation. Though it often lent itself to wooden performances, audiences did not mind greatly, as local stock companies increasingly existed to feed lines to the visiting star.[41]

Stock companies underwent a change from the 1870s onward, adopting longer runs. This allowed for greater study of parts and a refinement of acting. Beginners could now expect more thorough instruction in the finer points of performance, particularly if they were fortunate enough to study under the dean of stock-company managers, Augustin Daly. Daly's company, housed first on Fifth Avenue and then after 1877 at 30th and Broadway, was one of New York's most prominent, a regular stop for tourists to Gotham. It also was the greatest stock company school for actors America has known. Daly, sitting five rows back in the theatre, scrutinized his rehearsing cast with an unerring eye, demanding rereadings until the act suited his taste. His martinet manner drove off some, but his survivors included many future stars: Clara Morris, Otis Skinner, Fanny Davenport, and Henry Miller, to name only a few.[42]

By 1880, however, the traditional stock company was already an endangered institution. Though it would continue in the form of popular-priced stock, the future belonged to emergent combination companies. But who would train the legion of actors needed to fill the scores of combinations taking to the road every fall? Not the managers of the combinations, for they were preoccupied with the details of booking and travel. They expected to hire performers already versed in their trade. This expectation proved unrealistic. The number of qualified actors simply did not keep up with the demand, leading to the forming of the touring "snaps" (fly-by-night companies with shoestring budgets), which featured actors for whom the label amateur might have been generous. Already by 1881 the *New York Clipper* complained that the combination system "offers no school of progress to the young actor, but tends, on the contrary, to dwarf his facilities and belittle his art."[43]

At the same time that the craft system's decline created a need for alternative actor training, the pervasive ideology of professionalism compelled consideration of systematized instruction. As early as 1879 *The Illustrated Dramatic Weekly* called on universities to train actors, just as they did lawyers and doctors.[44] And the *Dramatic Mirror*, which initially showed uncharacteristic reserve about professional training, displayed wholehearted conversion in an 1895 editorial:

> The theatre is an institution in which exact knowledge is as necessary as it is in other institutions. This profession can make no better headway without schools of instruction than can the profession of the law, or that of medicine, or that of painting. In fact, the transition from the old system to a new one will involve just such formality, if the new one is to be permanently successful and to maintain dignity.[45]

The early acting schools issued from the elocutionary tradition of voice instruction. Elocution—the science of speech and declamation—played an important part in a nineteenth-century culture that relied so much on the spoken word. Especially in the theatre of early and mid-nineteenth-century America, before the dazzling visual effects of the later century were seen, did speech dominate. Declamatory acting necessitated strong vocal projection, clear articulation, and pronounced inflection. Instructors of the elocutionary art were many, most of them second-rate itinerants who combined teaching with public readings; others, like James Rush, were notable contributors to the science.[46] Actors and actors-to-be formed an important clientele for elocutionists. Tragedians Edwin Forrest and James E. Murdoch studied under elocutionist Lemuel G. White, and Mary Anderson worked with George Vandenhoff, to mention just a few. In the final decades of the century prominent elocutionists, such as Lewis Baxter Monroe, J. M. Shoemaker, S. S. Curry, and Joseph Frobisher, began opening schools of speech, providing systematic training to actors and others who felt the need.[47]

But schools of speech were not acting schools. Focusing only on voice and gesture, they ignored the other aspects of production. The man who fused elocution to formal acting instruction was Steele MacKaye. Not only the pioneering figure in thespic education, MacKaye also stands as one of the true geniuses of the American theatre—as actor, playwright, director, and inventor of stage machinery. MacKaye was also the great American disciple of François Delsarte's system of philosophical elocution. In MacKaye's translation Delsartian techniques became a series of "harmonic gymnastics" intended to impart graceful movement and expressive characterization to actors. MacKaye taught informally while a stage manager, then in 1877 launched his School of Expression in New York. He purposed, through the Delsartian method, to instill a "thorough discipline in practical Pantomime, Stage Business, and Vocal Gymnastics," with the ultimate aim of endowing the actor with complete "spontaneity." That MacKaye's claims were not idle was attested to by John McCullough, already an accomplished player of tragic roles, who stated that MacKaye "has taught me more in three months than I could have learned otherwise in twenty years."[48]

The School of Expression was short-lived. But it prepared the way for another, more enduring acting school, the Lyceum Theatre, founded in 1884. Here again, MacKaye led out, though his early departure left the Lyceum's operation in the hands of the other important pioneer of acting instruction, Franklin Sargent. The Lyceum Theatre School combined the functions of stock company and school, maintaining a professional company that put on plays in its own theatre, and also having a host of distinguished instructors (including William Seymour and noted elocutionist Alfred Ayres) to drill members in the Delsartian method. The curriculum included stage business and deportment, pantomime, vocal expression, and character study. The school experienced some heavy weather at first: student complaints, faculty firings, and finally a financial scandal that drove MacKaye from the school. But by 1886 Sargent headed up a reorganized and renamed institution, the American Academy of Dramatic Arts, which still operates.[49]

The founding of the Lyceum was symptomatic of a larger movement to establish acting schools in major cities. New York, the theatrical center, naturally had the most. The Empire Theatre Dramatic School, the McKee Rankin School of Acting, Proctor's School of Acting, and the Stanhope-Wheatcroft Dramatic School were among the many founded between 1884 and 1900. But Chicago, Boston, Philadelphia, Cincinnati, and St. Louis also boasted conservatories. In many cases such former players as D. P. Bowers or Rose Eytinge opened them, and other notables, such as David Belasco and May Robson, taught in them. The proliferation of acting schools bespoke the breakdown of stock as an entree to the stage as well as the continuing large numbers of people who aspired to the stage.[50] At Sargent's American Academy of Dramatic Arts, 370 people applied for just 23 openings in 1887; by 1898, 2,480 sought acceptance. Entrants averaged twenty-one years of age and many had had some experience, if only on the amateur boards. The Academy's graduation roster showed that it attracted students from all parts of the country.[51]

Instructional content varied from school to school. A number of them remained elocutionary strongholds, particularly of the Delsartian persuasion. S. S. Curry's School of Expression in Boston shunned makeup, costuming, and stage business, focusing solely on Delsartian aesthetic gymnastics and vocal training. But the trend in most schools was clearly toward a broadening of the curricula and elevating other aspects of technique to a par with elocution. The American Academy of Dramatic Arts probably offered the most complete course of study. A full program there lasted two years (though most students contented themselves with one), with terms running from October to May. Sargent had a staff that by 1898 had grown to twenty-four teachers and six lecturers, many of them stage veterans.[52] The school's commitment to systematic instruction, a hallmark of a profession, was evident from the first issue of its *Dramatic Studies*: "Trained knowledge and skill are the power of the true professional which distinguishes him from the amateur. Body and voice are the actor's instruments. Mechanical expertness in playing upon these instruments must precede the art of acting. The one thing a dramatic school can do thoroughly is to cultivate proper technical habits." [53]

Coursework concentrated on technical aspects of acting, correcting bodily movement and expression and striving for poised, controlled movement of hands, arms, legs, and face. Students analyzed the voice and production of sound. They had exercises to improve resonance and articulation. Basic acting skills were stressed: stage business, pantomime, fencing, French, dialects, dancing, and singing. Pantomime study incorporated the basic Delsartian idea of liberating inner feelings. Instructors criticized any lack of sincerity or concentration. Stage business, which for a time was taught by David Belasco, covered the mechanics of movement on stage, such as entrances and crossings. Particularly interesting were the "life study" courses. Students went out during the day to observe people. They picked a subject, examined him closely, then in class mimicked his gestures, facial expressions, and speech. The "life study" exercise illustrated the replacement of traditional acting techniques by an imitation of life itself. [54]

Students who returned for a second year concentrated on play production. The senior class was organized into a stock company, giving students a taste of actual stage discipline. During the latter half of the year a company of students was sent out to small towns, usually playing classic drama such as *Elektra* or *Antigone*, occasionally doing some Ibsen. Second-year students were also expected to take bit parts in commercial plays. This was facilitated when the academy and the Empire Theatre Dramatic School merged in 1897. Students then had access to the many Charles Frohman productions at the Empire Theatre, some in important understudy roles. [55]

In its first twenty years, 1884 to 1903, the academy graduated 278 people, 161 of whom were women. It counted among its alumni such future stars as Ida Conquest, Elsie Lombard, Robert Tabor, Blanche Walsh, George Fawcett, Alice Fisher, and George Foster Platt. Graduation ceremonies were august occasions, with eminent persons of the theatre, such as Bronson Howard, Joseph Jefferson, and Richard Mansfield, delivering addresses on the actor's art and the actor's reponsibility. To the most talented graduate went the gold medal of the Belasco Prize, established by Belasco himself. The academy initially had trouble finding positions for its graduates. Students grumbled that they were lured to the school by the promise of jobs that did not materialize. By 1899, however, Sargent boasted that the school could not fill all the positions offered by managers. The school became a talent pool for Charles Frohman productions, and Sargent attempted to keep the best in the Frohman fold. On at least one occasion, though, David Belasco stole the prime talent by offering starting salaries of forty to fifty dollars a week.[56] The competition for acting school trainees suggests that the school turned out a worthy product.

Among actors themselves, however, there lingered skepticism about the new route to the stage. In part, this reflected the tradition-bound nature of their calling. The legendary performances of Lear, Hamlet, and other classic characters set the standard by which later interpretations were measured. Edwin Booth styled himself after his father, and Edwin Forrest copied Edmund Kean. To a generation accustomed to apprenticeship as the only conceivable means of learning the trade, acting schools seemed patently ridiculous. Players' caustic remarks about the new schools filled newspapers and magazines through the 1880s and '90s. "Training must be essentially practical," remarked Lawrence Barrett in a typical judgment. "No School of Elocution, no training outside the theatre can I regard as valuable."[57] Players also complained that the schools flooded an already overcrowded field with novices willing to underbid veterans, exacerbating unemployment.[58] Elocutionists as well griped that acting schools were graduating a generation of performers unskilled in vocal delivery. Alfred Ayres, the shrillest of the traditionalists, waged war on those teachers and actors who in his mind were lowering standards, keeping a two-year vigil on the front row of Broadway theatres, notebook in hand, recording verbal miscues by players which were then published in the *Dramatic Mirror*. But it was a losing battle. The onset of realism rendered the declamatory style obsolete. Preparation for the stage would mean less the exercise of the lungs than the attention to the multiple facets of performance, to which would be added in the twentieth century introspective studies of the character to be portrayed.

But if the traditionalists lost the battle over elocution, they at least gained a draw in the war over actor training. Though acting schools had by 1900 become a well-used path to the stage, they did not attain the monopoly on training that other professional schools achieved. The resurgent popular-priced stock companies opened up new oportunities for stage training within the older craft tradition. Their rigorous schedule and frequent change of bill instilled a stage savvy that many actors still felt no school could teach. Some players took a tour of duty in stock to sharpen their skills. Jane Cowl was a Belasco leading lady when in 1909 she decided to leave New York and join the Hudson Theatre Stock Company in Union Hill, New Jersey. Her two seasons there enhanced her acting and led to critically acclaimed performances on Broadway.[59] Popular-priced stock also served as a kind of farm system for the New York touring companies. Managers kept their eye open for precocious players in the provinces. Alfred Lunt, Grace George, Francis Starr, Edward G. Robinson, Fay Bainter, Laura Hope Crews, Warner Baxter, and Pauline Lord were just a few of the many actors who learned their trade in stock. Thus, in the first two decades of the twentieth century dramatic training was divided between the traditional and the new, stock companies and acting schools. Most likely, through the 1920s at least (after which time they declined precipitously) stock companies were more important in training Broadway performers than acting schools. Not until the mid-1920s did drama departments become an accepted part of university curriculum and give evidence that the professionalizing impulse was still strong.

Even then, the commercial theatre kept its distance from the educational establishment. As recently as the 1960s theatre educators decried the split between the educational and professional theatres, complaining that there was no systematic preparatory training for the professional actor.[60] The mandatory training that characterizes modern professions was never realized in acting, and in that failure lay a compromise to claims of professional standing. The reason for the failure, in part, resided in the loose structure of the theatre; opportunities for breaking into show business could come in many ways and on many levels, and the theatre had no central authority to check credentials. It also bespoke a pervasive conservatism that resisted full embrace of a new system. Most important, though, the limited success of institutionalized training resulted from the nature of acting itself, a vocation grounded in distinctiveness and nonconformity. Success on the stage was not measured by technical knowledge but by the degree to which the player could establish that magical relationship between himself and the audience. No course of study, no academic degree could confer what in the final reckoning is a gift.

* 4 *

The keystone of the drive for professionalization was the establishment of a professional association. Such an organization clearly was vital both for engendering group self-consciousness and channeling it along constructive lines. "If the player's art and the player's dignity have halted in the march," Fiske's *Dramatic Mirror* stated, "it has been largely due to the lack of artistic fellowship, and the absence of just such associations as that which has given other professions the power to improve themselves."[61] The logic of Fiske's reasoning found tangible application in the late fall of 1892 when four of the day's preeminent tragedians—Wilson Barrett, James O'Neill, Frederick Warde, and Louis James—proposed an actors' convention, the first of what would hopefully be annual gatherings to discuss mutual problems.

It took another year and the impact of a serious depression to get the wheels moving. In the winter of 1893–94, with the theatre feeling the ripples of a nationwide depression, a group of actors met to consider collective action. Out of this meeting came the Actors' Society of America (ASA).[62] Its founders—F. F. Mackay, William Courtleigh, George McIntyre, and Israel Washburn—were not stars, but solid journeymen performers.[63] Mackay was the most noteworthy, a man whose versatile career began in the 1850s. He had acted with the redoubtable Mrs. Drew at the Arch Street Theatre and managed Philadelphia's Chestnut Street Theatre for three years. Mackay could handle all types of roles and was an accomplished dialectician. He distinguished himself after leaving the stage as a teacher and writer on the art of acting.[64]

The ASA grew slowly at first, attracting only a hundred members its first year. But in the spring of 1896 membership shot up to six hundred, and formal organization took place in May. The only qualification for membership was three years' stage experience (though foreign players had a six-month American residency requirement). By 1904 membership reached 1,770. Some of the stage's biggest names belonged: Mrs. Fiske, James K. Hackett, Dustin Farnum, Maxine Elliott, Virginia Harned, and Henry Miller. It survived a scandal in 1897 when John Malone was forced to resign as president following accusations of self-aggrandizement. The society also had to overcome fears among many players that membership meant unionization. "This is not a trades union," the *Actors' Society Monthly Bulletin* explained, "but a professional association which aims to assume such magnitude as to make membership in the association tantamount with membership in the profession."[65] The spector of unionism would similarly hang over organizers of Actors' Equity in the next decade and impede their work.

The Society stated its purposes broadly as seeking to "improve the actor's calling by artistic, dramatic, economic, social, mutual benefit and financial means."[66] This rhetoric can be reduced to two essential goals of the organization: first, creation of a professional image for actors; and second, attention to very practical issues that vexed players in their work. The ASA's attempt to polish a public image and confidently assume a professional stature fits the pattern often followed by striving occupations. At its founding it issued two resolutions expounding actors' social and professional virtues. They declared acting to be a "fine art," rebutting a common inference that it was inferior to the established arts of music, literature, painting, and sculpture. The resolutions also asserted that the "practice of acting is an entirely honorable profession," one "worthy of the support of the best social influence." Responding to lingering prejudices toward amusements, the ASA also resolved that all public amusements that "entertain and do not demoralize are legitimate." [67] In short, the ASA began its work by defending players' honor against the still-frequent charges of disrepute. Recognizing the increasing importance of entertainment in American life, it entreated the public for a corresponding respect toward its providers.

Hortatory pronouncements would not change reality, however, and the ASA did not shrink from tackling some long-standing problems plaguing actors. The chief thorn in the actor's side was incompetent and sometimes double-dealing managers. With the proliferation of touring companies in the 1880s and 1890s came the "snaps." Ambitious managers lured actors with promises of fat salaries, and since few players could afford to turn down an offer, even a chancy one, they signed with managers of dubious reputation. Members of Wallack's Company, for example, agreed to tour California under the tutelage of Tom Maguire, a manager who had stranded the Leavitt Company, Nat Goodwin's Company, and others.[68] Frequently a troupe would leave New York and begin its tour, box-office receipts would slump, and the manager not only could not pay his company, but frequently did not have enough funds to give them train fare back to New York. Actors were stranded all over the country. On one occasion manager Charles Parsloe wanted his actors to pay their train fares from Cleveland to New York for a two-week layoff while he attended to personal business. Julius Kahn, a member of the troupe, stood up to Parsloe and forced him to pay the fares; but Kahn observed that "actors are too often afraid to assert their rights. They seem to lack moral stamina to stand up before a manager and speak out their grievances." [69] A leitmotif running through theatrical fiction was the actor's dilemma when the "snap" disbanded on the road. The all-too-real frequency of this occurrence led to ASA bylaws stating that if a player's salary fell two weeks in arrears he should quit the company and apply to the society's secretary, who would furnish his train fare home.

In contrast to the Actors' Fund show of cooperation between actors and managers, the ASA admitted only players. Yet it denied any adversary relationship between the two. "The interests of the managers and actors are the same," it stated. "There is no cause for antagonism in seeking to arrange business relations between actor and manager upon principle of equity."[70] The disparity between practice and rhetoric revealed a realistic appraisal of the divisions between the two combined with an idealized hope for change. The ASA worked toward a resolution of player-manager conflicts in several ways. It encouraged actors to contract with reliable managers by publishing a list of those guilty of nonpayment to players and advising members to avoid them. It also attempted to end the frequent and well-publicized lawsuits between actors and managers by setting up an arbitration board. Actors, who had been suspicious of the managers' arbitration league in the early 1890s, now found managers just as leery of this proposal. A number of disputes, however, were adjudicated in the following years. Finally, the ASA sought legal protection through a bill introduced to the New York legislature which would have established sanctions against those who defrauded actors. Managers would be fined not less than $250 or sentenced up to one year in prison for either failing to pay actors or stranding them on tour.[71] Like most of the ASA's legislative initiatives, this one died in Albany.

The Actors' Society tried to be evenhanded toward actors and management alike and was not above punishing those who violated their contracts. It suspended William Pascoe when he broke his contract with M. J. Jacobs, manager of Newark's Columbia Theatre. Pascoe had left the company on only one day's notice, unhappy that his wife had been fired. The society recommended that Pascoe pay Jacobs a $194 reimbursement. Members were occasionally suspended from the society for appearing onstage intoxicated.[72] But lacking coercive authority over even its members (apart from threats to disfellowship from the society), the ASA could only resort to moral suasion in seeking to uphold its standards.

The society also set out to reform theatrical employment agencies. Few things in the player's life equaled the humiliation of trudging from agency to agency, seeking a job. Minor players, like pawns, were ordered about at the whim of agents and managers. Plainly incompatible with pretensions to professional standing, this situation prompted the ASA to organize its own agency, one that would show no partiality and charge only enough to pay expenses. The agency, after working through a controversy over its availability to non-ASA members, became an established if small concern. But like the Actors' Fund employment agency, it proved unable to compete with private agencies and eventually closed.[73]

A more ominous issue for the theatre as a whole was the endemic play piracy. In the early nineteenth century stars would often memorize their own lines and give the supporting stock company their cues. This prevented rivals from stealing the precious dramatic vehicle. As published plays assumed greater importance, copyright laws were enacted for their protection. The Copyright Act of 1865 offered a measure of protection, but it had a major loophole: Only titles could be protected. Identical plays under different titles escaped the law. A popular production might spawn several unauthorized imitators. James Herne's *Hearts of Oak* (which itself smacked suspiciously of an earlier British play, *The Mariner's Compass*), inspired another version called *Oaken Hearts*.[74] Gilbert and Sullivan's *H. M. S. Pinafore* captivated America in 1879 as few plays have; yet because of no international copyright law most *Pinafore* shows paid no royalties, and the authors saw little of the money. Play piracy was especially common among the popular-priced companies, who by avoiding royalties could offer budget entertainment. Unscrupulous brokers traded in pirated manuscripts. Alexander Byers of the Chicago Manuscript Company sent stenographers to theatres to record dialogue and stage business. These were mimeographed and sold at a fraction of royalty costs.[75]

Such rank thievery reflected poorly on the theatrical profession, and the ASA determined to end it. Members were forbidden to appear in pirated versions of plays, and it disciplined four offending members by suspensions in 1902.[76] By itself, however, the ASA could hardly hope to solve the problem. Actors who joined were those most concerned about professional ethics and the ones least likely to act in a stolen play. Those who did not belong, and thus were outside its sanctions, included many actors who wanted work badly enough to overlook the fine details of copyright.

A reform that attained greater success was the campaign to improve dressing rooms. No aspect of the theatre better symbolized the player's status. While many theatres hosted the spectator in splendor, their dressing rooms usually offered the performer only cold, dirt, and an occasional rat. With few exceptions actors in their autobiographies expounded on the atrocious conditions they suffered through while making up for the show. Books and articles discouraging stage hopefuls commonly pointed to the danger to health that dressing rooms posed. It was said that the great Rachel's death resulted from a cold caught in a drafty Philadelphia dressing room. The stars, of course, got the best rooms, but often that was saying little. Poor lighting made it hard to apply makeup, and no running water made removal difficult. The dressing rooms presented special problems for actresses, whose long, expensive gowns soiled easily in the accumulated filth. Moreover, the dressing rooms were often pockmarked with holes, convenient for peeping Toms. Actors sometimes had to share the blame for unkempt quarters. Dressing-room walls served as billboards for many actors who scribbled their names and addresses on them; graffiti and greasepaint art work decorated somber walls, in some cases perhaps brightening the room, but usually cheapening the player's environment. Generally, provincial theatre dressing rooms rated below those of New York. Gotham's Lyceum Theatre was reputed to have the best. Located near the stage, the rooms opened into a wide hallway, allowing for rapid stage entrances. Each room had a sink with hot and cold water, a wardrobe, cupboard, large mirror, and both gas and electric lights. But these conveniences were exceptional.[77]

Actors put up with these conditions for years, as they did with all the other uncomfortable features of their life. But in the 1880s, concern for their professional environment led to a demand for dressing room reform. In a Pennsylvania town a company refused to use the dressing rooms given them, and the performance was canceled. The significance of this issue was underscored by a letter to the *Mirror* in 1887: "the dressing-room question is for the profession one of the most absorbing of the hour."[78] Ever willing to seek legal redress, actors rallied around the Sullivan Bill introduced to the New York legislature in 1896, setting minimum standards for dressing rooms. They would have to be at least eight feet by ten feet, supplied with gas jets for lighting, and have toilets. Predictably, managers reacted strongly to this interference in the operation of their theatres. The bill failed. The ASA had more success in encouraging actors to report unsanitary dressing rooms. The ASA would then notify local boards of health about miscreant theatres. Making as many as 119 complaints one year, the ASA proved effective in upgrading dressing rooms.[79] Later, under Actors' Equity rules, more stringent requirements were enforced.

The ASA provided other services in its *Actors' Society Monthly Bulletin*, published from 1899 to 1908. In its first two years the *ASMB* was primarily a list of member actors, their line of business, and their company if engaged. By the third year it had added many features as it sought to be the complete professional magazine: a report of its business meetings, regular articles on leading actors, a column of stage gossip, theatrical short stories, and sundry articles of interest to the actor. It also carried many advertisements of hotels, boardinghouses, tailors, costumers, and makeup companies. Actors placed personal ads, some of them full-page portraits, announcing their availability.

The most ambitious undertaking of the ASA was its lobbying for legislative standards for stage performances. This call for licensure—the ultimate test of professional recognition—had reasons beyond simply those of professional emulation. The intense competition for acting jobs was aggravated by managers who set out on tour with a cast of low-salaried amateurs. Then there were individuals who had made a name for themselves in other fields or who had become notorious through scandal and tried to exploit their fame on the stage. Professional boxers seemed especially susceptible to the call of the footlights. John L. Sullivan, who started the trend, went on the stage in the 1890s to try and recoup his lost fortune. The great Irish pugilist was a tremendous drawing card, but an insipid actor. Even more of an affront to the professional dignity of actors were people seeking to capitalize on scandal. A women tried for murder in New York announced her intention of going on stage in 1896 and expected to command a thousand dollars a week.[80] By excluding these inept actors dramatic standards would be kept high, while more jobs would be available to qualified players. "We ought to be more careful about the fitness of those who enter the profession," said Lawrence Barrett in 1882. "Those who are admitted to its lower ranks should be subjected to the same scrutiny that candidates for college are obliged to undergo."[81] The *Mirror* advocated this same step a few years later. "Why should not an actor or playwright be obliged to give a taste of his quality to a legally appointed bench of judges who could hear with patience and give just judgment? . . . Let actors pass an examination and be licensed to practice as other professional men are."[82] The *ASMB* picked up the theme in 1905. "The actors can do as the other learned professions have done, get themselves actually professionalized by legislation. . . . You have your organization ready to your hands, or the nucleus of it at any rate. It is called the Actors' Society of America. It could easily be to the actors of America what the New York County Medical Society is to the physicians of New York."[83]

In 1902 the ASA managed to get a bill before the New York legislature defining a minimum standard of excellence for actors to meet before they could act in the state. To those who protested the impossibility of setting such a standard the society responded: "Has the aspirant for honor in dramatic art a better right than the student of painting and sculpture to thrust his untried and underdeveloped power upon the public and to demand money for it? Such an assumption is impudence."[84] The bill would have put the theatre under a state board with power to examine and license all who would be actors. The ASA itself considered imposing more stringent membership requirements, testing professional competency instead of simply demanding three years' experience.[85]

But the ASA once again met failure in its request for legislated standards. Its unfulfilled hopes for restricted membership further attested to the marginal position of acting as a profession. Licensure depends upon accepted standards of knowledge and performance that must be met. Engineers must calculate stresses in exact degrees, and lawyers have to learn cases that serve as important precedents. But acting requires little theoretical knowledge. The numerous amateur productions and the many amateurs who acted with professional companies suggested that acting relied on natural ability, perhaps needing cultivation, but not necessitating formal training or legal standards. "The actor's art," wrote a thespian in 1897, "is one that the novice can master after a brief course of drill to the satisfaction of the speculative manager."[86] The test of adequacy came from the audience. Good attendance certified worthy acting, while a falling off at the box office would soon reflect incompetency. And despite the society's stricture that "bad science in medicine may sicken the body but bad acting perverts the mind," few Americans feared that performances presented a clear danger to the public welfare.[87] Moreover, acting resisted rationalization. Acting involved a stepping out of everyday life into the realm of fantasy; it implied a spontaneity that defied strict control. The actor's freedom onstage extended to his life off the boards. Rigid canons of professional behavior could never be imposed on the idiosyncratic player.

The kind of professionalization envisioned by leaders of the Actors' Society consequently was impossible. But if players could not restructure their vocation along classic professional lines, nothing prevented them from at least adopting professional ideology. Sociologist Everett C. Hughes points out that to professionalize means less to conform to an ideal occupational type than it does to adopt a desired conception of one's work.[88] This more flexible, ideological definition of professionalism was already being used by many groups in the early twentieth century. "The kind of work one does is not what makes one a professional," commented educator George Herbert Palmer in 1914, "but rather the spirit in which one does it . . . for professionalism is an attitude of mind."[89] A "spirit of professionalism" began to inform the players' self-image in the later nineteenth century, and through The Players, the Actors' Fund, acting schools, and the Actors' Society they sought to shape their occupation according to its dictates. That, of course, was not to be. But their success in engendering a new dignity among players must not be minimized. Actors could no longer think of themselves as the carefree strolling players who gave little thought to the future. What the *Brooklyn Times* had in 1892 called "the most gullible, near-sighted and unbusinesslike set of mortals under the sun," became a good deal shrewder and tough-minded, promoting their interests through collective action.[90] The ASA's campaign against swindling managers anticipated the upcoming war against the Theatrical Syndicate. In time, the genteel professionalism of the ASA would yield to the more strident trade unionism of Actors' Equity. Yet even then the professional ideal persisted as the controlling image of self-identity.

*   *   *

While players took their fate in their own hands and thought to improve their social standing through professionalization, changes went on around them less amenable to their control. The actors' own efforts at uplift were just half the story; the other half concerns a society in the midst of a transformation that would earn players unprecedented public appreciation—an appreciation quite different from that envisioned by the profession's leaders.

Mary Anderson: classic beauty of the American stage. COURTESY OF THE BILLY
ROSE THEATRE COLLECTION.

Julia Marlowe and Edward H. Sothern: a commitment to Shakespeare.
COURTESY OF THE BILLY ROSE THEATRE COLLECTION.

Edwin Booth: a prince of players. COURTESY OF THE BILLY ROSE THEATRE COLLECTION.

Joseph Jefferson: the quintessential "Rip Van Winkle." COURTESY OF THE BILLY ROSE THEATRE COLLECTION.

Ethel Barrymore: model of the sophisticated life. COURTESY OF THE BILLY ROSE
THEATRE COLLECTION.

Maude Adams: dispensing charms of the heart. COURTESY OF THE BILLY ROSE THEATRE COLLECTION.

William Gillette: calm intensity; eloquent silence. COURTESY OF THE BILLY ROSE THEATRE COLLECTION.

Minnie Maddern Fiske: an intellectual Tess of the D'Urbervilles. COURTESY OF THE BILLY ROSE THEATRE COLLECTION.

John Drew: drollery in the drawing room. COURTESY OF THE BILLY ROSE THE-
ATRE COLLECTION.

Five 🌺

Actors and Society: I

*T*he theatre has reached the most prosperous era in its history," proclaimed Arthur Hornblow in 1916, "and the actor has prospered with it. No longer is he a social outcast. The stage is a recognized profession. Society no longer despises the actor, but greets him with open arms." [1]

Hornblow's glowing tribute would appear a testimony to the successful efforts of Harrison Grey Fiske, Edwin Booth, and the leaders of the Actors' Fund and Actors' Society in transforming a motley collection of players into a respectable profession. And to some degree it was. But Hornblow, who was himself a champion of the theatre's social advancement, spoke too glibly of the actor's rise. Old prejudices lingered, and even as society embraced the player and his work, this acceptance was due less to the actor's professional aspirations than to a complex set of cultural changes. These changes, which nurtured a new relationship between actor and society, shed an interesting light on both the theatre and American culture. I shall begin by outlining the main social changes that affected the actor's status, then look more closely at two groups—America's religious community and polite society—which partly out of free will and partly out of necessity were forced into uneasy acceptance of actors.

* 1 *

To appreciate the social advance of the actor in the late nineteenth century one must recall his origins. For centuries to be an actor meant a life outside the framework of established society, a life circumscribed by regulations and prohibitions. We remember the greatness of Shakespeare's plays but forget that they were performed by the "rogues and vagabonds" of Elizabethan law. Even during the great ages of Restoration and eighteenth-century drama,

English performers found themselves at the whim of patrons, licensing laws, and audiences, any of which could unexpectedly turn on them. Moreover, touring remained central to the actors' lives, an itinerancy that continued to mark them right down to the twentieth century as a vagabond people, people outside the social order.

In the face of this checkered history it should not seem strange that actors constantly sought greater security and esteem. One discerns an anxious desire for respectability in the constant protestations of social progress among actors. A Frenchman in 1701, for example, lauded Gallic performers as "truly decent people, who are frequented and respected by gentle folk in many quarters."[2] This incantation of respectability would be repeated through the next two centuries, intensifying in the last few decades of the nineteenth century. Yet one also finds repeated examples of insult, condescension, and social exclusion through the years, and actors realized that talk of social advancement was often wishful thinking more than descriptive reality. The actors' "rise," then, was a labored path bespeaking the marginal role of the theatre and its performers in society. The leading figures of the stage, of course, always commanded a certain respect and admiration. But even this was a tenuous possession. It was the actor's privilege to be "petted and pelted," remarked the great David Garrick, a truth the two biggest stars of the English stage in the early nineteenth century, Junius Brutus Booth and Edmund Kean, sadly learned, having had their acclaim punctuated by outbursts of public indignation.[3] The public's regard for its performers ran to extremes, from unbounded affection to unbridled scorn. These excessive reactions were in part a logical consequence of the histrionic art, which trades in the evocation of powerful emotions, but were even more so a result of a society's not yet having learned to distinguish fully the mirror of the theatre from the reality of life. As later audiences became accustomed to the conventions of the theatre, their response to the players grew more predictable.

The American actor of the early and mid–nineteenth century shared the problems of his English counterpart: frequent travel under difficult conditions, low pay and reccurrent unemployment for most players, the reputation as drunkards and irresponsible profligates, and the long-standing Puritan prejudice against players. Suspicion lingered about players because they touched a comparatively small number of Americans through most of the century. America was overwhelmingly rural, and commercial amusements played a smaller part in people's lives than they would to the urbanites of a later age. Actors were not yet the familiar figures they would become at the turn of the century, when popular magazines carried their pictures and told their stories to people across the nation.

It would be a mistake to think that actors generally encountered an active hostility. William Wood observed in the mid–nineteenth century that social scorn for actors was more often a verbal platitude than a driving conviction.[4] Outside the hard core of church people who viewed actors as the devil's minions, probably most Americans had no overt hostility toward them. Prejudice toward actors was generally latent rather than active. Periodically it would be called forth, boldly, as after John Wilkes Booth's assassination of Lincoln, or more often the case, mildly, as when a notorious divorcee such as Mrs. Leslie Carter went on the stage. More significant during normal times, however, was that actors lacked an acceptable social function. To a people concerned with building a nation, players' work served no productive end. They spent their life playing. The exceptional actor, such as Edwin Forrest, transcended this triteness in a display of American bravura. Toward the common player, however, Americans extended indulgence, even applause, but not respect.

With the expansion and comparative prosperity of the later nineteenth-century theatre both English and American players began a more insistent drive for social acceptance. In England, even more than America, discussion of the actor's social status filled genteel reviews. The *Saturday Review* complained in 1885 of these endless debates, and the *Scot's Observer* sarcastically noted in 1889 that "a review without an article on the actor's social status will sell high some day." That actors felt compelled to continually solicit public opinion on their status, observed the *Saturday Review*, indicated an uncertainty about their advance, as if they needed constant reassurance.[5] American actors labored in a society where class distinctions were less finely drawn, but their ambitions for social advancement were no less keenly felt. The appearance of the Actors' Fund, Actors' Society, The Players, and a dramatic weekly dedicated to theatrical uplift, all in the span of roughly fifteen years, attested to a lively hope that a new day of social opportunity was at hand.

It is difficult to assess the impact of these organizations' efforts at social advancement on public attitudes. Certainly the Actors' Society failed to achieve a high public profile. References to it in contemporary newspapers and magazines are few, and it probably did little to affect public attitudes. The Actors' Fund, especially through its popular Fund Fairs, attained greater success in letting the public know about its work for the retired or disabled actor. But not until the founding of Actors' Equity and in particular the strike of 1919 did the American public become fully aware of players' self-help efforts. More important, the Actors' Fund, Actors' Society, and *Dramatic Mirror* reinforced actors' self-esteem by constantly exhorting actors to take pride in their profession.

Although these measures may have instilled group confidence, they had only marginal effect on public opinion. Actors' social status would be shaped, ultimately, by more fundamental changes within American society and culture.

*   *   *

Without question the change of greatest portent for the theatre and its performers was America's urbanization. America's great metropolises had grown throughout the nineteenth century, but it was in the 1880s, as Arthur Meier Schlesinger long ago noted, that they "became a controlling factor in national life."[6] Most significantly, American culture was becoming urbanized, with the triumph of the city coming through its purveyance of material objects and styles of life to the rest of the nation. It is no coincidence that the magnificent flowering of the American theatre corresponded to the epic period of urban growth. Amusements of all types flourished in the burgeoning cities, in part simply because of the proximity of a huge patronage, but more fundamentally because of an essential characteristic of urban culture: a pervasive specialization that altered even the leisure moments of life.

Recreation had posed no problem for rural peoples of an earlier age, who found diversion in informal contests of skill—shooting matches, horse races, wrestling matches, logrollings, and the like—and in social gatherings with neighbors; only occasionally were they treated to a show by an itinerant theatre company or minstrel group. But there was no distinct break between the rural work and play environments. The specialization of factory and office changed this pattern, as the repetitiveness of factory work and the monotony of office routine compelled both kinds of employees to look outside their work for fulfillment. The workday became something to be endured, redeemed only by leisure hours. The constraints of office and factory labor prompted workers to "let loose" in their free time. Entertainment was no longer sought in one's home or place of work, but in specialized venues of pleasure: the billiard parlor, racetrack, dance hall, baseball field, theatre. Leisure time, moreover, lengthened considerably. The average workweek in nonagricultural industries decreased by almost ten hours between 1850 and 1900, from 66 to 56 hours, then fell even more sharply from 1900 to 1920 to about 45 hours.[7] Both opportunity and inclination, then, encouraged a quickened pursuit of amusement.

In the wake of this social change wrought by urbanization there followed a cultural awakening to the value of recreation. This occurred on many fronts. Organized spectator sports expanded, led by professional baseball and intercollegiate football; dramatic arts flourished on the legitimate and vaudeville stages and in the ubiquitous movie houses; outdoor life found many new enthusiasts; camping, mountain climbing, canoeing, fishing, and hunting were pursued avidly by urbanites with the means to get out of the city. Newspapers and magazines reflected a growing ethic of pleasure. In the 1890s, sports pages appeared in newspapers, and such popular periodicals as *Harper's Weekly* and *Colliers'* featured sports news.[8] Magazines of the day also chronicled the new enthusiasm for outdoor recreation. The *Review of Reviews* found the "open-air movement almost revolutionary in its degree. . . . People are bicycling, yachting, running, jumping, fishing, hunting, playing baseball, tennis and golf, to an extent which is new in this generation."[9] Foreign travelers commented on the new spirit. In the 1830s and '40s Frances Trollope, Charles Dickens, and others had observed America's obsession with work and indifference to recreation.[10] By contrast, James Bryce's 1905 visit to America left very different impressions. He noted the recent passion for "looking at and reading about athletic sports," an enthusiasm exceeding anything he knew in Europe.[11]

Cultural leaders reluctantly came to agree that Puritan animosities toward recreation were inappropriate to modern life, and a gospel of play began to be heard. Americans were now instructed that periodic amusements were not only harmless, but positively beneficial. "The people wish, need and should have recreation," wrote Michael Davis in a 1911 study of commercial recreations in New York. "They will have it."[12] Even a conservative spokesman such as Richard Henry Edwards, who condemned most forms of commercial amusements, conceded that serious drama served an important function: "The purpose of drama is primarily to give recreation in the full sense of the word. . . . It releases them in flight beyond the stern borders to which life has brought them, and thrills them with some bit of the human study which might be their own."[13] A symposium entitled "Christianity and Amusements," published by *Everybody's Magazine* in 1904, featured eight of America's leading churchmen, who agreed that innocent diversions, if not carried to extremes, played an important part in the well-balanced Christian life.[14] Similarly, Howard Palmer Young's

1915 treatise entitled *Character through Recreation* posited a close relationship between piety and play. Recreation, said Young, "may
be one of God's chosen avenues for the introduction of ethical and
social virtues. The ministry of amusement to man's higher life must
not be overlooked."[15]

These views implied (though their advocates might have
balked at admitting so) that entertainers provided an essential service. Although many Progressives would have preferred that citizens find recreation in such things as community drama and participatory recreation, the public clearly showed its preference for
the professional entertainers of stage and screen.[16] When America
became involved in World War I the extent of this preference became apparent. Actors' ability to help maintain morale at home and
on the front lines was an acknowledged contribution to the war
effort, and they were exempted from the rigid "work or fight" rule.
In a society that increasingly defined the "good life" in terms of leisure pursuits, the actor's labor was no longer a senseless frill, but
had become a job as essential as any other.

But urbanization and its cultural changes (what might be
called the deep structure of change) were only enabling conditions
for the actor's rise. At closer range the undifferentiated terrain of
social attitudes resolves into a remarkably variegated landscape of
shifting dispositions toward the player. Two groups illustrate the
complexity of this change. The religious community and polite society, different as they were, were both forced to come to terms
with the acting profession in these years. Their response to a
group they found enticing and threatening illuminates American
culture's gradual—and sometimes begrudging—surrender to the
charms of its entertainers.

* 2 *

Of the many challenges facing American churches in the late
1800s, none was more serious than that of the city. And of the
many aspects of urbanism which bedeviled traditional Christian
mores, few were more vexing than the theatre. As Protestant and,
to a lesser degree, Catholic clergy witnessed the increasing rush to
the theatre's door, they realized that its growing influence would
have to come at their expense. But the hope persisted among some
that the actor's power might be appropriated for religious ends.

Religious hostility to the stage, of course, is one of the venerable truisms of theatrical history. The Puritan prejudice toward drama
was as deeply engrained in America as it had been in England.[17]

The first published broadside against the theatre, Princeton president John Witherspoon's *Serious Inquiry into the Nature and Effects of the Stage* (1757), was published just a few years after the Hallam family introduced professional theatre to America, and over the next century and a half similar manifestos warned the faithful of evils lurking inside the playhouse. A chronicling of such evils generally included the unruly behavior of the pit and gallery, the active presence of prostitutes, blasphemous language, indecency of costume, immorality of the plays themselves, plus their expense and waste of time.[18] Through much of the nineteenth century clerical prestige dissuaded many Americans from attending the theatre.

But the urban milieu of the post–Civil War years fostered the theatre's growth and eroded inhibitions against attendance. Religious writers, consequently, stepped up their attack against a surging foe. The theatre, in their writings, became a visible symbol for the evils that stalked the city; innocent youth and concerned parent were warned of the dangers of apparently innocent shows.[19] "Vicious habits and sinful propensities," wrote Ellen White, prophetess of the young Seventh-day Adventist church in 1881, "are strengthened and confirmed by these entertainments. Low songs, lewd gestures, expressions, and attitudes, deprave the imagination and debase the morals. Every youth who habitually attends such exhibitions will be corrupted in principle."[20] While a few liberal ministers were already arguing that the theatre could be reformed along Christian lines, most denied this possibility. "A divergence so great as would be necessary to render the theatre no longer obnoxious to Christian condemnation," judged J. M. Buckley in 1875, "could not be brought about in many ages unless all the laws which have obtained in other departments of progress should fail."[21]

The theatre was said to corrupt its performers as well as its audience. Charles Parsons, who had left the stage for the ministry, described the acting profession as "intellectual prostitution" because players threw away their considerable abilities to chase a fleeting prize.[22] A more common argument against acting was that it deadened moral sensitivities. "How can they mingle together as they do," Herrick Johnson questioned, "and make public exhibition of themselves as they do, in such positions as they must sometimes take, affecting such sentiments and passions—how can they do this without moral contamination?"[23] Reverend Perry Sinks voiced similar concerns about the actor's work: "The life of an actor is a fictitious one, being made up of the personation of other characters, often gross and immoral, even diabolical. It is a subtle law which governs in all histrionic art that one must have sympathy for the role he plays or the character he paints in his acting; hence the danger of personating evil characters."[24]

The public politely listened to these warnings—but then, more often than not, ignored them. Sarah Bernhardt's 1880 American tour, for example, occasioned many attacks from moralists. Her flaunting of conventional morality offstage and the racy productions in the theatre led to a storm of protest in the press and from the pulpit. Ministers denounced the "perverted Parisienne" and exhorted their charges to stay away from her performances. Yet Bernhardt played to full houses everywhere.[25] The phenomenon of Sarah Bernhardt and the popularity of "leg shows," such as the *Black Crook*, indicated that urban audiences increasingly took their pleasures as they wished regardless of clerical condemnation. These changes are hard to document, but one piece of evidence indicates that even Christians were frequenting the theatre. The Cleveland Y.M.C.A. surveyed its members in 1907 regarding theatre attendance. The results showed a familiarity with the theatre by nearly all and frequent attendance by a sizable number, suggesting that at least the younger Christians of the city were shedding the traditional animus toward theatricals.[26]

Yet outside of the urban centers active opposition to the theatre continued strong. The *Dramatic Mirror*, which frequently reprinted clerical references to the theatre, reported in 1890 that there appeared to be no softening in churchly attitudes.[27] Indeed, in the last few decades of the century the more conservative churches stepped up their attack on sinful amusements in a futile attempt to stem the tide of worldliness. Formal declarations against certain pastimes were issued, a step not felt necessary earlier in the century. At an 1889 session of the Baptist Association a resolution was adopted requiring church members to abstain from attending theatres.[28]

The most sweeping statement against amusements came from the Methodist Episcopal Church, the denomination that best reflected small-town, middle-class American values. The Methodist amusement ban was instituted in 1877. The *Discipline* stated that a member could be reproved or even expelled from membership for patronizing certain amusements, including the theatre.[29] The rule was enforced, at least in its early years. When Frederick Warde's company played in Ohio sometime in the 1880s, a group of students from Ohio Wesleyan slipped away to the theatre disguised in wigs and beards. Unfortunately, their makeup lacked conviction and college authorities were not fooled; the underclassmen were disciplined, seniors expelled.[30]

By the turn of the century, nevertheless, Methodist laymen attended the theatre in great numbers. After the disastrous Iroquois Theatre fire in Chicago in 1903 it was discovered that many Methodists had been present.[31] Few pastors enforced the amusement ban, leading the *Northwestern Christian Advocate*, the Chicago organ of the church, to comment that the ban was "just less than impotent. No pastor is going to enforce the law when sentiment is so evenly divided; and no law under such circumstances can have much moral or restraining force."[32] After 1900 the amusement ban was discussed at every quadrennial General Conference session. Many bishops wished to repeal the rule, realizing its divisive impact on the church. However, at every General Conference a vote on repeal was defeated, and as late as 1920 a senior bishop of the church, replying to a query from Actors' Equity Executive Secretary Frank Gilmore, stated bluntly that neither actors nor those that attended the theatre were wanted in the church.[33] Not until 1924 was the ban removed from the *Discipline*.[34]

While the more conservative churchmen either refused to compromise with the stage or did so only at last resort, another group of clergy, usually identified with the Social Gospel, viewed amusements in a different light, recognizing that an urban population needed diversion.[35] Lyman Abbott, for one, once an adamant opponent of the theatre, later championed healthy amusements in his *Christian Union* paper and called for a more tolerant view of Sabbath pleasures. He envisioned an ennobled stage as "useful not only in affording tired brain-workers the very best recreation possible to them when they live in towns and cities, but also affording intellectual stimulus of a moderate kind, and often stirring the heart and quickening the emotions by noble ideals, nobly presented."[36]

Although liberal Christian leaders accepted the theatre as potentially beneficial, they had little good to say about what was seen on the commercial stage. Washington Gladden charged that "the business of diverting people is largely in the hands of men and women whose moral standards are low, whose habits are vicious, and whose influence upon those with whom they come in contact must be evil."[37] The nagging doubts of even a liberal mind were displayed by Phillips Brooks, prominent Episcopal bishop, who once turned down an invitation to a benefit simply because it was to be held in a theatre. He explained: "The trouble with the theatre is its dreadful indiscriminateness. The same house which gives good Mrs. Vincent her benefit to-day may have almost anything to-morrow."[38]

The stage, then, had to be reformed. Once reformed it could

become an ally of religion in advancing civilization. Millennial hopes were expressed of the theatre's power. Otto Peltzer believed Christianity alone could not cure the many social ills of America, but combined with the influential medium of the theatre a social revolution could be produced.[39] Likewise, Charles Sheldon, who authored the fabulously popular *In His Steps*, suggested in 1902 the possibility of establishing a Christian theatre, complete with its own school for Christian actors, managers, and playwrights. His Christian theatre would be a place "where men and women of consecrated, devout, earnest Christian character would act only good plays."[40] A minister in Buffalo put such sentiments into practice, authoring a romantic drama entitled *The Dagger and the Rose*, which had its first (and probably last) performance by a local stock company in 1894.[41]

But if certain religious leaders anticipated a rapprochement between church and theatre, American actors were less sure. They had, after all, known nothing but religious disfavor. They recalled their humiliation in 1870 when actor George Holland was refused a Christian funeral at a New York church. Chronic religious disapproval evoked an arrogant withdrawal by many actors. Players maintained their distance from the elect, sheltered within the comradeship of their community. Actors did not always suffer meekly in the face of churchly criticism. At a Lotos Club dinner, for example, a clergyman praised Joseph Jefferson for maintaining his integrity amid the temptations of stage life. Jefferson got up and replied curtly that he could not accept a compliment that implied a reproach on his profession.[42] And when Francis Wilson put on a one-act play, *The Father of the Wilderness*, at Lake Chautauqua in 1910, he astounded the audience by denouncing the Methodist amusement ban.[43] Raymond Hitchcock poked fun at his accusers, working up a fifteen-minute routine given between acts satirizing Billy Sunday's attacks on the stage, where he even got down on the floor and talked to the devil. The stunt was such a hit that he received an offer (tongue in cheek though it may have been) to become Sunday's evangelistic partner.[44]

One cannot with certainty estimate the percentage of players who were believers. Actors' biographies and autobiographies give the impression that religion, at least the kind of religion characterized by regular church attendance, played a small part in most of their lives. Several prominent actors dabbled in spiritualism. Edwin Booth tried to reach his first wife, Mary Devlin, through the spirit world. Joseph Jefferson was a confirmed spiritualist and occasionally visited spiritualist mediums. Richard Mansfield twice had psychic experiences and at least once reported seeing an apparition. E. A. Sothern, too, believed in spiritualism for a time, but later decided that it was a fraud, and like Houdini, enjoyed duplicating spiritualists' feats.[45] A number of other players, particularly actresses, subscribed to Christian Science beliefs. Overall, however, players remained noncommittal toward organized religion. The *Dramatic Mirror* chided players for their apparent apathy, and encouraged church attendance, thinking it would improve the actor's image. "As clergymen should attend the theatres," it editorialized in 1881, "so actors and actresses should attend the churches . . . every professional should make it an invariable rule to go to church every Sunday. Where they are settled in stock companies they should take sittings or pews; where they are traveling they should accept the hospitality of church members. Few persons can realize what a change it would make in the profession, in their social standing, in their moral influence, if this advice were taken and persevered in for five years." [46]

To bridge this alienation between church and player the Actors' Church Alliance (ACA) was founded in 1899, modeled after a similar organization that had appeared the year before in England.[47] The ACA, though interdenominational, was largely composed of Episcopal clergymen. Its founders included Henry Potter, bishop of New York, veteran player F. F. Mackay, and most important, Reverend Walter E. Bentley, a former actor who had left the stage to enter the Episcopal ministry. The first chapter formed in Boston, and by 1902 the organization had 400 branches and a membership of 2,250, including 850 chaplains.[48]

The ACA's aims were threefold: to minister to actors and welcome them into the Christian community, to alleviate the prejudice of church and society against the theatre, and to reform the commercial stage. It sought these ends through a variety of activities. The Boston chapter for example, one of the largest and most active, headed by the Reverend George Wolfe Shinn, held religious services once a month and sponsored receptions, lectures, essays, and social gatherings. Additionally, each week ACA chaplains across the country received postcards telling them which alliance members would be in town so that they could visit them.[49] In effect, the itinerant player became a temporary parishioner of the chaplains. Which actors took advantage of this unique program and why they did so remain unknown. That so many apparently did indicates a latent religious interest among players. On the other hand, the ACA's failure to mention any prominent stars among its members indicates that the leading performers kept their distance.

The characteristic feature of the ACA was its sympathy to the player and to the great value of his art. At the organization's first mass meeting in 1900 Walter Bentley alluded to the "heartbreaking trials" of actors and to their subservience to greedy managers. Likewise, at the same meeting the Reverend Howard Wilbur Ennis sympathetically characterized players as "the most misunderstood and the most grossly abused people in the world." If the stage was too often immoral, he continued, blame not the player but the audience.[50] The ACA zealously proclaimed the gospel of drama, prophesying that actors—once freed from the shackles of commercial bondage—would minister to the dramatic craving of humanity. It went so far as to compile a list of creditable plays that it sent to its chaplains, encouraging them to attend and then to commend them to their congregations. Through all of this, though, ran an implicit and probably unrecognized note of condescension. The ACA was to "uplift" the theatre. "The time has come," Reverend Bentley announced, "for the Church to save the stage from the blight of mere triviality and pure commercialism."[51] If the ACA reached out its hand of fellowship to the religiously proscribed actor, it was not without a favor to ask in return. The uplifted actor was to take his place alongside the clergy in fulfilling its task, which was to be, as Bentley grandly concluded, "one of the great ethical forces in society."[52]

It was a task that would remain unfulfilled, and for the actors' part a loss they scarcely noticed. The reconciliation between church and stage envisioned by the Actors' Church Alliance, like the increasing liberality of most churches toward the theatre in the early twentieth century, was an accommodation to social changes beyond their control. Although the ACA clergymen may have felt they were doing actors a favor with their attention, in reality it was the ministry which was struggling to keep up with the times. Players were no longer the socially scorned figures of the past. Despite clerical denunciations and official amusement bans the public flocked to the theatre. Traditional arguments against the stage no longer carried the same conviction. If the moralists could not stop the flood, they hoped at least to channel the theatre's growth into areas compatible with the Christian tradition. But that proved a hopeless task, and one not favored by many actors. Comedian Stuart Robson skeptically eyed the ACA, thinking that the theatre could do without the church's help. "The stage has now become so strong that it is respected by the pulpit," Robson insightfully observed in 1902. "Clergymen are now making terms with actors."[53]

This inversion informed Harold Frederic's minor classic of American fiction, *The Damnation of Theron Ware*, published in 1896. The story revolves around Theron Ware, a fundamentalist Methodist minister, who finds himself awash in the breakdown of Victorian verities which accompanied his immersion into the higher learning and aestheticism of fin-de-siècle America, and ultimately drives him to collapse. By contrast appear the Soulsbys, former barnstormers who have become church fund raisers. Frederic's portrait of them embodies the usual stereotype of actors: manipulators of human emotion, masters of dissemblance and deceit. But there is a difference. Frederic presents these traditional foibles in a positive light. The Soulsbys use their professional tricks in a benign way—they are "good frauds," in their own description. They exhibit a sensitivity to and understanding of human nature that make them, not the church, the redemptive force of the novel. Theron Ware himself will in the end owe his healing and fresh start to the ministrations of the Soulsbys, a fitting commentary on the reversal of roles occurring in American culture.[54]

Actors (as will be discussed later) had emerged as the prophetic figures in the shift from the Victorian ethic of self-discipline and restraint to the twentieth-century celebration of self-realization. By the early decades of the twentieth century they knew they had little to fear from clerical denunciation. Though American churchmen desperately tried to tame the actor's influence, they must have sensed it was a losing cause. Entertainment had been legitimized on its own terms, without the need for religious justification. The actor, first on stage and then on the screen, upstaged the minister as a model for attitudes and behavior. Indeed, age-old Puritan fears had been realized: The competition between church and stage for the public's loyalty had been won by the player. There could be no ultimate reconciliation between church and commercial theatre— only an uneasy truce forced upon a churchly minority whose prestige had been compromised.

* 3 *

The accommodation of the church to the theatre finds an interesting parallel in polite society's acceptance of the player. The details of the two stories are very different, of course, but an underlying dynamic links them together. As the nineteenth century gave way to the twentieth both clergyman and socialite found their social leadership undermined by forces beyond their control, and they witnessed the sudden prestige of a group long assumed to be subordinate to them.

* * *

Extending far back into European history, to the days when the first professional players performed Interludes in the great halls of the aristocracy, a special bond has existed between actor and patrician. The patronage of the great was often essential, not just for financial support, but for the very right to perform. On the Restoration and eighteenth-century stages trod courtesan-actors who mirrored the foibles and grandeur of aristocratic life. But if players enjoyed an intimacy with the great which few others knew, it was a familiarity based on the indulgence of the wellborn. The favor extended to a troupe or individual performer could be withdrawn at a whim. The applause and fine clothing did not conceal the fact that actors were little more than glorified servants.

Without a court or aristocracy, American society obviously could not offer its actors as regal an audience. Yet in the post–Civil War years, as the nation's newly minted millionaires affected the manner of an ancient nobility, they assumed a similar posture toward their favorite players. The high spirits and good conversation of actors made them ideal people to enliven a party. Indeed, actors' major contact with society outside the theatre came as entertainers at dinner parties, where they were hired to sing, tell stories, or give readings. In these situations it was always clear that they were hired workers, not invited guests. Usually they would remain downstairs until dinner finished, then be brought up to perform. Occasionally a player would rebel at this humiliation, as when Marshall Wilder, after being kept alone for over an hour in the parlor of a millionaire, simply walked out.[55] But actors generally knew their place and kept to it.

This servility was shed first in England and then in America. According to historian Michael Baker the status of the English actor in 1850 was no different than it had been in 1800. But by 1880 the situation had changed considerably. Not only did English society embrace theatricals as never before, but its scions began pursuing acting careers. The rise of the gentleman-actor revolutionized relations between stage and society. Such notable West End players as the Bancrofts became fixtures in fashionable London society.[56] American stars could only envy such intimacy. During his tour of England in 1881, Edwin Booth noted that "with us [American actors] only the very distinguished ones are invited, while here I've met many of subordinate positions in the best houses."[57]

The English player who did the most to upgrade his profession's status was Henry Irving, unquestionably the greatest actor of the English stage in the last half of the century. Where Garrick or Kean were concerned primarily with self-aggrandizement, Irving manifested a conscientious concern about his responsibility to the theatre. His Lyceum Theatre, where he costarred with Ellen Terry, became a source of national pride, prefiguring the much later British National Theatre.[58] In 1895 Queen Victoria knighted Irving, and that same year he had become the first actor invited to speak at the Royal Institution banquet. The knighting of Irving bestowed a new eminence on the player's profession and opened the way for other actors to be similarly honored in the following years: Sir Squire Bancroft, Sir George Alexander, Sir Johnston Forbes-Robertson, Sir Herbert Beerbohm Tree, and Sir Gerald du Maurier.

Supporters of the American theatre hoped that Irving's celebrated knighthood would signal a new day for their actors as well. But polite society in America, perhaps less sure of itself than the English upper class, manned the barricades longer. The exclusion of actors from gentlemen's clubs has already been established. Further evidence of prejudice comes from a British player who resided in America in the 1880s and experienced society's snub. From a prominent family, he had done well on the amateur stage and subsequently turned professional. He came to America with letters of introduction to prominent clubmen and expected a cordial welcome. Yet despite his theatrical achievements, his social connections in England, and his acknowledged gentility, he was never invited to the homes of the men he met or even put up at their clubs. "As disagreeable as the fact may appear," this anonymous and embittered player wrote in *The Theatre*, "it is, nevertheless, true that the actor is not considered proper enough to be admitted into New York 'society' simply because he is an actor."[59]

This observation proved true time and again. Proper society delighted at the capering comedians and lyrical sopranos; they wept at renditions of bathetic ballads. But let the performers overstay their welcome a few moments or otherwise trespass the invisible boundary between themselves and their hosts, and the visible signs of exclusion appeared. The *Dramatic Mirror* claimed in 1888 that no actor had penetrated society and pointed to the example of Kyrle Bellew, who, although a matinee idol and a well-bred Englishman (the son of a minister), was nevertheless ejected from elite Tuxedo Park.[60] Similarly, when Lillian Russell visited Chicago's Washington Park racetrack on Derby Day in 1893 and ventured into the clubhouse, the haunt of Chicago society, her presence so upset the Chicago aristocrats that the president of the racing association asked her to go to the grandstand.[61] A final example comes from that theatrical event so resonant with cultural meaning, Sarah Bernhardt's 1880 American tour. The fascination the American public had for Bernhardt led not only to sold-out performances, but also to a public scrutiny rarely seen. Her arrival in each city was an occasion. Women's pages carried accounts of her every move and described her attire in detail. Manufacturers cashed in with Sarah

Bernhardt perfume, candy, cigars, and eyeglasses. New York's haut monde was not immune to the excitement, paying up to forty dollars a ticket to see her on stage. But after the curtain went down and the audience went home, its doors were tightly shut to the Divine Sarah (though she had earlier been welcomed by London's elite). Her notoriety made her good box office but unfit for association with the women of the Four Hundred, and the reception given her at the Century Club was attended only by men.[62]

What lay behind these episodes of pointed rejection? Novelist Edith Wharton, chronicler of New York society in this era, gave one answer, recalling in *The Age of Innocence* that the social elite felt timid around actors and other artists, and though they mingled with them occasionally at the Century Club, they were not willing to invite them into the sanctuary of their homes. The unpredictable artistic temperament made them uneasy. Performers "were odd, they were uncertain," Wharton wrote, "they had done things one didn't know about in the background of their lives and minds."[63] The reluctance of high society to embrace actors, moreover, bespoke its general sense of being besieged by social climbers, immigrants, and other undesirables in the late nineteenth century. New York high society, in particular, with its mass of nouveau riche clamoring for admittance, felt compelled to establish rigid tests of certification. Such social arbiters as Ward McAllister and the *Social Register*, started in 1887, identified those who belonged and those who did not. Country clubs and residential areas, such as Pierre Lorillard III's Tuxedo Park, provided secluded recreational and residential areas for the rich. Ancestry, too, became a mark of distinction, with genealogical investigations undertaken to establish families' European roots, founded out of the desire to maintain ethnic purity. In short, it was an exclusionary era, when society sought to preserve its domain against unwelcome intrusions, including those by actors.[64]

But even as some actors were suffering the slings and arrows of patrician insult, others were beginning to insinuate themselves into society's inner circles. They accomplished this in part through society's vogue for amateur theatricals in the last half of the nineteenth century, a passion, *The Theatre* reported in 1886, which had become an "epidemic."[65] The amateur stage offered New York's stagestruck elite an opportunity to indulge their passion without jeopardizing their social standing. Even better, these "amateur" productions often featured professionals in leading roles, giving matrons and debutantes a chance to play out their fantasies opposite reigning matinee idols. Some of the more audacious (and wealthy) amateurs bribed managers to give them a night on the professional boards. Both the money and the advertising value of having a prominent socialite on their stage generally convinced managers to give the fledgling performer his or her wish. A few well-heeled amateurs made the transition to the professional stage. Usually these were women who had fallen on financially hard times and found their peers sympathetically willing to forgive their adventures. One thinks of Anna Cora Mowatt, who conquered the New York stage in the 1840s (appropriately in the play *Fashion*), the vivacious redhead Mrs. Leslie Carter, who became a Belasco star in the 1880s, and Cora Urquhart Potter, who sacrificed a marriage into one of New York's most prominent families for a successful fling on the legitimate stage in the 1880s and '90s. Polite society did its best to ensure that association with professionals in amateur productions did not go beyond the theatre, but bridges were built that both actors and socialites began to cross.

Even more critical for the relationship of actor and society were changes in the behavior and outlook of the gentry itself. At the same time that the old guard withdrew into a cocoon of privacy a younger set of socialites led by Mrs. Stuyvesant Fish displayed an inclination for exhibitionism and publicity. This group had tired of the dreary balls and dinners. It preferred a livelier, gayer form of expression, and began in the 1890s to adopt a more gregarious and publicly expressive behavior. The construction and patronage of elegant hotel dining rooms and restaurants in New York attested to a sociability not seen before.[66] A new social grouping was in fact being formed—what would later be called cafe society. Stolidity and respectability gave way to pursuit of the interesting and lively. Popular (and, it should be added, suitably refined) players such as John Drew, Ethel Barrymore, Elsie De Wolfe, and Annie Russell were received as guests and not simply as after-dinner entertainers.[67]

Ethel Barrymore's experience is particularly revealing. A member of America's most distinguished theatrical family, the Drew-Barrymore clan, she first attained stardom on the London stage. She scored an even greater success in English society, being the only actress invited to Queen Victoria's Jubilee Ball and being wooed by a bevy of suiters, including Winston Churchill. New York papers covered her triumph in full, and on returning to America she found herself welcomed into the finest homes of Boston, New York, and Philadelphia.[68]

Players were not only found to be congenial company; they were taken as objects of romance. In the 1890s young blue bloods could frequently be seen escorting actresses and chorus girls about the town, perhaps to an after-show bird and bottle supper at Rector's on Broadway. Such dalliances were not without effect; in more than a few cases marriage followed. Edith Kingdom, a supporting actress in Augustin Daly's company, won the heart of George Gould, son of the rich and ruthless Jay Gould. Their rapid engagement met the opposition of the Gould family, but once overcome the marriage took place at the family estate on the Hudson. The new Mrs. Gould kept her promise to leave the professional stage, and she became a society leader in her own right. Eleanor Robson had a more difficult time deciding if she wanted to give up the stage for love. The English-born beauty had created the role of Bonita Canby in Augustus Thomas's *Arizona* in 1899, and her career had been a series of popular and critical achievements. She finally accepted one of multimillionaire banker August Belmont's repeated proposals, left the stage, and was immediately accepted into society, becoming one of the queens of New York society and later a noted philanthropist.[69]

By the turn of the century the double standard shown toward actors—feted as performers, excluded as individuals—was becoming untenable. High society was enamored of the player and his plays, and attempts to compartmentalize associations with him were failing. In fact quite the opposite was happening. Theatrical companions became objects of pride and envy. "The actor of today enjoys a fashionable prestige unknown in the annals of the past," wrote Margherita Hamm in 1909. "In many cases he is a social lion before whom all kneel in homage."[70] When actress Marie Dressler told Mrs. Fish that she would boast to her mother of having dined with the noted socialite, Mrs. Fish rejoined that she would be "proud to tell my children that Marie Dressler dined with me."[71]

Society's acceptance of actors in part followed its internal rivalries and changes in taste. Upstart social leaders of the 1890s rebelled against traditional formalities and decorousness as they pursued a more expansive lifestyle. But this acceptance also resulted from a more fundamental change in the actor's social role. Stars were becoming celebrities. The incipient mass media, initially incarnated in the popular press, was bestowing on actors an attention and influence unseen before. The result was something of a crisis of cultural authority for the social elite. In the previous few decades urban upper classes had established great cultural institutions—libraries, museums, symphonies—that served to validate their cultural hegemony. As patrons of the high arts the elite hoped to wield a social influence on the unwashed masses of the cities through the salubrious effect of culture.[72] It was not to be. Though these citadels of culture would remain, Americans turned elsewhere for standards of taste and value. The power of publicity was establishing new sources of authority. In the past the public had avidly followed the affairs of the Four Hundred. But beyond their prodigious ability to spend money, few society leaders were interesting. Players now captured much of the attention that had once gone to their patrons.[73] This curious reversal supports the observation of Erving Goffman that "curator groups"—groups that originally existed to enhance the status of an elite, fashion experts, models, architects, actors, for example—may on occasion manipulate their skills to usurp their patrons' position.[74] Actors, who for centuries had embroidered the cloth of privilege for the rich, began themselves to wear the ermined mantle. The penchant of society members to socialize with stars indicates that they sensed this change and strove to regain their authority through association with the newly powerful.

*   *   *

One sees in the evolving relationship of church and polite society to the actor evidence of important social rearrangements. Ministers and socialites were integral parts of the nineteenth-century cultural establishment, in their own sphere defining matters of value and taste for the public. The actor's rise was symptomatic of the decline of these two elite groups, not just because players took on their function as exemplars of morality and lifestyle, but because players were part of the larger machinery of mass culture which compressed the influence of these older groups. America's urban public had needs that neither the clergy, with its hopes for sanitized amusements, nor refined society, with its institutions of genteel culture, appreciated or fulfilled. The fin-de-siècle defiance of Victorian norms meant a questioning not only of traditional pieties and social amenities, but more fundamentally of authority itself. Ultimately no institution, be it church or fashionable society, would be granted the right of prescriptive guidance simply because of its social position. In the place of church and society came the media, which served not as cultural authority but as cultural mediator, allowing Americans to select among its varied offerings of taste and opinion. Paradoxically, this situation both centralized and diffused power—centralized, because it concentrated disproportionate power in one institution among the many of society; diffused, because the media purveyed assorted messages by the many groups that captured its ear. Authorities of all kinds would proliferate in the twentieth century, and Americans seemed more dependent on them for counsel than ever before. But in a Madisonian sense, these competing voices delimited the power of each, preventing any cultural strand from exercising the authority of the

Victorian leaders. The democratization of American culture, a tendency Tocqueville identified over a half-century earlier, was taking another leap forward as the nation entered a new century.

It was appropriate perhaps that actors, the celebrity creations of the media, should be in the forefront of the overthrow of older authorities. They, who for so long had suffered at the hands of a disapproving church and had been forced to scrape before a fickle gentility, now found their former masters in a supplicant posture. On the other side, the bearers of Victorian culture, a culture unusually authoritarian in the demands of behavior it made on those striving for respectability, witnessed their prestige slip away, in part to a group that had always symbolized the antithesis of these values. One could exaggerate the extent of this change by 1900, or even by 1910. Clergymen continued to denounce the stage from the pulpit to a still considerable if shrinking audience. High society, moreover, retained a certain authority in matters of taste. Theatrical managers never missed a chance to play up their star's social connections, confident that such news would boost the box office. But neither the approval nor the disapproval of high society was the critical issue any longer. The actors' legitimation came from a more direct appeal they made to middle-class culture. Actors had become celebrities in their own right, embodying images of personality and lifestyle that the public found immensely attractive. A new relationship between actor and society had been formed, aided by revolutionary changes in the field of journalism.

Six

Actors and Society: II

*T*he last fifteen years of the nineteenth century, observed historian of American journalism Frank Luther Mott, marked the rise of the magazine to a central role in American culture. The significance of this development may have surpassed even Mott's estimation, for with the popularization of magazine journalism came the beginnings of a national mass media, which in turn formed the heart of mass culture. The advent of the quality ten cent magazines created a huge new readership among the American public. Such periodicals as *Munsey's*, *McClure's*, *Ladies' Home Journal*, *Cosmopolitan*, *Colliers'*, and *Leslie's* proved tremendously popular with turn-of-the-century readers. They educated Americans regarding the rapid changes in the world around them. Magazine writers covered every conceivable topic and did so with a freshness and vitality generally missing from the more staid journals of the day. Their topical inclusiveness and huge readership contributed to a wholesale advance in public knowledge, helping make this era a time of social self-consciousness. Extensive illustrations made the magazines' impact even greater. The development of the half-tone photoengraving process in the 1880s enabled magazines to multiply illustrations and helped familiarize the public with the great people and exotic places of the world.[1]

A flourishing mass media was also crucial for the expanding social role of actors. The public's interest in the player did not end when the curtain fell. Indeed the actor's private life was even more compelling to his audience than his theatrical personations. When the footlights were dimmed, the greasepaint removed, and the player stepped out the stage door into the street—what was he like then? That this curiosity (an American trait European travelers had commented on decades earlier) should focus disproportionately on actors is perhaps the most important fact of all. The information revolution then getting under way bombarded Americans with multiplying wonders. Reports of exploration, of social reform, of scientific, medical, and technological advances reassured the public that a rational pattern of control was being imposed on the world. Yet at the same time and in the same magazines great attention was paid to a group whose lives seemed an open rebuke to the notion of an orderly and controlled life. Popular magazines were filled with commentary on the drama and illustrated features on the offstage life of players; many journals made this a regular feature.[2] Typically they promised glimpses into the players' private lives, with displays of their homes, accounts of their vacations, descriptions of their personalities, estimates of their incomes, and statements of their opinions on a variety of contemporary issues.

The collective portrait of the profession sketched by different journalists contained significant variety; some actors appeared nearly indistinguishable from the common run of humanity, while others were highly caricatured eccentrics. But overall the portrait displayed a group whose lives suggested a marked contrast with those of average people, a difference that compelled the public to stop and wistfully admire those who seemed exempt from the social restraints that bound others.

*   1   *

To players the press meant publicity and publicity meant stardom. The lengths to which actors would go to get their names in the newspaper were proverbial. They volunteered details and incidents in their lives to eager journalists, transforming mundane events into glorified escapades. Certain stories were overused and lost their credibility, actresses stopping a runaway team, or losing their jewels to robbers, for example. Not only aspiring thespians resorted to sensationalism, but even established stars. Genevieve Ward publicized her narrow escape in a carriage accident, while Rose Eytinge created a disturbance at the Bowery Theatre, then struck a dramatic pose before the enraged audience. And Fanny Davenport, who actually did have her jewels stolen, squeezed public-relations mileage out of the incident by publicly asking the governor of Tennessee to pardon the thief.[3] Occasionally a publicity stunt would backfire and injure a career. Comedian William Crane made a phonograph cylinder of his impressions of San Francisco for the *New York Times*. Trying to be funny Crane wisecracked about the city's climate: cold in the morning; very hot at noon; wind, dust, and fog in the afternoon; pneumonia at night. San Franciscans read his remarks in the newspaper but saw no humor in them, and for six years theatre managers discouraged Crane from playing the Golden Gate City.[4]

The lust for publicity was generally harmless entertainment for the public. But the self-promotion violated actors' concurrent wish for professional standing. The ban on advertising was credal among established professions, and the *Dramatic Mirror* tried to instill this standard in actors: "There is a general inclination to subordinate professional claims to extraneous personal ones. This spirit of cheap advertisement is damaging to the Profession."[5] A few of the more discreet professionals also thought actors erred in self-puffery. Marguerite Clark, for example, warned fellow players that an overabundance of personal interviews endangered their mystique should the public discover that their life was "just as ordinary and commonplace as anyone else's."[6] These admonitions did little good. Reticence was not common among performers. Moreover, acting by its very nature involves self-promotion, and the temptation to continue this outside the theatre was great.[7]

The business of publicity spawned a new professional in the late nineteenth century: the press agent. One of the first was Charles Emerson Cook. A Harvard graduate, he started out as a drama critic for several papers, but in the late 1890s he became David Belasco's full-time publicity agent. In 1900 he accompanied Mrs. Carter and the production of *Zaza* to London, where he introduced the zealous methods of American press agentry to the British. Cook recognized the value of magazines for theatrical pictures and articles, being a frequent contributor to *McClure's* and others. He also founded that venerable club, the Friars, as a retreat for theatrical pressmen. Another prominent press agent—later turned playwright—was Channing Pollock. He served as publicist for Florenz Ziegfeld, William A. Brady, and the Shuberts. While Cook once claimed that he never sent out a false story, Pollack described his own work as that of a "professional liar," and in some of his writings he detailed his more elaborate fabrications.[8]

A more respectable ally of the actor in the work of promotion and a more telling sign of the theatre's growing importance was the drama critic. Though dramatic criticism had begun with the Restoration stage, as late as the mid–nineteenth century it had not yet attained, in America at least, the stature of literary criticism. Newspapers often passed off theatre reviews to a neophyte journalist or a member of the staff with friends in the theatre. Even worse, honest criticism was often subverted by newspapers' reliance on theatrical advertising. Consequently, many reviews served as no more than eloquent press notices for a play.[9] Yet alongside the continued ballyhoo an increasing number of independent and informed critics began writing in the later decades of the nineteenth century. These American men of letters writing for the newspapers and journals of the day treated the theatre seriously. As guides for middle-class theatregoers, the new critics' unwavering commitment to genteel standards helped create a greater estimation for players. The very number of magazine and newspaper reviews plus the biographies and compilations of dramatic essays published near the end of the century further attested to the stage's heightened prominence.[10]

Preeminent among these genteel theatre critics was William Winter. Incredibly prolific, Winter authored a stream of lengthy biographies on leading players in addition to serving as the *New York Tribune's* drama critic from 1865 to 1919. Though never counted among the first-rank literary figures of his day and in later life subjected to caricature as "Weeping Willie" because of his lachrymose Victorian sentimentalizing, Winter up through the 1880s prevailed as America's most influential critic. He constantly exhorted the acting profession to be true to its duty, which was "to instill, to protect, and to maintain purity, sweetness, and refinement in our feelings, our manners, our language, and our national character."[11] Another of the Victorian moralists was John Ranken Towse, prominent critic of the *New York Evening Post* from 1874 to 1927 and contributor to many journals. Like Winter he resisted the wave of realism sweeping the theatre, wishing instead that it be "an elevator of the public mind and morals."[12] Henry Austin Clapp, Walter Prichard Eaton, Edward Dithmar, James Gibbons Huneker, and Andrew Carpenter Wheeler (known to his readers as Nym Crinkle) were among the other eminent newspaper and magazine critics who upgraded both their own profession and the stage in general.

In addition to the workaday critics, there were two writers who combined the careers of professor and critic. One was Brander Matthews, professor of English at Columbia University, who authored many serious works on drama and the theatre. Matthews's appointment to the first chair of dramatic literature in the country at Columbia University in 1902 symbolized the growing acceptance of drama by academia. Another of the scholar-critics was Clayton Hamilton. Lecturer in English at Columbia and critic for several magazines, Hamilton wrote some of the most insightful criticism of his day.[13]

But the genteel tradition of Winter and Towse and the scholarship of Matthews and Hamilton coexisted with another tradition of dramatic criticism, that of the "new journalism" ushered in by Joseph Pulitzer and William Randolph Hearst. These critics, typified by Alan Dale of the Hearst Syndicate and Ashton Stevens of the *Chicago Sun*, were clever and witty, valuing a well-turned phrase over thoughtful analysis. The reading public loved the chatty, gossipy style of Alan Dale, who became the most popular critic in the country by the first decade of the twentieth century and a celebrity in his own right. Dale felt no duty to instruct player or playgoer about the drama; he wrote simply to entertain his readers. "I have always held that the lighter, the frothier, the more amusing you make your reviews, the more you will be read and the more theatre will gain," he wrote.[14] Dale's columns were well suited for the mass audience of the Hearst newspapers and magazine *Cosmopolitan*. Employing a similarly "smart" style were critics Alexander Woollcott and George Jean Nathan in the second decade of the twentieth century. But where Dale and Stevens were clever and vacuous, Woollcott and Nathan combined colorful prose with shrewd theatrical comment.

As might be expected, critics and actors could have their differences, which at times escalated into pitched battles. Alan Dale was hated by many actors and managers for his vitriolic pen; at different times he was banned from virtually every theatre in New York.[15] But the more general story of their relationship was not one of enmity but of peace. History chronicles many close friendships between the two. Critics could be extremely loyal friends, providing constant support for actors' tender egos. William Winter's loyalty to McCullough, Booth, Jefferson, and Mansfield led him to boost their careers at the expense of his critical objectivity.[16] When Paul Potter of the *Herald* attacked Fanny Janauschek for her interpretation of a role, she turned to critic A. C. Wheeler to write her defense, distributing ten thousand copies of the apologia through the country.[17] Actors would also look to critics for technical advice on their acting. Actor John Emerson wrote to Pittsburgh critic Charles Bregg thanking him for his review of *Hedda Gabler*, in which Emerson had a supporting role: "I have always insisted that one of the chief, if not the chief function of dramatic criticism is to assist the actor in bettering his work. In this respect your article seems to me to be particularly helpful."[18]

In truth, the relationship of actors and critics offered mutual benefits. Actors received encouragement, advice, publicity, and entrée into the literary circles that could validate their pretensions to artistic accomplishment. In return critics enjoyed the pleasure of hobnobbing with the stars. They had an insider's access to the stage and its heady whirl of excitement. It was a privilege few had and many coveted.

Beyond the press agent and the critic lay another rank of individuals unconnected to the theatre except for their hope of using its glamour for self-gain. These were publishers, who capitalized on both the players' vanity and public curiosity by producing picture albums. Portrait albums of players appeared in the 1770s in England, and collections of lithographs and prints were seen in several European nations and Japan as well as America in the nineteenth century. The development of photoengraving multiplied the albums. Some of the volumes were collector's items, beautifully bound and expensive. But by the end of the century budget editions were made available to the theatre-happy public.[19] In addition to the albums, sales of individual photographs of stars became a lively business in the early twentieth century. Pictures of such wholesome actresses as Maude Adams, Ethel Barrymore, Maxine Elliott, Eleanor Robson, and Julia Marlowe sold well to the young matinee girls.[20] Bizarre variations on these photographs emerged, such as cigarette cards that pictured actors dressed in colorful costumes of the world. They dressed Lotta Crabtree in the costume of a Japanese lady, Joseph Jefferson as an Indian Mogul, and Dion Boucicault as a French knight.

Players, or at least players' names and pictures, were also subject to exploitation by less scrupulous publishers and newspapermen. Dime paperback albums featured cheap reproductions of actresses, including prominent ones, dressed in tights or other provocative outfits. Tawdry publications such as the *Police Gazette* put out illustrated supplements of actresses and dancers. The first girlie magazines, in fact, almost always identified their unclad nymphs as actresses.[21] Books reputing to be exposés of life behind the footlights were sometimes merely excuses for printing racy pictures and relating lurid details.[22] These books and pictures reinforced a long-standing connection in the popular mind between actresses and immoral women. Evidence of this prejudice was felt by a group of American actresses who tried to go to Canada in 1915 in search of work. The actresses, unaccompanied and without a contract, were assumed to be prostitutes, and Canadian border officials ordered them off the train and sent back to America. Even an actress under contract to a troupe in Montreal was denied entrance on similar suspicions.[23]

On the margins of the theatre, admittedly, there was a group of women who split duty between the chorus line and prostitution, their connection with the theatre probably helping them ply their trade. A 1912 survey of prostitution in New York City found that of the 487 women who gave their occupational history, 72 said they had previously been on the stage, and 16 claimed they worked on stage throughout the season. Only department stores and domestic service supplied more recruits to the trade than did the theatre.

Although few of these women may have ever spoken a line on the legitimate stage, their identification as actresses shaped the public's feelings about the morality of the stage and its people.[24]

Attacks leveled against individual players in the press posed an even more serious problem. These attacks could be vicious, and no actor was immune. A man notorious for accusation and innuendo was Charles Alfred Byrne. Byrne's career in the theatre included stints as theatrical and operatic manager, author, dramatic critic for the *New York Herald*, and—beginning in 1875—editor of the *New York Dramatic News*, which for several years was the sole theatrical newspaper in New York. His tenure at the *Dramatic News* was stormy, punctuated by constant charges of libel and even a few lawsuits. He was regarded as a blackguard among professionals for his reckless attacks on their personal lives. On the eve of Edwin Booth's 1880 tour to England, for example, Byrne accused him of drunkenness and shady financial dealing. He also referred to William Winter as a drunkard and charged E. A. Sothern with licentiousness and bribery. Byrne's motive for the attacks—whether he was personally vindictive or thought scandal was a way to sell newspapers—remains unclear. At any rate, when Ernest Harvier founded the *Dramatic Mirror* in 1879, he wasted no time in launching a crusade against Byrne, charging him with blackmail and finally forcing him out of the *Dramatic News* in 1881.[25]

But Byrne's silencing did not spell the end of attacks on actors by other newspapermen. Divorce or illness often occasioned sensational stories about players. Georgia Cayvan, one of America's popular leading ladies of the 1890s, was named as the "other woman" in an 1896 divorce case. She went to court to defend her name and was eventually exonerated. But the strain of the scandal ruined her health and virtually ended her career.[26] When Sarah Jewett had to undergo treatment for nervous disorders in 1887 the *New York Sun* printed rumors of opium use. Fortunately for Jewett, many of her friends in the profession rushed to defend her reputation.[27] Even the beloved Mary Anderson was not spared. When she suffered a nervous breakdown in the spring of 1889, Louisville and St. Louis papers made unflattering suggestions about the origins of her problem. Possibly the newspaper reports contributed to her decision not to return to the stage. Certainly such vicious journalism distressed all sensitive players. Kate Rankin told of the effect of a "shameful article" about herself in Pulitzer's *St. Louis Post-Dispatch*: "You cannot imagine how this malicious, disgraceful falsehood has preyed upon my mind. I can think of nothing else. . . . If it was to continue I should leave a profession where one's name is to be handled as commonly as the lowest of God's creatures."[28]

Not all players were innocent victims. Occasionally the reality lived up to the headline. Henry Rose, actor and stage manager for Charles Frohman, shot and killed his wife, whom he accused of unfaithfulness. James B. Gentry, a member of the Willie Collier company, shot actress Madge Yorke three times through the head in a fit of jealousy in 1895. Less seriously, actress May Buckley was shot at and two of her male companions wounded by a jealous, deaf-mute member of a prominent Southern family.[29] All of these incidents, newsworthy in themselves, were reported with special relish by the press because they involved actors. Similarly, newspapers habitually identified women in morally compromising situations as actresses, prompting the *Rochester Democrat and Chronicle* to rebuke the Actors' Society for not protesting a practice so injurious to the profession's image.[30]

A related problem was the lawsuits that brought discredit on the profession. Most concerned broken contracts between actors and managers or accusations of play piracy. But there were also a number of libel and slander cases. In one, McKee Rankin publicly accused playwright Bartley Campbell in 1880 of stealing his play and turning it into the popular *Galley Slave*. Campbell responded by a libel suit against Rankin. In another case, thespian Frank Keenan filed a $75,000 slander suit against William Faversham in 1913, claiming that his plan to produce Shakespeare had been blighted by Faversham's defamatory remarks about him in the *Kansas City Journal*. Attacks on actors became a serious enough problem to merit a lengthy article in the *Dramatic Mirror* in 1881 advising players of the legal definition of libel. Unfortunately for aggrieved actors, legal redress was difficult, and most cases proved futile.[31]

Unknown to them, actors were caught up in one of the important legal questions of the day: definition of the right to privacy. The advent of privacy as a social and legal concern issued from the increasing density of urban life—which made people more sensitive to personal privacy—and as a reaction to the growth and character of late nineteenth-century journalism. Newspaper circulation ballooned and, more critically, was accompanied by the sensationalistic style of Pulitzer and Hearst. Papers included interviews and personal investigations by "Paul Pry" reporters who dug up as much gossip and scandal as possible. People found their names bantered about in newspapers and other publications, perhaps linked to a notorious affair of which they knew nothing. Photography and the halftone reproductions added the possibility of having not only one's name but one's picture displayed to thousands of readers.[32]

In this atmosphere of wide-open journalism, when anyone was fair game to the prying eyes and acidic pen of the reporter, dissenting voices began to be heard. The genteel editor E. L. Godkin distastefully observed that newspapers had made curiosity a marketable commodity, putting scurrilous gossip at a premium.[33] John Gilmer Speed wrote in 1896 that the right to privacy was essential, for without it "civilization must deteriorate, and modesty and refinement be crushed by brutality and vulgar indecency."[34] But the most direct call for legal sanctions against invasions of privacy came in in an influential *Harvard Law Review* article of 1890, "The Right to Privacy," by Samuel D. Warren and Louis D. Brandeis, which remains a landmark in the modern formulation of the legal doctrine of privacy.[35] Warren and Brandeis argued that the common law could be extended to protect the rights of a person "to be let alone." Recent inventions and trends in business, they pointed out, had made the issue of privacy a compelling one. In a scathing indictment of the press they wrote that "instantaneous photographs and newspaper enterprise have invaded the sacred precincts of private and domestic life; and numerous mechanical devices threaten to make good the prediction that 'what is whispered in the closet shall be proclaimed from the house-tops.'"[36]

No occupation found itself more often the object of journalistic prying, rumor, and scandal than acting. Exposés of actors' private affairs sometimes reached the absurd. For example, the *New York Sun* reported in detail a legal dispute between a prominent actor and his plumber over a repair bill, even printing interviews with both.[37] "One would think," the *Mirror* editorialized in 1888, "that actors and singers are the only people worth talking about in all this great, busy, active, pushing, enterprising world, and that newspapers are published for the express purpose of perpetuating the doings of actors in private life, rather than their endeavors upon the public stage."[38] Notwithstanding this admonition, the *Dramatic Mirror* ran its own column on the personal doings of players, "The Usher," and later, "The Giddy Gusher." And Deshler Welch's *Theatre*—which appeared in 1886 with the disclaimer that "with the private affairs of actors, with the cheap gossip which seems to drift about the stage, and thence into street and newspaper scandals, we have nothing to do"—bowed to journalistic convention with its gossip column called "Both Sides of the Curtain."[39]

Much of the publicity, of course, was encouraged by actors themselves. But what of the players who wished to keep their private affairs private: did they have that right? John Gilmer Speed said yes. Despite the "habit indulged in by so many actors of thrusting their portraits before the public, and filling the columns of daily newspapers with the most intimate as well as the most trivial of their private affairs," Speed said, this "does not take away from any member of the profession the right to be let alone when the curtain which hides his assumed character from the world is drawn close." [40]

Given the public's insatiable curiosity it is not surprising that two of the early privacy cases involved players. One of the first (and one cited by Warren and Brandeis) happened in 1890. The Broadway Theatre management of *Castles in the Air* wanted a picture of comic opera prima donna Marion Manola to use on its advertising posters. A photographer lay in wait until the actress, clad in tights, was onstage. Then without her consent he took her picture. The infuriated Manola went to court and got an injunction— upheld by the New York Supreme Court—prohibiting the management from using the photograph for any purpose without her permission. [41] Another case in the early 1890s involved actors from the Yiddish theatre. The editor of *Der Wachter* planned a popularity contest between Rudolph Marks and comedian Zelig Mogulesko by publishing pictures of both men and letting readers vote for their favorite. Marks refused to let his picture be used, perhaps sensing he would lose to the popular Mogulesko, but the editor ran it anyway. Marks went to court and obtained an injunction against the use of his picture, the judge ruling that those who desire privacy must be let alone. [42]

But these two cases were not indicative of the future course of privacy law, at least as it pertained to actors. A comparison of two treatises on theatrical law, one from 1892 and the other from 1907, illustrates an interesting shift. The 1892 treatise reflected the decision of the Manola case—that is, actors had the right to control exhibition of their photographs. By 1907, however, the courts had made an important distinction between private and public individuals. A private individual had the right to prohibit reproduction of his picture. But public characters—statesmen, authors, inventors, and actors, among others, those having asked for public recognition—surrendered the right to keep their pictures out of the press. They belonged to the public. [43]

Legal recognition of such "public figures" quietly signified the arrival of the "celebrity." In effect a new class of people had been recognized, a group whom the public was given the right to know intimately. That the courts were forced to deal with this issue testified to the impact of the mass media. That they acknowledged a public right to private information about highly visible people bespoke a new sense of public need. The complex story of one of America's most fundamental cultural changes, from the self-directed society of the eighteenth and nineteenth centuries to the other-directed mass society of the twentieth, has yet to be fully unraveled.[44] At the center of that mystery, however, will be the hunger for human images, which is perhaps the most characteristic feature of mass culture. And at the turn of the nineteenth century, when urbanization created the social conditions conducive to this craving and the media developed the means to fulfill it, celebrities—those in Daniel Boorstin's famous epigram "known for their well-knownness"—became a permanent part of the American landscape.[45]

There was a cost to be borne by those heralded few. Celebrities were the creations of the media and the captives of the public. Players had to realize that fame made them vulnerable to journalistic prying. Many actors of that day (as well as our own) resented the other edge of the sword of fame: the thrusts into the sanctum of their private lives. But the loss of privacy was the trade-off players accepted when they embraced stardom—it was the price of celebrity.

* 2 *

By the early twentieth century actors not only mixed with the "smart set," but gained wide exposure through newspapers and magazines, making them familiar figures to even America's non-theatregoing public. Observers inside the theatre and out commented on the players' rise to prominence in American society. But questions remain. To what use did actors put their new-found celebrity? And, more crucially, what was the basis of the celebrity itself?

*   *   *

The most common prerogative of the celebrity from any field is that of social commentator, and actors were no exception. As early as 1873 the *New York Times* noted that "the stage is asserting itself as an engine of reform in social uplift."[46] In the following decades newspapers and magazines printed interviews with or articles by players on many topics. Actresses usually restricted themselves to giving beauty tips or suggestions on interior decorating. Actors ranged further afield. In the Sunday supplement section of early twentieth-century newspapers one found articles by (or at least attributed to) David Belasco on beauty, the homely girl, life after death, the supernatural, the implications of bobbed hair, short skirts, and corsetless bodies.[47] But some players did more than repeat cant phrases on inconsequential issues; they spoke out on the political and social reforms of the day.

Political involvement was not completely new. Edwin Forrest actively campaigned for the Democratic party in the 1830s. But his famous political sympathies were exceptional among players of his day. As a rule, actors kept aloof from political issues. The *Dramatic Mirror* observed in 1880 that "it has generally been conceded that actors have nothing to do with politics; . . . it is one of the unwritten laws of the profession that actors shall take no part in political movements and display no partisanship on or off the stage."[48] Political noninvolvement resulted in part from the difficulty actors had in exercising their voting rights. Before the advent of absentee ballots the touring players had no chance to get to the polls on election day. Apathy followed political impotence. It took a seven-year fight, including efforts by Actors' Equity, before absentee voting was provided for in New York state in 1918.[49]

Perhaps a more important reason for players' lack of political interest was their legacy of social exclusion. Though their position became more secure in the late nineteenth century, a social group reaching for respectability would not likely risk its tenuous position by taking a strong stand on a divisive political or social issue. Moreover, producing managers such as Augustin Daly and Charles Frohman felt that actors compromised their appeal by prolonged public exposure and discouraged their stars from speaking out on issues, especially controversial ones.[50] When actors did express their social views, they were given to conservative sentiments. The *Dramatic Mirror* urged players to take their civic responsibilities seriously to prove that they were "reputable and respectable citizens" and had "a property interest . . . in good government and prosperity of the nation."[51] Social conservatism can be seen in a letter from Edwin Booth to a friend in San Francisco during the anti-Chinese riots in 1880: "I am glad to hear that peace is restored in Frisco, but they should not let Kearney (nor Kollack) off without a whipping at a public pillory on the sandlots. That should be the punishment for such d—d rascals! a good sound lashing, 'till the blood ran—then a bath of salt water' . . . there'll be no more nihilism in 'Frisco.'"[52]

Actors also helped promote the fervent nationalism that was so much a part of turn-of-the-century America. One could be sure of an enthusiastic reception by waving Old Glory. George M. Cohan built his career around a cleverly scored and choreographed patriotism.[53] The full potential of thespic patriotism only became apparent with World War I, when actors raised millions of dollars for the government through their staged promotion of war bonds.

While increasing prosperity and higher status inclined most players to political conservatism, a few players joined the forces of social reform. Mrs. Fiske, George Arliss, and Dudley Digges waged war on behalf of humane treatment of animals and antivivesection, and Lotta Crabtree willed $300,000 for an animal fund.[54] A more controversial social reform that attracted support among many actresses was women's suffrage. The alliance of actress and suffragette appears natural when one recalls that the stage was a place where women had attained equality with men and that the ambition and self-reliance necessary for a woman to forge a stage career would also incline her to demand full rights. Playwright Israel Zangwill saw the appropriateness of actresses being in the feminist vanguard. "The actress has long appeared to the crowd as the ideal image of freedom and spontaneity," Zangwill observed, and as a "pioneer of public works" she shook herself free from many "old-fashioned crampings and convictions."[55]

The first actress to promote feminism, and perhaps the pioneer of the social reform spirit among American players, was Olive Logan. Born in 1839, she appeared with Philadelphia and New York stock companies before leaving the stage in 1868 to devote full time to lecturing and writing. Her interest in women's rights sprang from the difficulties she had met in pursuing a career. She spoke at the American Equal Rights Convention in 1869, then continued in the feminist cause through newspaper articles and lectures.[56] Although Olive Logan left the stage, later proponents of women's rights combined their reform efforts with an acting career. These included Julia Marlowe, who was a close friend of Susan B. Anthony; Mrs. Fiske, whose feminism manifested itself with her promotion of Henrik Ibsen's *A Doll's House*; May Irwin, who had evangelists for women's rights lecture the audience between acts of her play *33 Washington Square*; Lillian Russell, born of a feminist mother, who actively joined the battle for suffrage; and Trixie Friganza, who led a march of militant suffragettes to New York's City Hall where they lectured Mayor McClellan and a crowd of several thousand from City Hall steps. A longer list would include Mrs. Potter, Elsie Janis, and Eleanor Robson.[57]

The theatre's most radical reformer in this era was James A. Herne. Herne's close friend, author Hamlin Garland, introduced him to the Single-Tax reform of Henry George in 1889, which Herne took up with a passion. For the next twelve years he worked tirelessly in its behalf. Herne felt that George's panacea of the Single Tax held the answer to players' problems of unemployment. Actors, Herne asserted, were wage earners at the mercy of an unjust taxation. Through a means that Herne could explain only vaguely, the Single Tax would free players from economic tyranny. As an agency for reform Herne proposed the formulation of an Actors' Single Tax League.[58] Herne's suggestion caused an uproar. Actors considered themselves professionals, and the notion that they join hands with the labor movement scandalized them. At the founding meeting of the Actors' Society in 1896 Herne criticized his fellow workers for their political apathy and for their failure to ally themselves with other laborers in the cosmic struggle between capital and labor. Herne's polemic only alienated other actors. The Actors' Society rejected any notion of unionism, and for his efforts Herne was shut out of The Players.[59]

Another hotly debated reform championed by a player was Richard Bennett's advocacy of the Wasserman test for syphilis. The elegant, mustachioed Bennett epitomized the matinee idol of the early twentieth century. But along with a number of other players of his generation, Bennett viewed the theatre as a vehicle for public education, and he took up the battle against veneral disease. Although state laws had been introduced calling for mandatory blood tests prior to marriage, discussion of the topic was deemed unfit for polite circles and legislation foundered. French playwright Eugéne Brieux wrote a play describing the effects of hereditary syphilis called *Damaged Goods*, which Bennett found and determined to produce, much to the horror of his producer Charles Frohman. Bennett had difficulty finding a theatre to use, as no owner wanted to lease his theatre for a play that might offend the public. With a theatre at last secured and Bennett and Wilton Lackaye set in the leading roles, Bennett encountered further problems in casting the remaining parts. Actors feared that an appearance in *Damaged Goods* might be professional suicide. The role of the prostitute proved especially hard to cast, with six actresses being hired and quitting before Bennett's wife, Mabel Adrienne Morrison, settled in the part.

The first performance, sponsored by the *Medical Review of Reviews*, took place in New York on March 14, 1913, with an audience of city officials, social workers, legislators, doctors, and ministers. The next performance came in Washington, D.C., a special Sunday matinee restricted to members of Congress and other government officials, foreign diplomats, ministers, and social workers. Whatever misgivings the public might have had about attending this kind of "problem play" ended with these two widely heralded performances. *Damaged Goods* returned to the Fulton Theatre in New York for a twenty-two-month run and later a successful road tour. The play continued to arouse controversy on tour; in Boston the mayor tried to ban it and in Chicago the city's chief censor forced certain deletions. Not content with letting the play's message speak for it-self, Bennett harangued the audience on the subject after each play. In 1915 his cast made a movie of *Damaged Goods* for the American-Mutual Film Company. Though Bennett's stage and film produc-tions of Brieux's play helped educate the public on the issue of ve-nereal disease, it remained until 1926 before any state adopted the Wasserman test.[60]

Actors not only expressed their opinions more freely on political and social issues; they increasingly kept company with the nation's political leaders. The most famous example of actor-statesman camaraderie was Joseph Jefferson's friendship with Grover Cleveland. Jefferson's vacation retreat at Buzzards Bay, Massachusetts, was near Cleveland's, and they frequently fished together. The much-publicized friendship was pointed to as signal-ing the advancing social esteem of the whole profession.[61] Come-dian William J. Florence counted a number of politicians among his friends, including theatre lover Cleveland. During his career Flor-ence portrayed a politician in *The Mighty Dollar* and burlesqued congressmen in *Honorable Bardwell Slate*. These roles were not mere acting, for he had political ambitions of his own; he had been con-sidered for the post of Ambassador to France until the fear of up-setting America's religious element caused Cleveland to drop the appointment.

Other players—William H. Crane, Richard Mansfield, John Drew, and Elsie Janis—visited the White House between Cleveland's and Theodore Roosevelt's administrations.[62] These associations ap-pear modest now, in an age when the White House regularly hosts entertainment celebrities. And the handful of actor-reformers seem insignificant when compared to the political activism and social concern of a considerable number of modern entertainers. But the turn-of-the-century era was significant as a beginning, with actors taking their first tentative steps from the stage to the rostrum. It heralded the future age of media politics, when the celebrity of the person espousing a cause would be nearly as significant as the opinion stated. Today, of course, far from being a political hand-icap, acting careers have given some the public recognition to ac-quire high office. In a media-dominated society the requirements for success in politics and acting are not dissimilar, and it has be-come a truism that the politician must carefully craft his public im-age, much as an actor uses his talents to create his stage role.

There was initially little public controversy over actors' in-volvement in social issues, probably because it had not yet attained major proportions, nor were actors involved in hotly debated po-litical issues (with the exception of women's suffrage) as they would be in the 1960s. The ease with which actors assumed the role of public spokesman, though, is striking; it is as if it were perfectly natural that their opinions mattered greatly. Only much later would society display a critical awareness of the phenomenon and even then simply register a cynical resignation to the fact. The modern blending of roles—actor, politician, celebrity—into a single type has rendered old distinctions obsolete, creating a political culture that is as theatrical as anything seen on the stage.

*   *   *

How, finally, was the actor viewed? What images of him did the media create that were so appealing?

There were two contrasting characterizations of actors, one more significant than the other, both in its pervasiveness and in its suggestiveness for a wider cultural perspective. The lesser of the two portrayed players as no different from other people, sharing the same hopes, fears, joys, and loves. The stress on domestic pleasures, as already seen, was common—likewise the love of outdoor life, an appealing thought to a generation that was getting back to nature. Maude Adams, the country was told, spent every moment she could at her country home in Ronkonkoma, Long Island, surrounded by her horses, pigs, chickens, and Saint Bernard.[63] This actress (the favorite subject of the moralists), as well as others such as Viola Allen and Julia Marlowe, were described as the quintessence of Victorian womanhood and enjoyed reputations based on upright behavior onstage and off. Moreover, certain actors themselves debunked the myth of exceptionalism. John Drew maintained that there was "little extraordinary" about the actor. When he shed his costume he became again "plain, honest citizen."[64] And even in *Equity* magazine, official organ of Actors' Equity, a note appeared in 1920 informing the public that the actor "is a regular human being, as you and I."[65]

These allegations of normality, however, were the minor key, pressed by those seeking genteel respectability for the stage. They failed to see that the actors' fundamental attractiveness resided in their difference, their uniqueness. Better than most, Cicely Hamilton, a British dramatist and suffragette, recognized the self-defeating efforts of some actresses to become models of domestic propriety. What attracted the public to players was not respectability but raffishness. "Tales of drink and divorce court were whispered about him," she wrote in 1912, "and those who heard and those who told the tales alike decided they must have a look at him."[66]

In spite of their hopes for social acceptance and esteem, many actors clung to a belief in their own distinctiveness, even though certain of its aspects might not flatter them. Players, admitted the *Actors' Society Monthly Bulletin*, were egotistical people, standing before an audience each night seeking the applause that reinforced their feelings of self-importance.[67] Richard Mansfield boldly proclaimed the actor to be "SUI GENERIS," "extraordinary," so that when he returned from his theatrical fantasy land, where he had transformed into "king, begger, lover or criminal," it could not be surprising that he remained "tinged with some clinging color of his living dream."[68] Mansfield expressed more forcefully than most the sense that actors' access to the potent magic of impersonation left them marked even away from the footlights. It was a conviction so deeply held by most of the profession that it did not require iteration. It was also a belief shared by the public, one so cherished that any denial by actors could only be ignored.

This predilection was both nurtured and reflected through a journalistic stress on actors' chronic nonconformity, a characteristic understood as nearly congenital. "There was never a Thespian," wrote Ida McGlone in 1911, "that could, by any stretch of the imagination, confine his life to conventional standards."[69] A short story appearing in the *Dramatic Mirror* in 1892 made the same point. It described a society girl involved in amateur theatricals, who became acquainted with a professional actor hired to direct the production. Though she was already engaged, she fell in love with him. Every Sunday he had dinner with her and her family and charmed them with his gracious manner. But she soon discovered that he had a wife and son to whom he was devoted. She was stunned. "What then had he meant by his looks, his attentions, his intimacy? Like a flash of lightening she understood that, being an actor, he had meant—nothing. He lived in a different world from her own, and was not to be judged by the same standards."[70]

A characterization of unconventionality implied an affectionate appreciation of actors' quaint behavior, but frequently it also carried an undercurrent of distrust. Eccentricity could verge on immorality. Speaking of English players, Henry De Halsalle declared that actors assumed a nonmoral attitude toward life. "He had his own manners, his own morals, and in his mode of life he differs widely from his brothers in the learned and business professions," De Halsalle wrote in 1907. Moreover, the actor was insensitive to the emotions he portrayed onstage and over the course of time "the practice of his art seriously impairs his capacity for the natural emotions of daily life."[71] Elocutionist S. H. Clark offered a psychological explanation for actors' weakness for erotic temptation. Artistic people dwelt in a realm of emotion and imagination, he said, and emotion, if not carefully channeled to noble impulse, would weaken the will. Thus actors had to take extra care lest their highly charged emotions undermine their moral sense.[72] In the same vein, Hartley Davis bluntly stated in the pages of *Munsey's* magazine that the stage weakened morals. It did so by imparting an artificiality to players' lives, leading them to strive constantly for effect —by isolating them from the prosaic workaday world, and by inducing a hunger for praise and personal aggrandizement. Few players could retain naturalness in thought and expression after a decade of acting, Davis felt, which would forever cause a suspicious public to keep its distance from them. Conversely, actors, "content in their isolation, their artificiality, and their emotional astigmatism, will live in their make up boxes, talk their own peculiar language, and work out their own salvation."[73]

This image of actors was summed up through their frequent description as "Bohemians." Such references are sprinkled through both theatrical and nontheatrical publications. The *New York Times*, for example, commented in 1884 that the rootless life of the actor encouraged this Bohemian lifestyle.[74] An 1888 article in *The Theatre* harshly denounced the dramatic profession as indecent, one which cast aside the conventionalities of the refined. "The greater number of the women of our stage are proved integrants of the blazing cauldron called Bohemia," it said.[75] Further, the *Dramatic Mirror* featured articles describing the "Bohemian" apartments of well-to-do players, dark and exotically furnished, hinting at a languorous lifestyle and an improper intimacy.[76]

The identification of actors as Bohemians linked them to an important cultural impulse of the nineteenth century. The Bohemian idyll originated in France, largely a creation of Henri Murger, who vividly described the exploits of Parisian demimonde in his *Scènes de la vie bohème*. From the Left Bank of Louis Philippe's Paris the spirit of artistic revolt against bourgeois culture spread to New York in the 1850s, where a group of free spirits, including Walt Whitman, Ada Clare, and Fitz-James O'Brien, sang the anthem of social freedom. The Bohemian spirit languished for the next several decades, though the word did gain currency in America as a synonym for outlandish behavior and a Bohemian Club composed of rakish journalists formed in San Francisco in 1872. But it was not until the last decade of the nineteenth century that the Bohemian virus infected the nation.[77]

The virus accompanied what one historian has termed a "cultural reorientation" of the 1890s.[78] This was a decade that witnessed an erosion of certain restrictions and confinements of behavior, while spontaneity and a more relaxed propriety gained acceptance. Manifestations of this new spirit were numerous. On college campuses the fight songs epitomized the competitive impulse as intercollegiate athletics—baseball, track, wrestling, and especially football—were becoming focal points of national interest. The "strenuous life," in Theodore Roosevelt's phrase, became a national ideal, illustrated by the bicycling craze and a new concern for fitness, which led to the popularizing of physical culture and the building of gymnasiums and playgrounds. Outdoor recreation and a heightened interest in nature led millions of Americans to the mountains or seashore or to the new national parks. And finally, the seaside amusement parks and resorts such as Coney Island and Atlantic City attracted thousands daily to their sandy beaches and seamy sideshows, inviting their patrons to shed genteel decorum in favor of a vivacious informality.[79]

Assertiveness marked the decade not only in sports and recreation but also in popular fiction, such as Owen Wister's bestseller of 1902, *The Virginian,* which exalted manliness and virility, and Jack London's adventure tales of the Klondike. Aggressiveness also characterized the "New Woman," who no longer content with the passivity prescribed by Victorian society began to pursue activities formerly considered indelicate or masculine and stepped up her crusade for suffrage. The feminine revolt against constraints extended to the intellectual class, who, anxious that life might be passing them by, preached a gospel of experience and scorned conventions of middle-class life. The 1890s was also a decade of remarkable ferment in American literature. Novelists, poets, and short-story writers experimented with new forms and subject matter. Stephen Crane, Hamlin Garland, Ambrose Bierce, Kate Chopin, and Edward Arlington Robinson were just a few of the authors whose works reflected the social tumult of the era. Such avant-garde magazines as *The Chap-Book* and *The Lark* appeared, tinged with the culture of decadence from fin-de-siècle Europe. Taken together, these literary manifestations represented an alternative to the genteel tradition in American letters.[80]

A common thread tied together all of these cultural expressions: a rebellion against the confined and sedentary life imposed by modern industrial society. This is John Higham's description:

> From the middle of the nineteenth century until about 1890 Americans on the whole had submitted docilely enough to the gathering restrictions of a highly industrialized society. They learned to live in cities, to sit in rooms cluttered with bric-a-brac, to limit the size of their families, to accept the authority of professional elites, to mask their aggressions behind a thickening facade of respectability, and to comfort themselves with a faith in automatic material prog-

ress. Above all, Americans learned to conform to the discipline of machines.[81]

In the 1890s Americans began reacting against the decorum and restraint of the Gilded Age in an attempt "to break out of the frustrations, the routine, and the sheer dullness of an urban-industrial culture. It was everywhere an urge to be young, masculine and adventurous."[82]

The fascination with Bohemianism represented another aspect of this breaking with old constraints. Bohemian freedom in lifestyle—from conventions of dress and speech, and from the eternal quest for money and respectability—proved attractive to a generation growing weary of excessive proprieties. "On these latter days, when so much of life is made up of work and care responsibilities," commented a writer for *Overland Monthly* in 1906, "it is not to be wondered at that all the world is ever ready to reach out for anything that seems to promise even momentary relief."[83] The American public saw in the Bohemian message a symbolic freedom from the Victorian restraints and confines of industrial life. The rage for Bohemianism was highlighted by the Trilby craze of 1894–95, inspired by George du Maurier's popular novel of studio life in Paris. Du Maurier's heroine became an exemplar of the modern woman and excited a vogue for nude modeling among the many young women who wished to follow the Trilby life. The massive book sales and multiple road-company theatricals of *Trilby* were soon followed by other sorts of commercialization. Trilby shoes and foot accessories, bathing suits, cigars, cigarettes were marketed. With the Trilby craze, said historian Albert Parry, "Bohemianism became the sensation and the rage of America. . . . Everyone talked about it and strove to be considered a Bohemian."[84]

The Bohemianism exemplified by the Trilby craze was, of course, something of a sham. In truth, Murger's *Bohème* had itself been a rather congenial defiance of bourgeois standards, and later Bohemianism continued to carry an air of affectation, a posturing by members of the leisured classes. William Dean Howells, whose civilized mien permitted only an amused tolerance of the denizens of vagabondia, authored *The Coast of Bohemia* in 1893, which portrayed the revolt as merely pretense. For the well-bred female, Bohemianism meant a studio in careful disarray, foreign chocolates, popcorn, and exotic drinks, a forbidden smoke, and conversation about psychology and the supernatural.[85] The shallowness of the Bohemian spirit was epitomized in a 1904 Philadelphia publication called *Bohemia*. Handsomely bound and lavishly illustrated, containing four hundred pages of photos, cartoons, lithographs, articles, and poems by such authors as Dorothea Dix,

Edward Bok, and William Jennings Bryan, it was a testimonial to the exalted position of a domesticated la vie bohème. Improvidence and unconventionality were downplayed. Bohemianism, wrote Julia Ward Howe, "desires to conform to all the healthful decencies of life, to all social ordinances which are truly refining." The book's dialectical blending of revolt and propriety appealed to middle-class buyers, making the album a commercial success.[86]

Not all Bohemians were poseurs. There was the community in the San Francisco area composed of talented and truly eccentric writers and artists such as Joaquin Miller, George Sterling, Jack London, Ambrose Bierce, and Mary Austin. The midwestern Bohemian circle in Chicago included those in the vanguard of American letters: Vachel Lindsay, Carl Sandburg, Margaret Anderson, Harriet Monroe, Floyd Dell, and Sherwood Anderson. And of course there was Greenwich Village, which in pre–World War I days became the symbol of the Bohemian revolt. But that is another story, for these thinkers anticipated the more serious alienation from American culture characteristic of twentieth-century artists and intellectuals, an attitude from which the genteel pretenders of the Latin Quarter would have shrunk in horror.

Popular Bohemianism may have been frivolous and devoid of serious content, but it was not inconsequential. It should instead be viewed as a sort of Victorian counterculture. Its attractiveness indicated a faltering of genteel culture and the stirring of a new sensibility, one less dogmatic about social conventions and more open to the possibilities of various lifestyles. It was a qualified rebellion to be sure. Bourgeois adaptations of any style have always harmonized with society's deepest values, and the pale copy of Bohemianism that emerged was no exception. Just as the Victorian middle classes had emulated the form of high culture, filling their parlors with cheap statuary and lithographs, many now affected a veneer of unconventionality. But that image of revolt, insipid as it might be, marked a step away from the controlling values of discipline and sobriety and toward an ethic of spontaneity and pleasure.[87]

Actors found themselves the beneficiaries of this change in national mood. Traditionally they had stood outside the pale because they were thought not to conform to the prescriptive values of morality, practicality, rootedness, and a host of others. When respectability reigned unchallenged among social attributes, players had little hope of acceptance or respect. Repeated tales of inebriety, divorce, immorality, excessive conviviality stamped them as social misfits. Actors seemed to deny the seriousness of life. Understandably then, concerned actors and patrons of the theatre sought the

elusive prize of respectability by upgrading the image of their profession. But as Americans began to chafe against the routinization
and constraints of modern industrial life, the players' image underwent a change. Their freedom from conventionality, once a source
of suspicion, now became their strength. Though in fact few actors
moved among the true Bohemian circles of artists and writers, they
became quintessential Bohemian figures in the public mind.

This change was bound up with the larger transformation of
Victorianism into modernism, a development historians have more
successfully identified than defined.[88] Behind the manifest changes
of style and behavior lay a bargain the American public struck with
itself. In exchange for submission to a highly structured and disciplined economic and social order—the fruits of an urban-industrial
society—it demanded a personal freedom for its members from
traditional restraints. Matters of personal behavior were removed
from public scrutiny, as historian Paula Fass has noted; rather than
being issues of morality they were to be matters of individual
taste.[89] Rigid canons of propriety were relaxed, even as the disci-
plining forces of modern society imposed themselves ever stronger
on the American public. The private realm of the individual was
granted wider latitude of behavior in exchange for a necessary conformity of social organization. Not all citizens adhered to this bargain, of course. The sizable minority of America's religious community continued to view issues of sex, drink, dance—all manner of
social and personal behavior—under the traditional category of
morality and subject to public control. The "noble experiment" of
prohibition throughout the 1920s and the sophisticated political activism on many issues by evangelicals decades later indicate that
the trade off was never accepted by some. Even people not driven
by religious conviction seldom used the more relaxed proprieties
of the new age for radical change. Most Americans then, as now,
remained tied to conventional behavior.

For that majority of middle America weary of the older constraints but too timid to cross the limen of respectability themselves, actors offered a safe release. Through the well-publicized
lifestyle and exploits of players they could vicariously violate cultural taboos and experience the exhilaration of social freedom. Society appreciated actors' nonconformity as an antidote to the ration-
alized life of industrialized America. Players, in effect, were given
license for unconventional behavior. Actors and audience con-
spired for mutual benefit: in their freedom to perform actors received the psychological fulfillment of self-exhibition in a variety of
roles, while the audience gained satisfaction in watching the make-
believe. The fantasy stretched even beyond the theatre as the pub-

lic indulged players in a continuation of exhibitionism, make-believe, and even immorality.[90]

Marxist and other radical social critics have charged that mass culture gives only an appearance of freedom to its participants while in fact holding them in the tightest bondage, and the relationship of actor to public at first glance seems to confirm that judgment. There was no threat, after all, to the underlying social order, and fascination with the exploits of a few appears the perfect way to diffuse serious self-examination of society. But this critique misses the fundamentally conservative nature of the crossover from the Victorian ethos to the modern one. Despite the demands for personal freedom and self-enhancement, few sought license for self-indulgence. The continuities of culture and the instrinsic wish to hold fast to social conventions tempered passage into the modern age. The vicarious enjoyment of the actors' revolt, then, should not be seen so much as bourgeois culture's form of social control as the natural inclination of a public that wanted the form of social liberation with little of its content.[91]

Symbols of freedom, actors were also paragons of success. Their manipulation of the material rewards of success is well understood. Through ostentatious display of all kinds, players became shills of the consumer culture. But their significance as exemplars of achievement went even deeper, as Roger Caillois has pointed out in his brilliant study of play. Equalitarian societies, he notes, are subject to a pervasive irony. As they have made social advancement more dependent on merit and less dependent on the chance of wealth and family background, many people feel less able than ever to compete. Consequently, they choose to find their success through identification with the stars. The choice is significant, for stars are determined by neither the accident of birth nor by the possession of personal merit. Rather, their good fortune seems to be a gift of the gods, something available to all, which may fall upon the most humble individual. Thus there are the endless stories recounting an actor's fortuitous rise to stardom. "It does not climax a conventional career," says Caillois, but "is the renewal of an extraordinary and mysterious convergence in which are compounded one's being magically gifted from infancy on, perseverence that no obstacle could discourage, and the ultimate test presented by the precarious but decisive opportunity met and seized without hesitation."[92]

Caillois's theory addresses itself well to turn-of-the-century America. The stresses and anxieties of competition for the ring of success made the indirect enjoyment of the stars' achievements an appealing alternative. The pleasures were secondhand but the path to them was safer and easier. One could settle for imitating actors' dress, manner, and attitudes, content in the illusion that it could just as easily have been oneself that fate had smiled upon. This vague and superficial identification, claims Caillois, "constitutes one of the essential compensating mechanisms of democratic society."[93] In recent years we have seen the darker side of this phenomenon. What is usually a harmless identification with celebrity can become a vicious obsession with the fame of others. The ephemerality of celebrity is matched by its incandescent intensity that can block out the perspective of reality. In such cases this "compensating mechanism" becomes a source of social pathology, leading in extreme examples to violent attacks on public figures. This problem goes deeper than the theatre, of course; yet in an age dominated by the media and its celebrated few, theatricality has become the controlling metaphor of social analysis and actors the models of modern success.

*   *   *

By the turn of the century the actors' social role was finding its modern definition. Actors had attained a prominent place in American society, as the entertainment business thrived and as even moralists recognized entertainers' right to perform. Players rendered a service now acknowledged as valuable. They also moved among polite circles as never before and suffered fewer blatant displays of prejudice. Their public profile was matched by few other groups, with their every idiosyncrasy recorded by the press. In one sense, then, the hopes of Booth, Fiske, and the other champions of uplift found fulfillment in an improving social status for players.

But such a statement must be carefully qualified, for actors' social position remained ambivalent. The ambivalence sprang from two sources. First, the strict moral standards of Protestant America continued to be used by many in their evaluation of the players' work and behavior. Traditional suspicions of actors persisted among many Americans and made complete social acceptance impossible. Second, and more fundamental, the actors' work itself created tensions and ambivalencies. Actors traded in the creation of multiple roles. They specialized in inconstancy and impermanency. Moreover, by their portrayal of dissolute characters they discredited their integrity in the eyes of many. While no longer an issue today, as late as 1915 Francis Hackett pleaded in the *New Republic* that the actor not be constrained by the same moral principles as the common citizen. To subordinate their acting to the conventions of everyday life, he argued, would weaken their art.

Actors must portray all the realities of life—whether healthy or repellent—and to do so they had to suppress private principles. "The principles by which an artist lives are necessarily in conflict with the ordinary routine morality," Hackett reminded his readers, and "it is the duty of all who love art to stand by the artist in his revolt."[94]

Ironically, however, these compromises of respectability did not hinder the more fundamental achievement of actors. Indeed it was actors' marginality that gave them much of their public appeal. As the dictates of genteel culture began to be questioned in the 1890s and the possibilities for new conduct opened, actors served as examples of freedom from societal convention. Both onstage and off they typified the "modern," offering alternatives of attitude and behavior to the public. To some degree actors had always performed this function. Jean Duvignaud argues that a troubled relationship necessarily exists between the actor and society; the actor, in a sense, remains outside of society because he is creating a new order.[95] But this function, more latent than real during most ages, burst forth in full bloom when the rays of the media showered attention on the player. The attention has never wavered, and if anything grows more intensive. And the actor, ever the outsider, has by virtue of that fact insinuated himself tightly inside the modern psyche as the other half of the alienated self.

* * *

The gift that bestowed stardom, significantly, was generally not a profound talent. Instead, it was the more modest element of personality, the kind of personal resource that anyone might possess. Mannerisms of speech, gesture, expression, and dress became the distinguishing features of the most popular actors in the early twentieth century. The replacement of histrionics by personality was in part a consequence of a drama that dealt with contemporary life. Theatrical realism demanded a more subdued and lifelike style of acting in its attempt to portray a convincing illusion.

Seven 🌸

The Illusion of Life

O*ne* trend overshadowed all others to theatregoers of the late nineteenth century: the striking increase in stage realism. Realism pervaded all the dramatic arts. Scenery and settings were designed to give the illusion of life. Gone were the crude interchangeable backdrops of the earlier nineteenth century; they were replaced by the box setting with authentic furnishings and stage props. Elaborate stage machinery was devised for moving props and for producing special effects. Improvements in lighting—first from oil to gas and finally to electricity, which could be easily modulated—aided realistic presentation. Close attention was paid to details of historical verisimilitude in costumes. Not only were productions staged more realistically, but the plays themselves took on a naturalistic quality. Although melodramatic by modern standards, the plays of Steele MacKaye, James A. Herne, Clyde Fitch, Edward Sheldon, Augustus Thomas, among others, strove for believable plot and characterization. The exoticism of older drama, though it never quite disappeared, increasingly gave way to plays reflecting the contemporary American middle class. Characters discussed the social issues that preoccupied Americans of the day.

Along with stagecraft and playwriting, acting styles took on a realistic manner. In place of the "grand and lofty," to use theatre historian Alan Downer's description of theatrical performances during the first three quarters of the nineteenth century, came what he called the "natural mode" in the final decades of the century.[1] This change, important in itself for the history of the theatre, also bore testimony to other cultural developments of the day and reflected a fundamental alteration of the actor's social role.

*   1   *

The "grand and lofty" (or traditional) style consisted of two major strains: the classic and the heroic. The classic school, which found its greatest early proponent in the English actor John Philip Kemble, was characterized by a faultless declamatory delivery, controlled emotion, and a thoroughly dignified stage presence. American actors in this tradition included Mary Ann Duff, James E. Murdoch, Edwin L. Davenport, and Edwin Adams in the mid–nineteenth century, and Fanny Janauschek, Helena Modjeska, Mary Anderson, Edwin Booth, Lawrence Barrett, Richard Mansfield, E. H. Sothern, and Otis Skinner in the late nineteenth and early twentieth centuries. A brief glance at the list reveals that it includes many of America's eminent actors and that this kind of acting continued well after naturalistic styles had become popular.[2]

A second branch of traditional acting was the heroic school, rooted in the Romanticism of the late eighteenth and early nineteenth centuries. The heroic style was popularized by the mercurial Edmund Kean, whose violent fits of energy and sudden shifts of tone inspired Coleridge to observe that watching Kean was like reading Shakespeare by flashes of lightning. In place of the classical actor's well-cadenced reading of blank verse, Kean substituted many breaks and changes in tempo. The great exemplar of the heroic tradition in America was Edwin Forrest. Forrest's muscularity and robust vocal power appealed to audiences of Jacksonian America. He magnified nature with exuberant bursts of passion that "made the pit tremble."[3] The popularity of Forrest and others who acted in the heroic mode—Thomas Abthorpe Cooper, Charlotte Cushman, and John McCullough notably—resided in their ability to create characters larger than life, heroic figures for the public to admire.

For purposes of this study the differences between the classic and heroic styles are not as important as their affinities, and the two can be grouped together as part of the traditional approach to acting, distinguished by its extensive use of pantomime. The sweeping gesture and studied pose, today associated with the ham, were standard techniques through much of the nineteenth century. While it seems stilted and artificial to modern viewers, players were then judged by different criteria. It was not that "naturalness" was unimportant. Indeed, eighteenth-century observers applauded David Garrick for his natural performances, and actors took seriously Shakespeare's admonition that they should "hold, as 'twere, the mirror up to nature." But the word "natural"

then had a different meaning. Players gave an Aristotelian interpretation to this principle: acting was to be an imitation of an action,
not the action itself. Characterizations were not meant to be real in
the sense that all the qualities and manners of an actual human
would be portrayed; rather, the actor presented a refinement or ide-
alization of a character, a type.[4] Traditional players were "thinly clad
with the vestures of human nature," said Willa Cather.[5] Like the
poet, the actor did not pretend to closely copy nature, George
Henry Lewes noted, "but only to represent nature sublimated into
the ideal."[6]

Traditional actors expressed emotion through pantomime.
Each emotion had its appropriate gesture and facial expression,
which were passed down from one generation of actors to the next.
Every actor could draw upon a set of poses or attitudes to convey
aggression, fear, defiance, supplication, self-assurance, and other
feelings. Books were written analyzing, classifying, and breaking
down gestures and expressions into their component parts.[7] Two
important manuals of dramatic acting, both English, were Henry
Siddons's *Practical Illustrations of Rhetorical Gesture and Action* (1882)
and Gustave Garcia's *Actors' Art* (1882), a text richly illustrated with
poses, gestures, and expressions. But not all acting guides were
English. An American manual on the art of acting published in the
1850s described the expression of love:

> Love, when successful, lights up the countenance into smiles; the
> forehead is smooth and enlarged; the eyebrows are arched; the
> mouth a little open and smiling; the eyes languishing and half
> shut, or gazing on the beloved object. The accents are soft to win-
> ning, the tone or voice persuasive, flattering, pathetic, various,
> musical, rapturous, as in joy. Kneeling is often necessary in all sup-
> plicant passions; but it is only necessary to bend one knee in case
> of love, desire, &c., which must never be the one that is next to the
> audience.[8]

The acting manuals all reflected an approach to acting at once
inflexible and unambiguous. The audience was to be able to immediately recognize the emotion portrayed. Joseph Jefferson proclaimed: "There must be no vagueness in acting. The suggestion
should be unmistakable; it must be hurled at the whole audience,
and reach with unerring aim the boys in the gallery and the statesmen in the stalls."[9] The conservative nature of the theatre helped
preserve the methods of traditional acting until well into the twentieth century. F. F. Mackay's influential *Art of Acting*, published in
1913, devoted considerable space to conventional techniques of
gesture and pose. Nevertheless, several decades earlier an ineluc-

table trend towards a more restrained and realistic acting style had begun.

*   *   *

The acting traditions that had endured for generations in England and America broke down during the last few decades of the nineteenth century. The change partook of the theatre's growth as urban middle-class entertainment with an audience that wished to see reflections of itself on stage. Modern dramas, which increasingly replaced classic fare, demanded that actors look to life for their inspiration instead of to stage traditions. The larger-than-life player of the traditional stage, who with his rant and broad gesture made no effort to conceal his theatricality, gave way to the comparatively subdued player of the new school, who sought to give the illusion of real life on the stage. "For the majestic dignity of the latter old school actor," wrote E. J. West, the modern actor "had substituted decorum; for the latter's voice of thunder he had substituted the ripple or chatter or mumble of colloquial conversation; for the knowledge of technique and tradition, he had substituted good looks and fine fashions."[10] A Paris critic commented about Daly's company during its European tour in the 1880s that "the propensity for naturalism shows itself in a thousand details. The fashion of entering, sitting, taking a chair, talking, taking leave, going out, coming in,—it is the usage of everyday life."[11]

Theatre historians generally credit the English playwright T. W. Robertson and the acting couple of Squire and Lady Bancroft as being the pioneers of stage realism, performing the "teacup" comedies at the Prince of Wales Theatre beginning in 1865. Robertson's plays replaced bombast and melodramatic sensation with clever dialogue and refined sensibility. *Society*, *Ours*, *School*, and *Caste* were set in the familiar environs of England's genteel middle class. Scrupulous attention was paid to details of setting, with draperies, fireplaces, pieces of sculpture, and other authentic properties dotting the stage. The drawing-room comedies required restrained performances from the cast, the traditional style of acting being unsuited for such productions. Rather than having a feature star who delivered a virtuoso performance, the entire cast had to work together as an ensemble. Character acting replaced bravura; actors developed distinctive character roles with an attention to detail far beyond what the melodramatic types had required. The Robertson-Bancroft style introduced almost continuous byplay among both the leads and supernumeraries; players seemed always to be picking something up or laying it down.[12]

It must be mentioned again that traditional acting continued to be seen on American stages through all of this era, particularly in the cheaper stock companies and tent-rep shows. But to believe many contemporary theatre critics one would think that the great age of acting had already ended by 1880. George Henry Lewes, an English critic whose 1875 volume, *On Actors and the Art of Acting*, was one of the finest studies of the dramatic art, objected to the idea that acting ought to be given in "a conversational tone and a drawing-room quietness." Although himself an advocate of a moderate realism, Lewes felt that realism had been confused with "vulgarism": "It is not consistent with the nature of tragedy to obtrude the details of daily life. All that lounging on tables and lolling against chairs, which help convey a sense of reality in the *Drame*, are as unnatural in tragedy as it would be to place the 'sleeping fawn' of Phidias on a comfortable feather-bed."[13] H. Burton Baker, another English critic, complained in 1879 that the new acting dealt with "the superficial phases of an overripe civilization," which could "never rise to the dignity and grandeur of the old school, the object of which was to analyze and depict all that was noble, sublime, terrible, and tender in human nature."[14]

Some American theatrical observers were similarly unimpressed by stage realism. Joseph Frobisher, director of the College of Oratory and Acting in New York, decried the loss of manliness and vigor on stage, which he attributed to realism. "Can't one be a gentleman and manly at the same time?" he asked. "Yet not a single gentleman as represented on the stage is manly. . . . His ways are what the boarding-school misses call 'refined,' his voice is of the 'sucking dove' modulation and of the 'Ta-ta, George' timbre."[15] Frobisher displayed the prejudices of an elocutionist against the deemphasis on vigorous oratory, but his lament was a general one. Actors who retired around the turn of the century repeatedly asserted in their autobiographical reflections that modern actors did not compare with the older ones.[16] Hearkening back to a golden age is a familiar tendency, of course. But these players recognized that a major change had taken place in the histrionic art; time-honored traditions of acting had broken down; the heroic figures of Spartacus and Virginius yielded to the gentility of John Drew's society personations and to William Gillette's intense low-key Sherlock Holmes.

The earliest proponent of a thoroughgoing realism in American drama was James A. Herne.[17] Actor, author, director, producer, Herne was the complete showman and an innovative force in the American theatre who deserves greater recognition than he has received. His popular plays, *Shore Acres, Hearts of Oak*, and *Sag Harbor*, foretold a dawning dramatic realism, but his relatively obscure

Margaret Fleming, first produced in 1891, may be said to have introduced Ibsenite realism to America. Just as Herne advocated "art for truth's sake" in drama, so did his acting embody an appropriate naturalism. His 1893 portrayal of Uncle Nat in his own *Shore Acres* was acclaimed by Boston critic Henry Clapp: "Mr. Herne showed the whole man, as if he had entered into the very body and nature of his hero." Clapp observed that Herne's impersonation "seemed to be from the inside out, not from the outside in." [18] Herne felt that repose was an essential quality in acting. He encouraged his actors to think about what their lines meant before delivering them, and to convey emotion through suggestion, using minimal facial expression and gesture.[19] These traits typified the realistic style.

Like Herne, William Gillette succeeded both as dramatist and actor. Gillette was born into the Connecticut home of a United States senator in 1853. After displaying a love for theatrical play as a child, he left college in 1875 to join a New Orleans stock company. Gillette spent a few years in supporting parts while learning the trade before he appeared in the title role of his own play *The Professor* in 1881. The play was the first of twenty he authored, including the extremely popular *Esmerelda* (1881), *Held by the Enemy* (1886), *Secret Service* (1896), and *Sherlock Holmes* (1899). Gillette's interpretation of Conan Doyle's sleuth became his most famous role. After a career that lasted into his eighty-second year, Gillette received honorary degrees from Yale, Columbia, and Trinity College in Hartford and was elected to the American Academy of Arts and Letters, one of the few actors so honored.[20]

Gillette cannot be described as a versatile actor, for his range of acting was narrow. He specialized in underplaying his parts, gaining the audience's attention by his very calm. Rather than "taking the stage," in the tradition of the great tragedians, he came onstage almost stealthily. His stage movements were deliberate, with economy of gesture. Yet he conveyed an intensity through nervous mannerism, twitching his fingers and hardening the muscles in his face. Phrases such as "calm intensity," "nervous quietude," and "the perfect example of excitement under a cloak" were used to describe him. "He seems to be doing nothing, but he is doing many things," said Norman Hapgood, "making a hundred subdued movements of his frame or head or face to reflect every change in the situation." [21]

Gillette outlined the principles of his acting style in an address before a joint session of the American Academy of Arts and Letters in Chicago in 1910, entitled "The Illusion of the First Time in Acting." Gillette made the address a declaration of the imperative to simulate life. The actor, Gillette declared, must play his part to give the illusion that he is moving or speaking his line for the first time. Since actual people do not act with perfect continuity or speak in smoothly flowing lines, the player must not behave, speak, or gesture too correctly. "Drama can make its appeal only in the form of simulated life as it is lived," Gillette insisted, "not as various authorities on Grammar, Pronunciation, Etiquet, and Elocution happen to announce at that particular time that it ought to be lived." [22] Each night the audience should feel that the player was living his role for the first time. Gillette's own acting was faithful to this doctrine; he moved naturally and delivered his lines in a halting manner.

Gillette's tenet, that the audience ought to be looking at life rather than at a performance, became the view of an ever-growing number of players and critics. Heywood Broun called him the "Father of the Modern School of Acting," and Charles Collins, a Chicago critic, said that Gillette "gave acting a nervous system, whereas before his time it was largely a matter of tongue and lungs." [23] It is difficult to assign credit to the "first" or the "most influential," but certainly William Gillette gave the most articulate statement on acting realism of any contemporary player.

Even more than Herne and Gillette, Minnie Maddern Fiske became publicly known as the champion of realistic acting. A recent historian of American acting has credited her with being the major transitional figure between the traditional acting of the nineteenth century and modern techniques. [24] Mrs. Fiske anticipated Constantin Stanislavsky's revolutionary psychological naturalism. In both method and aim she represented an intellectual approach to acting, attempting to plumb the psychological depths of her role and convey its personality to the audience.

Mrs. Fiske's views on acting matured during a temporary retirement from 1890 to 1893, following her marriage to Harrison Grey Fiske. She studied the techniques of Helena Modjeska, Ellen Terry, and Eleanore Duse and incorporated elements from each of them, as well as ideas of George Henry Lewes. She learned to prepare roles by analyzing the character's motivations, much as Method actors were taught to do decades later. The result was an idiosyncratic style which, according to Lewis Strang, "absolutely refuses to be classified." Like William Gillette, she underplayed her parts. Her way of speaking broke radically with the declamatory stage tradition in an attempt to speak as people actually did in life. She had a "hard, staccato, and even monotonous histrionic style, speaking with a voice that is unmusical and incapable of varied colouring," wrote her contemporary Strang. Moreover, she freely committed the unpardonable stage sin of speaking with her back to the audience. But through these techniques she succeeded in conveying the inner life of her character, which dialogue alone only suggested. Fiske's main stylistic technique, according to Elizabeth Neill, consisted of psychic repression followed by a sudden release of energy.[25] Her performance as Rebecca West in Ibsen's *Rosmersholm* exemplified this. Throughout the play she remained passive and in the background. Although she showed no outward change, the audience sensed something ominous about her silence and constantly focused its attention on her. Near the end of the play her performance reached its peak. While being cross-examined she continued to be passive; then suddenly she let loose the torrent of emotion that had been building throughout the play. Her previous reserve made the scene terribly effective.[26]

Mrs. Fiske triumphed in some of the most challenging roles of the day: Thomas Hardy's *Tess of the d'Urbervilles*, Langdon Mitchell's *Becky Sharp* and *The New York Idea*, Paul Heyse's *Mary of Magdala*, and of course in her roles in Ibsen and Sheldon. The public responded by making her a leading box office attraction from the late 1890s until the 1920s. Admirers of her realism lauded her work as "the art that conceals art." Players sang her praises as well. Blanche Bates testified that Mrs. Fiske "has always been 'the actor's actress' even more than the public's favorite, for her art has a breadth, a subtlety, and perfection that makes its study a postgraduate degree to any player."[27] Her unique style had its detractors, however. Some critics were put off by her cold, intellectual approach and indicted her for lacking emotional power. This charge reoccurred so often that at a press interview in 1901 she begged reporters not to concentrate on her intellectuality for fear that the public would begin to think she had no feelings or emotional expression.[28]

Although few actors attempted to copy the styles of Gillette and Fiske, realism became the code word for more and more actors in the early twentieth century. In the same way that players proudly proclaimed themselves to be Method actors in the 1940s and '50s, players of earlier decades announced themselves to be realistic actors. In her declaration of loyalty to realism Carlotta Nillson explained that "when developing parts I play I have looked within rather than without," anticipating what would later become the litany of Method actors.[29]

Realistic acting, with its subdued and simple gesture, natural speech, and concentration on the character's inner feelings, was a logical concomitant of the contemporary drama that became so popular. Plays about ordinary people in everyday surroundings required a scaled-down technique. Critics who denigrated the modern players' histrionic ability failed to see this. But Brander Matthews (writing in 1914), who conceded that his generation of actors may not have been capable of the tragic power of Cushman, Forrest, or McCullough, did not believe that fact made them inferior to actors of the past. He saw the close relationship between drama and acting technique:

> They [modern actors] may not succeed always when they attempt the plays of an earlier day, but their failure is not as complete as the failure of the older actors would be if it were possible to call upon them to appear in our modern realistic drama, where every part is more or less of a character-part, and where the actor, standing on a fully lighted stage, is expected to get his effect sometimes by his speech, but also often merely by a gesture or only by a look. Our actors are now less rhetorical and more pictorial—as they must be on the stage of our modern theater.[30]

* 2 *

Just as naturalistic acting was part of a realistic trend in the theatre generally, theatrical realism partook of a realistic impulse in literature, painting, social thought, and elocution.

Warner Berthoff has written that the most significant event in American letters during the 1880s and 1890s was the growing dominance of literary realism.[31] This movement involved a stress on regional themes and dialect and the honest treatment of contemporary subject matter, often centering on the conflicts in late nineteenth-century American culture, such as labor and agrarian unrest, problems of the city, depression, the new immigration, and the corrupting influence of unbridled materialism. However, American realism retained an optimism about the possibility for reform that European writers surrendered. The quintessential American realist, William Dean Howells, did not doubt that America's democratic spirit would prevail. Henry James wrote to Howells in 1884 conceding that he was "the great American naturalist," but adding, "I don't think you go far enough, and you are haunted with romantic phantoms and a tendency to factitious glosses."[32] What James said about Howells could be applied in a greater degree to the American theatre, where the happy ending remained obligatory for most plays through 1920. Theatrical realism was manifested more in stage settings and acting techniques than in critiques of society.

Realism in American art, pioneered in the nineteenth century by Thomas Eakins, emerged full blown during the first decade of the twentieth with the canvases of the "ash-can school." Led by

Robert Henri, such painters as John Sloan, George Luks, and William Glackens sought a more authentic art through portrayal of low life. The tenements, saloons, dance halls, and back streets formed the venue of these artists. Just as realistic acting stripped away the older conventions of stage pantomime, realist painters passed over the convention-bound rich to record the vital and direct activities of the working class. And like the writers of a similar conviction, realist painters were less social critics than artistic reformers, seeking new subjects and fresh perspectives in hopes of creating artistic truth.[33]

Theatrical realism was also related, if only as a distant cousin, to what Morton White called "the revolt against formalism." Such social thinkers as Oliver Wendell Holmes, Jr., John Dewey, Charles Beard, and Thorstein Veblen rejected the a priori deductive method of earlier philosophy and social science and replaced it with instrumentalism, pragmatism, economic determinism, and legal realism. They hoped to get beneath surface appearances to identify the forces shaping the social order.[34] In journalism this attempt to uncover the actual locus of power and corruption sent the muckrakers from political back room to meat packing plant. The suspicion that the deepest level of reality lay beyond mere appearance infused the Progressive spirit.

The belief that reality resided in the subsurface of affairs was not confined to the social or political realm. Influenced by psychology, elocutionists began teaching that outward expression had its origins in the speaker's inner self. The transformation of elocution from a study of sound production and pronunciation to a concern with the psychology of expression had its beginnings in the 1890s and was pioneered by two men: S. H. Clark and S. S. Curry.

Solomon Henry Clark, public reader and professor at the University of Chicago for twenty-nine years, advocated a marriage of elocution and psychology. Psychologists taught that expression flowed from an internal feeling, which stimulated the body. Consequently, Clark believed, an actor should use his imaginative faculty to help him feel his part and then guide its expression by his intellect and technical ability. Proper delivery required both emotion and technique, but of the two emotion was the more critical. "Unless a pupil can conceive the thought behind the gesture, the expression as a whole will have the appearance of affectation," Clark wrote.[35]

Perhaps an even more pivotal figure in the transformation of elocutionary style was Samuel Silas Curry. During his ministerial training at Boston University Curry studied under Lewis B. Monroe at the School of Oratory, and his interests soon shifted from preaching to teaching elocution. In 1885 he and his wife organized the School of Expression in Boston, which in the following decades trained America's leaders in speech education. Curry traveled to Italy, England, and France to study with leading elocutionists. None of the systems satisfied him so he set out to develop his own eclectic system, which he defined in his fourteen books, the most important being *Province of Expression* (1891), *Imagination and Dramatic Instinct* (1896), and *Foundations of Expression* (1907).[36]

Like Clark, Curry's technique owed much to the theories of contemporary psychology. Rather than starting with the voice or with pantomime, he centered attention on the mind. "The great center of consciousness must be upon the thought and action of the mind," wrote Curry.[37] Effective delivery required more than the mechanical reproduction of words; it required the possession of the ideas at the moment they were spoken. In other words, the speaker must be able to create spontaneously the idea he wished to convey. Expression was the objective manifestation of something subjective.[38] Curry drew upon William James's "stream of thought" theory, which postulated that within personal consciousness thought is continuous and always changing. Curry taught that thinking consisted of concentration upon one point, then leaping to another point, and so on.[39]

Curry developed a set of exercises to aid control of voice and body. He stressed breathing exercises, gymnastic exercises similar to Delsarte's, and exercises to improve "tone-color." The voice and action must be flexible mechanisms, able to express any thought of the speaker, Curry reiterated. Ideally, if one put oneself in a subjective mood the muscles and voice would respond automatically.[40] But Curry, who criticized mechanical approaches to speech, left room for "artistic spontaneity" in expression. He saw all human action as unions of conscious and unconscious, voluntary and involuntary elements. An analogous situation to expression, Curry felt, was the movement of the arm. Man consciously initiates the movement of his arm, then an unconscious force takes over. "Consciousness and will act at the initiation and at the climax, but between the great spontaneous impulses of the soul are aroused and dominant." "True spontaneity," according to Curry, "does not mean an absence of deliberation. . . . It is coordination of the deliberate with the unconscious that is the glory of human expression. . . . Every artist must have a long, deliberative, conscious struggle to secure truthful execution, but if this struggle does not rise above technique and secure and develop the unconscious impulses of the soul, the man can never become an artist."[41]

Although he trained few actors directly, Curry's books undoubtedly were read by members of the profession. His *Imagination and Dramatic Instinct*, a plea for the observation of life and disciplined concentration, prefigured acting theorist Constantin Stanislavsky's notion of "emotion memory." [42] In both Curry's and Clark's writings and to a lesser extent in the theories of other elocutionists, one sees the beginning of a psychological attitude toward speech. Concern shifted from purely technical matters of pronunciation, tone, and gesture to an understanding of the subjective elements of communication.

The roots of this change go beyond the field of elocution to developments in academic psychology and psychiatry. The last two decades of the nineteenth and the first of the twentieth century marked the beginnings of modern psychology and psychiatry. The "New Psychology" of G. Stanley Hall, William James, George Trumball Ladd, and others sought to understand the mysteries of consciousness. It abandoned deterministic neurological explanations and looked instead at the unconscious motivations, habits, instincts, and sexual drives that informed human emotions. The field of psychiatry took this approach a step further, dwelling completely upon the subconscious components of behavior. The belief in nonrational drives and hidden motivations characterized much social thought of the day, notably in the European writings of Nietzsche, Bergson, and Freud, but also among Americans. Psychic phenomena became a topic for popular discussion, evidenced by William James's 1890 article in *Scribner's*, "The Hidden Self," which helped rekindle interest in the occult, mysticism, automatic writing, and faith healing, by endowing them with the legitimacy of science. On an even more popular level the advent of mind-cure religions, such as Christian Science and New Thought, also indicated the appeal of a psychologizing approach to reality. [43]

These new theories and beliefs affected the theatre in two ways. First, some popular plays of the day reflected the vogue for hypnotism, suggestion, and other manifestations of the unconscious. The biggest success was Paul Potter's dramatization of du Maurier's *Trilby*, first performed at New York's Garden Theatre in 1895. The story concerned a young woman's ambition to become a concert singer. Under the hypnotic spell of the malevolent Svengali she achieved great success, but became his slave. The original cast included Virginia Harned as the heroine Trilby and Wilton Lackaye, whose Svengali became the capstone of his career. *Trilby* was an immediate sensation in Boston and New York and then throughout the country, with twenty-four *Trilby* companies touring in 1896. [44] But *Trilby* was not an isolated case. Critic Walter Prichard Eaton observed in 1910 that "just now the fashion is 'realism,' dashed with 'psychology' and 'new thought.'" Where an earlier generation found an emotional outlet in the old romances, "now we take it out in 'telepathy,' 'suggestion,' 'thought transference,' and the like. We hail *The Witching Hour*; we thrill when Glad, in Mrs. Burnett's *The Dawn of a To-morrow*, declares that if you keep on asking for anything hard enough you will get it." [45]

Second, awareness of life's psychological dimension clearly had an impact on styles of acting. New plays that explored internal moods and conflicts encouraged realistic acting. Yeats observed that when "modern educated people" are deeply moved, "they look silently into the fireplace." This mood of introspection influenced actors to adopt a quieter style. "The inner space that Ibsen and his successors were concerned with," Michael Goldman writes, "had to be charted by a repertory of pauses and indirections, by small details of gesture and expression. . . . The construction of plays, the technique of the actors, the age's growing interest in psychological science and in detection of all sorts, invited the audience to listen for movements beneath the characters' public performance, beneath even their consciousness." [46] Even in plays that offered only superficial characterization (as most plays continued to do), actors added touches of psychological realism. Mrs. Fiske's stage speech —with its sudden starts and stops, frequent tempo changes, and long pauses—suggested Jamesian influence.

The influence of modern psychology can also be seen in the debate it inspired over acting technique. The debate, whether or not actors should feel the emotion they portray, was actually an old one. Denis Diderot formulated the classic statement against the reality of stage emotion in *The Paradox of Acting*. The paradox, according to Diderot's dictum, was that to move the audience the actor must remain unmoved. Although penned in the 1770s, *The Paradox* was not published until 1830 and did not appear in English translation until 1883. Its publication in England and America renewed the debate over head versus heart, and in the next few decades it became a major issue among actors and drama critics. [47]

Opposed to Diderot's assertion that the actor remains untouched by the emotion he portrays was the view of the emotionalist school, which found its most articulate statement in English critic William Archer's *Masks or Faces? A Study in the Psychology of Acting*, published in 1888. Archer's book was intended as an outright rebuttal of Diderot's position. He surveyed a number of British thespians, questioning them about the feelings they had when they acted. Archer found that most actors identified with their role, unable to remain as unmoved as Diderot alleged. To counter Diderot's most clever argument (how it was that in the middle of an emotion-laden scene an actor could maintain enough presence of mind to correct a miscue), Archer resorted to an overtly psychological explanation. He posited a dual level of consciousness (allowing even more) that an actor could draw upon. Thus, while on one level the player was totally engrossed in the impersonation, on another level of consciousness the player could maintain an objectivity toward his stage situation: "Severe suffering on one mental plane is quite consistent with perfect contentment, nay, with absolute beatitude on another. Happiness and misery reside in the deeps of consciousness; the upper strata are of small account . . . The surface of his [the actor's] consciousness may be tormented and tempest-tossed while the depths are unruffled." [48]

The head versus heart debate made its way into a leading psychological text, G. T. Ladd's *Outlines of Physiological Psychology* in 1887, indicating that psychology's influence on acting was not a one-way street. Ladd noted: "Recent inquiries have elicited the interesting and the important fact that, as a rule, great actors actually have feelings and ideas present in their consciousness, which their acting expresses with such wonderful results. Their power is the power to PUT THEMSELVES in the appropriate condition of mind, rather than the power merely to act a part." [49] Similar acknowledgments of emotion's place in elocution were made by S. S. Curry, who averred that the merely imitative elocution had given the art a bad name. Vocal expression should manifest the feelings of the soul, giving objective form to subjective feeling. Curry considered Edwin Booth an exemplar: "There is not the least hint of merely an exhibition of 'doing things.' We feel that there is an instinctive and intuitive assimiliation of a character." Booth, Curry wrote, displayed a "psychic link of unity." [50]

In sum, critics and actors came down strongly on the side of the emotionalists, and that is where the consensus has remained ever since. Popular psychological theories were not the only reason for the emotional argument to prevail. Diderot's argument overstressed the purely rational component of acting, whereas actors almost unanimously attested to a personal involvement in their roles. But the new awareness of multiple levels of consciouness provided a more sophisticated explanation for a player's simultaneous involvement and detachment than had previously been available. Care must be taken not to read back into this pre-Stanislavsky era a psychological realism obsessed with subtexts which did not yet exist. The early days of naturalistic acting merely involved a subduing of gesture and a less-cadenced speech. Although styles varied, by 1900 critics agreed that acting on Broadway stages was substantially different than it had been a few decades earlier and that realism had come to stay. Among the influences affecting the change, it is argued here, was a modern psychological outlook on human behavior. Freely expressed emotion and broad pantomime began giving way to restraint as actors conveyed emotions subtly. The pause became as important as the spoken word, and audiences had to scrutinize stage characters to discern the hidden motives of action.

* 3 *

At the heart of the new acting style was a reliance on personality. By this was simply meant that the actor infused his personality into the role he played—openly and without apology. This development did not meet with unqualified approval. Critics charged that modern actors lacked the highest form of histrionic artistry because they played every role in a similar fashion, making the author's character merely a vehicle for their individual personality. The versatility that had been displayed in the palmy days, some fretted, had given way to an era of typecasting, with outward appearance valued more highly than proven acting skill.[51] Critic Alan Dale grumbled that modern stars were products of the offstage publicity that surrounded them. "It is the personalities we go to see, not the actors and sometimes not the play."[52]

Complaints about the cult of personality belong partly to the general lament of the traditionalists over the disappearance of the grand style of acting. Though critics forgot that the great actors of the past had also stamped their personality onto each role, they were not wrong in believing that an increased emphasis on the personal characteristics of players accompanied the trend toward natural acting. Stock-company actors played a variety of roles, not all of which suited their particular build or personality. But the combination company rigidified casting as managers tried to find players who "looked" the part. The requirements for stardom changed, becoming a function not so much of an accomplished technique as of a magnetic personality. Actors needed an identifiable characteristic, said press agent George Lederer, some spontaneous charm, a trick of voice or manner. Sincerity, innocence, urbanity, wit, intelligence: these and other qualities did more to attract playgoers than the stentorian manner of an earlier day. Combined with good looks and attractive figure or physique, they became an unbeatable combination.[53]

Maude Adams's career exemplified how personality bestowed stardom. Though not considered a beauty, she had an elfin charm that audiences responded to warmly, making her perhaps America's most loved player in the first decade of the twentieth century. No drama critic considered her a great actress, and her attempts at Shakespeare were pathetic. But in the contemporary works of J. M. Barrie, particularly *The Little Minister* and *Peter Pan*, whose characters elicited her winsome charms, she scored triumphs. Walter Prichard Eaton meant it as a compliment when he remarked that Maude Adams's personality was her art.[54] John Drew also epitomized the actor's reliance on personality. His natural habitat was the drawing room, and he wisely did not stray from it, performing in a series of polite comedies. Drew was "an image of grace," said Lewis Strang, he possessed "repose, individuality, coolness, drollery, the talent of apparent spontaneity, and the faculty of crisp emotions."[55] His unvarying approach led Booth Tarkington to quip that "John Drew would play Simon Legree into a misunderstood gentleman."[56] While this trait led some critics to belittle his artistry, it did not diminish his popularity. One could give many other instances of personalities dominating the play. Mrs. Fiske's intellectual style, for example, transformed Thomas Hardy's Tess from a rough-hewn peasant into a fragile and sensitive woman. John Mason, Ada Rehan, Viola Allen, Ethel Barrymore, Doris Keane, and Charles Hawtrey were all players known for infusing a very personal style into each of their roles.

The critics who wanted to uphold traditional canons of acting resented the glorification of the stage personality, but the weight of public and perhaps even critical opinion seemed to favor the new system. Several writers, in fact, suggested that acting and personality were crucially intertwined. Consistent with his view that expression must originate in the mind, S. S. Curry believed that people ought to express themselves in accordance with their personalities. "Of all faults in expression the worst is for a man not to be himself." Curry wrote. He pointed to speakers who had faultless delivery and perfect elocution yet lacked intensity because they hid their character behind elocutionary perfection.[57] William Gillette took an even stronger position. In a *New York Times* interview in 1914 he stated that "it is a plain fact that personality is the most important thing in really great acting."[58] He felt that people who placed art above personality missed the issue entirely, for the actor fused his personality with the role the dramatist created. Personality, in Gillette's view, "is the most singularly important factor for infusing the Life-Illusion into modern stage creations that is known to man."[59] Gillette argued that the greatest actors of recent times had been universally acknowledged as great because of their compelling personalities. If they attempted roles not suited to their personalities, as when the elder Salvini attempted Hamlet or Edwin Booth essayed Othello, they failed.[60]

Drama critic Walter Prichard Eaton agreed with Gillette. Writing for the widely circulated *American Magazine*, Eaton attacked the idea that the expression of a strong personality was inferior art. Like Gillette, he thought the distinction between art and personality to be false. The aim of the actor was to bring the author's characters to life, and character could not exist apart from personality. The most interesting stage characters would therefore be created by those players with the most interesting personalities. The true test of an actor, Eaton thought, should be whether he presented the playwright's character in a consistent and convincing fashion.[61]

Both opponents and supporters of the new style agreed that in the final analysis the cult of personality resided in the public's preference. If the theatres have been filled with one-part actors, observed *New York Times* critic Adolf Klauber in 1905, it has been because the public encouraged it. "The person, not the artist," Klauber wrote, "is worshipped in our playhouses."[62] The personality cult must be seen as an integral part of the trend toward realistic acting. Audiences demanded—beyond realism in plot, characterization, scene design, properties, and in gesture and delivery of lines—an extra element of recognition from actors, some habit, mannerism, or way of speaking, any quality however indefinable that could establish a closer identity between themselves and the player. A distinctive personality rooted the actor in life. "The great, sensible, intelligent public," William Gillette commented, "goes on more or less consciously demanding that the 'behavior' of the theatre be the 'behavior' of ordinary life."[63]

*   *   *

The cultural significance of the cult of personality—and of realistic acting in general—becomes clearer when contrasted with the traditional acting style of mid–nineteenth-century America, exemplified by Edwin Forrest and Charlotte Cushman.

Traditional acting, to reiterate, did not seek a lifelike verisimilitude. It presented types that were larger than life. Charlotte Cushman possessed, in the words of William Winter, "extraordinary power to embody the highest ideals of majesty, pathos, and appalling anguish." "She made Shakespeare real," again quoting Winter, "but she never degraded her ideal to the level of the actual. She knew the heights of that wondrous intuition and potent magnetism, and she lifted herself—and her hearers—to their grand and beautiful eminence."[64] Cushman, and more particularly Edwin Forrest, personified the vigor and expansiveness of the new American nation. Both were muscular performers who could overpower an audience. Forrest's commanding presence resided in his massive torso and muscular limbs, a physique developed from years as a physical culture enthusiast. He radiated energy; his strength and fits of passion while acting frightened fellow players as well as audiences. His voice had few equals, capable of shaking the theatre's walls, yet always resonant, articulate, and capable of pathos. "He could sigh like a zephyr or roar like a hurricane," said the *Dramatic Mirror*.[65] Forrest embodied the Jacksonian spirit: aggressive, brash, and boisterous, thoroughly Democratic in his political philosophy (his sympathies with Jackson's party being well known).

The relationship that linked Forrest and his audience was significantly different from the one between Drew, Adams, or other stars of the turn of the century and theirs. The difference, in part, lay in the contrasting appeals of traditional acting and the newer realism. Donald Mullin points out that traditional acting was ritualized and community centered. "Its posings suggested an immediately translatable and unified 'ritualized' physical expression of emotion. Ritualization implies largeness of scale and action which may be identified with the more instinctive human behavior patterns."[66] But where traditional acting was culture or community centered, natural acting became individual centered. The dramatic focus shifted to distinctions of personality. The audience viewed players less as types and more as actual people with distinguishing personalities.

Edwin Forrest represented a special kind of traditional acting well matched to his time. A number of his greatest roles, notably Spartacus and Metamora, presented the struggle of the heroic figure against tyranny, a theme that harmonized with the young republic's self-image. Forrest's larger-than-life portrayals of heroic figures earned him a place among the pantheon of contemporary American heroes which included Andrew Jackson and Daniel Webster. His symbolization of the American community was dramatically illustrated in his confrontation with William Macready, England's leading tragedian, which led to the Astor Place riot in 1849.

Edwin Forrest was seen as a living embodiment of the American character. Yet that lofty status removed him from close identification with his audiences. His tragic roles were set in exotic surroundings far removed both temporally and geographically from the world his audiences experienced. He was a type of humanity, not humanity itself. By contrast, the turn-of-the-century players had been scaled down from Forrest's heroic proportions. They now talked and behaved more like ordinary people in plays that approximated modern life. If they lost some of the grandeur of an older style, their naturalism and personal charm invited audiences to a more intimate identification with them. Ada Rehan's sauciness, George M. Cohan's cockiness, Maude Adams's sweetness, all were traits that helped develop personal ties between actor and public. At the same time, magazines, newspapers, and books chronicled the details of players' offstage lives, helping to bridge the ancient chasm that had separated player and society. The basis of an actor's appeal no longer came from his symbolizing something greater than himself—as Forrest symbolized Jacksonian America—but now resided in attractive personal traits. The pictorial stage of the late nineteenth century required the player who cut a fine figure. Audiences preferred piquancy and a sense of style to virtuosity. If Forrest had been a symbol of the community, modern actors became models for individual lifestyle. Audiences identified with the actor as a personality rather than as an embodiment of community values.

This new preference was in no way arbitrary or simply a result of changing tastes; it followed naturally from public needs created by urban society. Urban life modified human existence in many ways, but probably none more fundamentally than in its effects on interpersonal contacts. The characteristic familiarity and intimacy of rural and small-town society bowed to the transitory and superficial relationships of city life. Interrelationships in the city's impersonal milieu took on aspects of a performance, with great care given to details of appearance and manner. As early as 1915 sociologist Robert Park observed that in an urban setting "the individual's status is determined to a considerable degree by conventional signs—by fashion and 'front'—and the art of life is largely reduced to skating on thin surfaces and a scrupulous study of style and movement." [67] The concern for fashion and front, for making impressions, for being "somebody," betrayed a new sense of self-definition taking hold in America. Warren Susman has suggested that an entirely new cultural order was inaugurated around the turn of the century. [68] In place of the nineteenth century's "culture of character," which emphasized self-discipline, moral development, and control, came a new "culture of personality," which had a different vision of self-development, one stressing fulfillment through an assertion of personal idiosyncrasies. Susman illustrates his argument with contemporary self-help manuals that taught the importance of setting oneself apart from the crowd through the training of the voice, exercise, control of diet, and careful grooming. Poise and charm became essential traits. The individual was seen as a performer, finding the role to which he felt best suited in the emerging mass society.

Just as actors exemplified freedom from social constraints they also, paradoxically, provided guidance for self-fulfillment within the prevailing social order. Gifted with the coveted physical and social charms, actors were logical models for the public to emulate. The great interest in the private lives of players, the concern for minute detail about their homes, hobbies, and ideas was a corollary to the personality mode of acting. Both onstage and off actors projected a well-defined image. By their naturalistic acting in roles that replicated contemporary life and by representation in magazines and books as people with a heightened sense of style, actors set forth an image with which the public could readily identify. Yet while actors' lives were of the same order as everyone else's, they somehow seemed richer, more fulfilled. "An actress is a woman intensified," wrote Ada Patterson in 1915; "in her the qualities of the average woman are raised to the hundredth power."[69]

In an age increasingly obsessed with images—visual images of photography and advertising as well as images of consumption and lifestyle, actors became human images. They represented a style of living at once unattainable yet inviting imitation. Dress, demeanor, speech, and of course love making could all be learned. A writer in *Cosmopolitan*, for example, encouraged the American male to pay closer attention to examples of the art of romance set before them onstage.[70] But such admonitions were largely unnecessary. The American public looked anxiously for models of the sophisticated life, and more often than not it found them in the lives of its acting heroes and heroines.

Actors became both exemplars and metaphors of modern life: exemplars in that the public followed their cues for personal development; metaphors in their role playing, which many social theorists (most notably Erving Goffman) now apply to the very definition of personality and human interaction.[71] The dramaturgical model of the "performing self," while not new ("All the world's a stage, / And all the men and women merely players," as a prominent dramatist put it centuries ago), gained conviction as urban life fostered a sense of continual performance. The obsession with personality and the image one projected betrayed anxiety not only about acceptance by others, but also about self-identity. Mass society threatened to overwhelm the individual, to destroy personal identity. Consequently, the new imperative was to distinguish oneself from the mass, a task accomplished through the conscious creation of a distinctive personality. Yet this definition of the self required constant outward attention to the changing nuances of public taste, for the self could only be understood and have meaning in reference to others. This dual focus on self and on society found analogy in the theatre, where the new psychological theory of acting commanded that the actor must first look within himself before playing his role to the public.

In sum, the early twentieth century witnessed the advent of what Philip Rieff calls "psychological man," a figure freed from the dictatorial authority of religious culture and given the promise of new life through cultivation of the inner self.[72] In both the theatre and in life awareness of this inner self reshaped beliefs about behavior. The knowledge has not been all to the good according to some social critics, who see it as the underlying cause of certain contemporary social pathologies. Richard Sennett believes the emphasis on emotion and personality nurtured a privatism harmful to a healthy public culture. Christopher Lasch in an even more thorough indictment of American culture takes the accompanying obsession with celebrities as evidence of a futile narcissistic search for self-identity.[73]

For better or worse actors have become the social type of particular appropriateness for our time. Skilled communicators, masters of appearance and personality, they exude the social qualities that in modern life mean success. At the same time they are perceived as individuals in touch with themselves, able to delve into the depths of soul and summon up the inner knowledge essential for their art. Actors combine, in other words, two primary elements of the modern sensibility: the need for social adroitness and the quest for self-knowledge. The anxieties peculiar to contemporary life find resolution in those who devote their lives to pretending to be others. A more telling—and more ironic—commentary on our culture is hard to imagine.

*   *   *

The new culture of personality gained an even stronger hold on the American public through a related art: the motion picture. While a trend toward realism characterized the late nineteenth-century stage, it could not match the realism of the movie camera. The movies offered new challenges and new opportunities for the actor, and as the cinematic art developed it created a distinctive image for the movie player.

Eight ❀

Hollywood's Wooing

*F*ew technological advances have influenced an artistic field as powerfully as motion pictures did that of acting. The movie screen intensified and extended the player's art, fundamentally altering the relationship between actor and audience. Understandably, its modification of the actor's craft evoked uncertainty and some suspicion from the theatre's performers. Broadway's stars responded to Hollywood's wooing in several ways: some resisted; some tried out the movies and failed; and a few succeeded. Stardom on Broadway did not ensure acclaim by movie audiences, and conversely, some of the screen's biggest stars had humble theatrical pedigrees. Though the movies continued trends that had begun on the stage, they brought new forces into play. The successes and failures of stage actors in the movies offer an interesting study of the implications of technological innovation.

* 1 *

The early history of the motion-picture industry is extraordinarily interesting, but well beyond the scope of this study.[1] Suffice it to say that the invention of Thomas Edison's Kinetoscope in the 1890s paved the way for the nickelodeons of the next decade and the subsequent expansion of the movie industry. Short one-reelers were replaced by longer feature films beginning in 1912, which allowed for development of plot and character. Moreover, film production, which originally centered in New York, had by 1913 moved to Los Angeles. Most important, movies transcended their working-class origins to become middle-class entertainment, increasingly viewed in palatial theatres. By World War I the film industry had reached significant proportions, and its stars—Douglas Fairbanks, Charlie Chaplin, Mary Pickford, William S. Hart, and

Fatty Arbuckle—had replaced the theatrical giants in the hearts of the American public.

But this eventual Copernican shift was not evident to stage actors during the early years of film. Rather, Broadway's actors, proud of their theatrical tradition, had difficulty taking the new medium seriously. The early movies, after all, were either arrant buffoonery or melodramatic vignettes intended for a class of people unschooled in Shakespeare. Players freely admitted their superiority to movie acting. This arrogance was not a recent affectation, for the entertainment world had long had a well-defined hierarchy based on the degree to which various forms were thought to be "art." Since drama had an established place among the arts, actors of the legitimate stage outranked performers in vaudeville, burlesque, the circus, or the movies. And within the theatre a similar social pyramid existed: actors who performed the classics received the most esteem, followed by those who performed more ordinary fare on Broadway and in first-class road shows, the stock company performers, and finally the 10–20–30 and tent-rep performers. Those not performing the "legitimate" drama were considered to be working in an inferior field, even though, as was the case with many vaudevillians, they might be making a good deal more money. This status consciousness was illustrated by an incident involving Mary Anderson. The driver of an omnibus in a small town inadvertently insulted Mary by asking her what time her show began. The indignant beauty responded that she was not in a "show," which to her carried connotations of a circus and its sideshow freaks; rather, her company presented "an intellectual treat." [2]

The initial avoidance of movies by stage stars opened the door for the legions of stock and cheaper road show performers, who suddenly found themselves in demand by the motion-picture companies. Many of these troupers began earning a regular paycheck for the first time, and an exceptional few stumbled into movie stardom. D. W. Griffith was an unemployed actor living on his last few dollars in New York when a friend suggested that he pick up five dollars a day acting in the movies. His celebrated career in film thus had its humble beginning.

A collective biography of the early movie actors, which examined their theatrical training, would be extremely valuable. It remains to be done, however, and for the moment one can say only that probably most of the pre-1915 movie actors began their careers on the stage. All the leading performers at Selig studio, for example, had come from stock-company backgrounds. Capsule biographies of Selig players indicated that most of them entered movie work on a temporary basis; then finding the experience rewarding and the pay good, they decided to remain. Betty Harte, for instance, after several years in stock, attempted to start a company of her own. Her leading man got drunk on the second night and the company disbanded. Desperate for work, Harte joined Selig as an ingenue in 1909, where she stayed. Charles Clary played stock companies and road shows all over America. While in Los Angeles he visited the Selig studio and became extremely interested in the whole process of movie making. Soon after, Clary joined Selig and contentedly remained.[3]

Most of the early players, however, viewed the movies simply as a stopgap measure until they received a reputable job on the stage. Actors would hang around the New York movie studios in the morning waiting for an assignment; then if nothing came, they would make the rounds of the theatrical agencies in the afternoon. It was a motley group of people who formed the movie stock companies. The genuinely talented players stayed only a few days before they left to go back on stage. Actors kept quiet about their forays into filmland and hoped that no one would recognize them on screen. For a proud man like Griffith, this continual association with the theatrical demimonde was humiliating. According to his wife, actress Linda Arvidson, his injured pride made it difficult for him to go to work many mornings. Even worse was his offering summer movie-acting jobs to his more successful theatrical friends, only to be turned down with flimsy excuses. These incidents reminded the Griffiths that they were in the movies only because they had failed in the theatre.[4]

The routine of the pioneer film makers was not conducive to professional dignity. Inside shots were filmed in cramped New York City studios. But the action-filled movies frequently required the crew to shoot in outdoor locations in the New York area. The woods, hills, meadows, and marshes of northern New Jersey were but a ferry ride from Manhattan and formed the setting for Westerns and other adventure films. Location shots provided players unusual experiences they would never have had in theatres, and the exposure to sunshine and fresh air solved an age-old objection to the theatre's deleterious effects on health. Nevertheless, the undefined nature of the movie-making venue compromised the actors' standing—they had no real artistic home. Players of the legitimate stage, by contrast, had a permanent and well-defined arena for their art. Be it a town hall or nothing more than a platform in a tent, it was an area set apart by agreement between player and audience for the creation of a new reality. The stage was a place where actors could feel at home and in charge.

When Griffith became a director at Biograph in 1908, he set

out to recruit better actors, visiting the Lambs and The Players and enticing thespians with offers of ten dollars a day. Griffith convinced James Kirkwood, who had finished acting in the popular *Great Divide*, to visit the Biograph studio, where he was given the grand tour and treated royally. The salary and deference convinced Kirkwood to join (though he disguised himself with a beard in hopes that his theatre fans would not recognize him), and he went on to a successful screen career. Other respected players followed Kirkwood into the world of the photoplay. The higher-salaried actors added dignity to the Biograph Company, but friction developed between the better-paid newcomers and the five-dollar-a-day screen veterans, who, though delighted at working with respected professionals, resented their preferential treatment. Salaries soon climbed to twenty dollars a day, making motion pictures even more attractive, and male actors found their way from the Rialto to the door of Biograph, Vitagraph, Edison, and other studios in increasing numbers. Actresses, however, were reluctant to try the new medium and proved more difficult to recruit.[5]

By 1913, movie salaries equaled those of stage stock companies. Beginners had to labor for $10 or less a day, but regular movie stock company players earned from $35 to $60 a week in minor parts and the leads made $75 to $250 a week. Moreover, where an actor in the legitimate theatre felt fortunate to get a full forty weeks of work in a year, the movie performer could be assured of year-around work and without losing four or five weeks of pay during rehearsal as Broadway performers did.[6] Walter Prichard Eaton in a 1915 article entitled "Actor-Snatching and the Movies" asked what actor could turn down a Hollywood offer of doubled salary: "Money for every day you work, no free rehearsals, and all your railroad and traveling expenses paid. Do you think twice about accepting it? No, you do not. You don't even think once. You pack your trunk and head for the coast."[7]

The early movie companies were modeled after theatrical stock companies. Roles in each film were parceled out to various members of the company by the director, who dominated productions even more than did his counterpart in the theatre. A form of equalitarianism ruled in the early days; a player might be featured in one movie and then become an extra in the next. Mary Pickford went from the juvenile lead in *The Lonely Villa* to an extra in her next film for Biograph. Film studios outdid theatrical stock companies in subordinating the player to the production. No screen credits were given at the beginning or ending of the films. The actors remained anonymous, as the film companies attempted to create an identity of their own as producers of a certain kind of film rather than to build an image for their players. Undoubtedly, the stage actors who were ashamed of their movie work preferred it that way.

The earliest compromise of this rule was the designation of Florence Lawrence and Florence Turner as "The Biograph Girl" and "The Vitagraph Girl" respectively, in an attempt to identify the actress with the producing company. The popularity of "The Vitagraph Girl" made Florence Turner the first actress to be put under contract by a film company. Yet even as a protostar she was hardly pampered. Besides acting she attended to the business affairs of Vitagraph, keeping the books and serving as cashier.[8]

American audiences were curious about their screen favorites. People wrote film studios asking about "the fat guy" and "the girl with the curls." Audiences wanted to know more about these actors and their backgrounds. This, of course, had been true with stage players as well, but the motion picture raised this phenomenon to a new level. It did not take the studios long to realize that they could exploit the star system for tremendous gain. By 1910 the names of the stars began appearing, and the next year some studios credited featured players. Carl Laemmle hired Florence Lawrence for his Independent Motion Pictures Company and immediately mounted a huge publicity campaign around her. She inaugurated the personal appearance; when in St. Louis she was surrounded by crowds curious about a planted newspaper report that she was dead. Likewise, when the identity of Florence Turner was made public, requests for personal appearances poured in from around New York.[9] Shortly after the beginning of her movie career, Mary Pickford was amazed at the recognition given her in public. It disconcerted her at first because members of Belasco or Frohman companies were not to be seen in public (theatrical producers feared that public visibility dissolved the star's aura).[10] But both the movie moguls and the stars themselves quickly learned that personal appearances heightened box-office value by adding a human touch to the larger-than-life screen image. James K. Hackett, for example, after returning to Broadway from filming *The Prisoner of Zenda*, found that he had the biggest business in years, and he determined to appear in at least one picture a year.[11] Actors' bid for publicity was abetted by the fan magazine, which first appeared in February of 1911 with the *Moving Picture Story Magazine*. Through this medium the happenings of the movie colony were related in vivid detail. The distinction between the public and private lives of stars blurred, with every aspect of their lives susceptible to scrutiny.

The emerging star system sent salaries skyrocketing as the

studios competed for the public's favorite actors. Only Biograph clung to the old policy of anonymity for its players, a policy which would doom the studio. Along with Florence Lawrence, a number of Biograph's most popular performers went elsewhere, and by 1913, when it jumped on the celebrity bandwagon, the studio had irreversibly declined.[12]

But movie producers were not content with the stars they created. The feeling persisted that stage stars were the only genuine stars, an attitude which reflected the moviemakers' sense of artistic inferiority. Consequently, a few producers set out to lure the stage luminaries to the silver screen, seeking to capitalize on the player's names while legitimizing the cinema. An example had been set in Sarah Bernhardt's film, *Queen Elizabeth*, which had attracted a wide audience during its 1912 American showing. The film proved that the discreet middle class would come to the longer features, especially if they starred established stage players.

Adolph Zukor, the man who imported *Queen Elizabeth* from France, devised the most ambitious plan to lure stage players to the movies. He formed the Famous Players in Famous Plays Company in 1912 with the aim of restaging for the camera the theatre's greatest dramas, performed by the players who made them famous. Zukor brought Broadway producer Daniel Frohman into the company to add prestige to the enterprise. As president of Actors' Fund and a greatly respected man of the theatre, Frohman's presence conferred a theatrical stamp of approval on the motion picture industry. Famous Players' films included Mrs. Fiske's *Tess of the d'Urbervilles*, James K. Hackett's *Prisoner of Zenda*, Lily Langtry's *Her Neighbor's Wife*, and James O'Neill's *Count of Monte Cristo*. Other companies followed Zukor's lead. Harry Aitken hired comedian Eddie Foy, Jr., and England's great Shakespearean Sir Herbert Beerbohm Tree for his Triangle Company; Vitagraph featured Edward H. Sothern. And there followed a number of others, the most important being the Jesse Lasky Feature Play Company, which hired David Belasco to provide the same kind of theatrical window dressing that Daniel Frohman gave Famous Players.[13]

Actors' decision to take the cinematic plunge was not made lightly. Traditional wisdom said that appearance in the movies would impair stage appeal. George Arliss, who resisted movie offers for several years before succumbing, admitted that an element of snobbishness had to be overcome by many players. They appeared before the "best people," and if they stepped down into the movies, the "best people" might no longer accept them as superior actors.[14]

Several factors convinced players to take the risk. First, there was the money. The scramble for Broadway's name players sent the asking price to unheard-of figures. Harry Aitken signed comedian Eddie Foy, Jr., for $1,200 a week, committed DeWolf Hopper to a one-year $85,000 contract, and paid Sir Herbert Beerbohm Tree an incredible $100,000 for thirty weeks of work.[15] Mary Pickford's 1916 contract with First National, of course, which paid $350,000 per picture, dwarfed even Tree's contract, but Pickford was a proven screen star. Movie executives took on faith the notion that their high-priced Broadway stars would prove equally attractive on film.

Another inducement was the incomparable exposure movies gave a player. The thought of playing to millions of people impressed the histrionic ego. Edward H. Sothern admitted as much in his justification for movie making: "Cheap amusement is popular amusement," he said. "Popular amusement gives one an immense audience." He estimated that after finishing his three movies he would play to three million people a day, and thus could give "entertainment and instruction and inspiration" to many who could not pay $1.50 for a theatre ticket.[16] Pauline Frederick admired the "universality of the language of pantomime" employed in the movies, by which she could reach millions.[17]

A third attraction of the photoplay was its permanence. The "poor player / That struts and frets his hour upon the stage, / And then is heard no more" had always been the epitaph of the actor. But film promised a more enduring legacy for his art. Sir Herbert Beerbohm Tree explained his decision to go to Hollywood in these terms: "The actor hitherto has lived but for his generation. The cinema has given him the enfranchisement of posterity."[18] Likewise, Sarah Bernhardt exclaimed at the conclusion of filming *Queen Elizabeth*: "I am immortal! I am film!"[19]

Broadway producers did not let their stars go without a fight. Although none of Broadway's actors planned to make a career of the movies, the producers feared that making even one film would greatly reduce the stage appeal of their players. Producer Joseph Brooks asserted that stars who appeared in movies cut their value 50 percent, and David Belasco, though he lent his name to the Lasky Company, refused to let his own stars appear in movies. He claimed to be able to identify an actor who had done film acting by a tendency to strike rigid poses and make artificial gestures.[20] In retrospect one might wonder at the inordinate concern of producers, for one can see now that movie popularity heightens box-office attractiveness in the live theatre. But in a more fundamental sense they had a right to fear. They sensed that motion pictures presented a serious challenge to the stage, if not at present, then in the future, and that the lifeblood of their business—the stars—had to be kept on the Great White Way.

The managers' stubborn efforts to keep their stars out of the movies upset their strong-willed players and provoked some heated battles. Both Al Woods and Charles Frohman stipulated in contracts that the actors could not make movies, leading Pauline Frederick to forsake the stage completely when Woods forbade her movie making. Billie Burke's $40,000 offer from the New York Motion Picture Company prompted Al Hayman to warn her that, if she accepted the film offer, her contract with the Charles Frohman Company would be at an end. Burke, in a move that left the theatrical establishment aghast, removed herself from the exclusive roles of Charles Frohman stars, announcing that she would make the movie, then return to the stage under the management of Florenz Ziegfeld.[21]

Like the theatrical producers, a few actors realized that motion pictures posed a genuine threat to legitimate drama and voiced their concerns. During his 1916 national tour, Louis Mann took every occasion to condemn the movies, indicting them for being a mechanical medium "without the red blood of life," for lacking literature, and for dwarfing the intellect of children and destroying their study habits. Mann did not fail to mention that his love of drama had meant the sacrifice of lucrative offers from movie makers.[22] Following his 1918–19 cross-country tour, George Arliss predicted that the movies would be the death of the road in America. Arliss observed that his audiences were composed almost entirely of the middle aged, people who went to the theatre by force of habit. Conspicuously missing was the younger generation, whose loyalties lay with the movie stars. He inquired of other touring thespians and they reported the same story: "Warfield and Skinner and Gillette and Maude Adams and Ethel Barrymore and Laurette Taylor . . . have come to mean almost nothing at all to young Americans. . . . In the smaller cities whenever the conversation is of the play—it is the stars of filmdom who are discussed to the complete exclusion of representatives of the spoken drama."[23] Frank Craven claimed that audiences of the postmovie era were "much harder to move to response than they used to be." "In spite of our best efforts," he continued, it seemed "that a pall has settled down over things. No matter how we exert ourselves before some houses, no matter how good the play, we are met with stony indifference—or what seems to be indifference."[24]

Not all actors answered Hollywood's call. Comedian and character actor David Warfield turned down a fabulous movie offer. "I'd rather be an actor than his photograph," Warfield explained when asked why he refused. "The audience is my confederate, my brother, my effect. . . . And I won't go to the screen because I can't take my audience with me."[25] Maude Adams, John Drew, Henry Miller, Grace George, Frances Starr, and Otis Skinner (though he succumbed in later years) also turned down movie offers. The holdouts soon became the minority however, as most stage stars found it impossible not to try the new medium at least once, especially when they were so handsomely rewarded for yielding. But the remarks of Arliss, Craven, and Warfield typified an uneasiness stage players surely felt as they beheld the rising star of the movie actor and realized it boded the setting of their own. A revolution was under way, and it threatened the hierarchy of status that had been well entrenched in the acting world.

* 2 *

The West Coast proved to be a congenial setting for the theatrical visitors from the East. After the crowded streets and hurried pace of New York, actors appreciated California's relaxed atmosphere. Dustin Farnum's evangelism concerning the pleasures of movieland helped convince reluctant players to make the westward trek, and by 1916 Paul Hubert Conlan announced that the Los Angeles Rialto rivaled New York's. Marguerite Clark, Mrs. Leslie Carter, Maclyn Arbuckle, Robert Edeson, Elsie Janis, Emily Stevens, Olive Wyndham, Constance Collier, Helen Ware, Billie Burke, DeWolf Hopper, and Willie Collier were some of the better-known stage players to be found on the coast in 1915–16. Hollywood Boulevard became the California equivalent of Broadway, albeit a more modern version. Where Broadway's habitants promenaded on the Rialto in the best fashion of nineteenth-century society, the screen's nobility drove up and down Hollywood Boulevard to and from the studios, Douglas Fairbanks in his green racing car, others in limousines, testaments to the emerging automobile age.[26]

The California movie colony quickly developed its own culture. Without the perpetual travel of stage shows, movie actors were free to set down roots in the community, and mansions and great estates of the movie stars began to dot the landscape, becoming regular stops for southern California sightseers. Yet the makers of the photoplay did not gain immediate entrance into established California society. With just the same experience stage players had had for centuries, the early movie actors found themselves outsiders, suspiciously viewed as gypsy inhabitants of movie camps.

Consequently, the movie colony was a self-contained society. Universal City, with a population of a thousand, governed itself, electing several actresses to municipal office, including Laura Oakley as chief of police. The communal life of the colonies continued even after the day's filming, with actors, directors, and technicians keeping company in leisure hours. The nightly ritual for many players included a trip to a movie theatre—the Hollywood, Iris, or Apollo—to view the products of their labor.[27]

Hollywood inherited the suspicions of immorality that had traditionally focused on the stage actor. The movie colony was widely reputed to be a source of licentiousness and corruption, especially for the movie-struck young girl. It was popularly believed that the only route to a movie career for the novice female was via the casting couch. To help guard the virtue of the young actress the Hollywood Studio Club was established, whose function paralleled New York's Three Arts and Philadelphia's Charlotte Cushman clubs.[28] The Studio Club housed about a dozen girls, held teas and lunches, and offered drama and dancing lessons.

Like the stage, the movies found their ready defenders. *Motion Picture Magazine* published the report of a university professor, who studied movie studios firsthand posing as an extra. This "Apostle of Comstockery" vigorously denied the rumors of immorality, stating that he found "no evidence of mental, moral or physical deterioration. . . . One saw the bright eyes, the elastic step, the quick movement," he wrote, "all the general indications of vigor that is co-existent with a temperate and moral life."[29]

But increasingly Hollywood did not need such defenders, as it began to create its special place in the public's imagination. Just as the stage star evoked visions of Broadway's glitter, the movie actor became identified with southern California, an association that enhanced his image. He symbolized the pleasure and vitality that California promised. New York still held an excitement, to be sure, but urban blight had tarnished the gloss. The next half century belonged to California and the suburban ideal. Film stars' estates with their swimming pools and gardens became as much of a fantasy environment as their movie settings, and the splendor of their private lives equaled anything that could be put on the screen. The ostentatious lifestyle of the early movie stars, in fact, went far beyond anything exhibited by stage players. Such lavish display of wealth had at one time been considered a major social problem. In the 1890s the mansions, extravagant dinners, and great yachts of the rich were seen as violations of the American code of equalitarianism and a precipitant of class hatred.[30] But sumptuousness seemed appropriate for the movie player. Hollywood was the venue of luxury and unmitigated consumption the mark of the film star. Actors could indulge their most extravagant tastes in dress, food, travel, and dwelling without exciting the resentment that others might. Public-relations agents nurtured the stereotype of luxuriousness, ensuring that the public's dream, which began in the theatre, would be continued without interruption.[31]

Stage actors in Hollywood made no secret of their feelings of superiority to full-time movie actors. Even Mary Pickford, who had once been the object of such condescension, was guilty of a similar snobbery. One reason she left D. W. Griffith in 1913 was his choice of Mae Marsh, a department-store clerk without the stage training that Mary valued, for the lead in *The Sands of Dee*.[32] But movie actors did not have to put up with the belittling comments of stage players for long. It became clear shortly after the Hollywood gold rush of 1915–16 that Broadway's favorites were not to be foisted upon the movie public. Audiences chose their own stars, and with few exceptions the stars of the legitimate theatre were not their pick.

Though the chemistry of stardom does not lend itself to exact analysis, the reasons for the failure of most stage actors in the movies are fairly clear. Primarily they trace to the unique demands of film, which the Broadway stars either failed to appreciate or refused to yield to.

The very earliest movie acting followed the pantomimic tradition of the stage. Moviemakers believed that without speech, attitudes had to be conveyed through exaggerated gesture and expression. As cinematic techniques such as the close-up developed, however, it became apparent that a restrained manner was more effective. Even more than the theatre, movies demanded natural movements and expressions. The theatre may have moved toward realism, but it could never equal the realism of film. Books for film hopefuls repeatedly stressed the need to act as one would in real life under the same circumstances.[33] Many stage players had problems learning how to subdue their expressions in the movies. One had to stop "letting one's face go," testified a leading actress. Facial expression and gestures common to the stage looked grotesque in movies. After seeing herself on film Virginia Harned became so upset by the way she appeared that she returned her contract check for five thousand dollars and refused to make the movie.[34]

Broadway stars came to Hollywood expecting simply to recreate their stage roles in front of a camera. An early name for the movies (and, significantly, one that did not endure)—"photoplays"—expressed a prevailing attitude toward the medium. Neither actors nor the producers who lured them west with fat contracts felt any change in technique necessary, aside from certain restrictions imposed by the camera. Consequently, most players came to the studios without an appreciation of or even an interest in cinematic methods. Once there the disjointed process of movie making baffled them. How could one build up to the climactic episode when the scenes were shot out of sequence? The directors constantly interrupted, making suggestions that contradicted a lifetime of experience on the stage. Even the daily routine was a complete reversal of custom. Filming days started early, and the Broadway regulars who were accustomed to a leisurely morning found getting up at six or seven in the morning a special burden.

In their memoirs stage players generally tried to look at their movie experience in a positive manner, although they usually noted the medium's intrinsic shortcomings. William H. Crane appeared in a few movies toward the end of his career and enjoyed the experience. At the same time he found it exasperating, having to learn how to cross a scene all over again to accommodate the camera—and having a scene end just as he was beginning to feel comfortable in it.[35] Otis Skinner had a similarly mixed reaction while filming *Kismet* in 1920. He concluded that the mechanical nature of film making contributed to the stage stars' difficulties. It lacked the presence of a live audience, which theatrical performers needed in order to give their best effort. Skinner also objected to the directors' common failure to explain the significance of each scene to their actors. On the other hand, Skinner personally claimed to have had no difficulty adjusting to film. In fact he found that his screen work helped his theatre work by enabling him to visualize his acting and see what the audience saw.[36] Similarly enthused, James K. Hackett planned to film the dress rehearsals of his stage productions and show the movie to his cast.[37]

Performers who depended on their rapport with a live audience found the new medium destructive of that relationship. Musical-comedy star Blanche Ring enjoyed an intimacy with her audience, a familiarity nourished by frequent asides. But the cinematic barrier destroyed this, and her appeal declined. Comedian Eddie Foy, Jr., traded on his sad features and rasping voice to achieve great popularity. But his humor just did not transfer well to film. Foy also chafed against the slapstick indignities to which Mack Sennett's writers submitted him. He stubbornly refused to go through with some of the stunts, holding up production until the studio suspended him. Foy made just one picture before he and Triangle agreed to terminate his one-year contract, and Foy returned to the boards.[38]

Perhaps the most resounding failure suffered by a major stage actor was that of Sir Herbert Beerbohm Tree. Nearing the end of his career in 1915, the eminent Shakespearean was undoubtedly the most distinguished actor Hollywood had attracted. The signing of his $100,000 contract with Triangle had been accompanied by great fanfare. Tree was to be featured in *Macbeth*, thought to be the most adaptable of Shakespeare's dramas to the silent screen. It soon became evident that the English tragedian had no conception of movie making. He continually moved out of the camera's range, turned his back to it, and exaggerated his pantomime. Tree's cinematic ineptitude brought production to a standstill. An exasperated D. W. Griffith finally decided to use stuntman Monte Blue as Tree's double in all scenes except those where the face would show. Blue eventually made most of the movie, but that did not save the film, which bombed even in London. Tree made only one film after that, *Old Folks at Home*, a second-rate sentimental tale far removed from the classics of Tree's realm. Well aware of how badly things were going, Tree volunteered to tear up his contract before the thirty weeks had ended.[39]

By the fall of 1916 the picture bubble had burst. Movie producers realized that the limited box-office draw of stage stars did not begin to pay for their inflated salaries. Film makers began relying less on Broadway's heroes and heroines and more on the proven stars of the screen. As the studios developed their own talent for minor roles, the movie market for lesser stage players also dried up. The generous yearlong contracts that required only occasional work and allowed for days of leisure at area clubs ended, and an exodus back to the stage began.[40] Harry Aitken's Triangle Studio learned the lesson too late. In addition to its unhappy experience with Foy and Tree it suffered high-priced failures with comedian DeWolf Hopper and the Weber and Fields duo. Triangle encountered all the problems that came from using legitimate players. Stage stars were paid high salaries, which caused friction with lower-paid movie veterans, and their inexperience required costly retakes. Moreover, some of the players were simply not photogenic; the camera revealed flaws and mannerisms unnoticed on the stage. Exhibitors also complained that Broadway's stars did not attract audiences, and they rebelled against the high rentals Triangle had to charge in order to pay for them. By April of 1916 patronage of Triangle movies dropped off precipitously, and soon after Aitken lost the studio.[41]

In fairness to the stage players it should be pointed out that few of them planned to make a career of the movies. They viewed them as a quick and easy source of money, and if they failed to set aflame the hearts of America's movie public, it did not greatly matter. They would soon be back onstage before the people who loved them, richer and without much loss of face. Connections between the stage and the movies were never completely severed, of course. Broadway stars continued to make occasional films, though no longer on the extravagant long-term contracts.

Historians of the movie industry invariably mention the failure of the famous players concept described above. Less often mentioned are the actors who made successful transitions from stage to screen. Notwithstanding D. W. Griffith's remark that "anyone has a much better chance in pictures if he has never been on the stage," it should not be thought that a stage career meant automatic failure in the movies. The theatre, after all, provided the training grounds for most of the early movie actors. And a fair number of featured Broadway players went on to equal or surpass their stage fame in the movies. Mary Pickford, Douglas Fairbanks, and William S. Hart—America's favorites—had attained recognition on the legitimate stage, and Charlie Chaplin had apprenticed in music halls and vaudeville.

Success in the movies required certain traits. Being an accomplished performer was not enough; one had to be photogenic, to have a "camera face," as Norma Talmadge put it. The unforgiving lens demanded a flawless visage. Makeup could not hide the marks of age to the degree it could on stage, so the female leads were youthful, often in their teens. Mary Pickford offers the prime example of an actress perfectly suited for motion pictures. The golden-tressed beauty grew up in the theatre, having been her family's breadwinner since the age of five. At fourteen she took a leading role in a popular Belasco play, *The Warrens of Virginia*, and received good reviews. Her mother first suggested that she apply at Biograph Studio. The idea of a Belasco actress working in the movies appalled Pickford, but the unsteady employment of the theatre left her little choice. Thus, in 1909, Mary Pickford became a Griffith-directed movie actress. Despite her ensuing popularity with the movie public, she let it be known from the beginning that she was only marking time until she could return to the stage. Her return came in 1913 as a leading lady in *A Good Little Devil*. The play was only fair, but Pickford received personal acclaim. The reception given her by the audience and by the crowds at her dressing-room door hinted at the unique nature of the movie appeal. Mary Pickford saw that her future lay in motion pictures, and she stepped off the boards for good.[42]

Other even more prominent stage actresses found equal acclaim in movies. Pauline Frederick's ability to project emotion with her eyes and hands made her more effective on the screen than on stage, and this led to a long career.[43] Alla Nazimova's exotic beauty cast her for the role of the temptress on screen. And Elsie Ferguson moved easily from starring roles on stage to similar roles in the movies.

Some of Broadway's leading men, likewise, made a smooth transition to the screen, although it sometimes took a modification of image. William Faversham had been known as a stylish actor of society drama. In his first movie he once again donned the tailored clothes, posed through five dreary reels, and was pronounced a cinematic failure. But Faversham's next director discarded the elegant apparel and fastidious manners and cast him as an heroic man-of-action. Faversham became a movie star. William and Dustin Farnum similarly abandoned the costume dramas of their stage days for the cowboy clothes of the movies.[44] America's first great Western hero, William S. Hart, had a twenty-five-year stage career behind him when he went into films. He had performed Shakespeare with Lawrence Barrett and other classical roles in support of Helena Modjeska. Hart moved into Westerns while still in the theatre, with *The Squaw Man* and the title role of *The Virginian*. Entering the movies in 1914 he introduced the low-key, taciturn cowboy type that has influenced Western heroes ever since. Triangle Films objected to what it considered a wooden performance by him and sold distribution rights of his films to another company. But American audiences vindicated Hart by making him a star.[45]

Besides having the necessary physical features, the stage players who succeeded in motion pictures did so because they were enthusiastic and eager to learn about the new art. They realized that motion pictures were not simply filmed stage plays but were a form all their own. Geraldine Farrar exemplified this open attitude. The Metropolitan Opera star signed with the Lasky Company in 1915 to film *Carmen*, the triumph of her previous season. Her Hollywood expedition was a journalistic feast. She traveled to the West Coast in a private railway car, was met at the station by a delegation of dignitaries, had the use of a beautiful home during her stay—in every way she was deferred to. The Lasky production crew probably anticipated headaches in instructing the prima donna in the ways of the cinema. But Farrar proved to be a diligent student of the movies, constantly asking questions about technique and camera angles. Her dark beauty and convincing acting led to a succession of popular movies over the next several years.[46]

Yet the magazines that fed dreams of a movie career talked less about these requirements for success than they did about the seemingly arbitrary conferral of stardom. Stardom, writers seemed to imply, might fall on anyone. Unlike the theatrical literature, which stressed the diligence and preparation of Broadway stars and only rarely recorded a shortcut to fame, sketches of movie actors often centered on how quickly and easily ordinary people were transformed into screen idols. The chance of being "discovered" became a part of the Hollywood mythos. The promise of instant fame and incredible fortune was unmatched. It all depended on whether one filmed well and—more important—if one had that indefinable quality called personality.[47]

The cult of personality had pervaded the stage to be sure, but the cinematic medium intensified its importance. Advice manuals for screen hopefuls stressed the trait's importance. "It is personality which wins popularity," wrote Francis Agnew. Inez Klumph agreed, stressing that personality was the key ingredient for movie success. Klumph suggested that screen candidates test their personality quotient by asking themselves whether in a large gathering people naturally gravitated toward them and if they commanded attention while talking. If so, they might have the magnetism to qualify for stardom.[48]

But the silent screen required a different means of revealing personality than the stage. The actor's chief means of expression on stage was his voice. Furthermore, the distance between stage player and audience required stylization, the resort to such theatrical devices as makeup, broad gestures, and voice inflection. This imposed a limit on the degree of realism which could be reached, and stylization covered actors' personalities with a layer of artifice. Motion pictures, however, encouraged a radical realism. The camera faithfully recorded the smallest detail and magnified it on the screen. Accordingly, movie acting had to be natural, a truth it took film makers a few years to realize. "I had always believed," George Arliss said, "that for the movies acting must be exaggerated, but I saw in this one flash that RESTRAINT was the chief thing that the actor must learn in transferring his art from the stage to the screen." Sincerity, restraint, the appearance of not acting at all proved the most effective techniques. And without the mediating conventions of stage techniques, the actor's personality could shine through unimpeded.[49]

Movies offered the most vivid revelation of personality: the close-up. An expressive face filling the screen conveyed direct emotion to the audience. Viewers felt an intimacy with screen characters never experienced with stage players. The "Intimate Photoplay," as Vachel Lindsay called it, was the vehicle of Mary Pickford's love affair with her public. A "certain aspect of her face in her high-est mood," apostrophized Lindsay, framed by the camera like a Botticelli portrait, lured the public to the theatre night after night to catch a glimpse of her.[50] John Emerson's and Anita Loos's checklist for cinema hopefuls underlined the importance of a distinctive, well-featured face: "Are my eyes large? Is my skin fine and well kept? Is my mouth small and are my teeth good? Is my nose straight? Has my face character, something which makes it not only beautiful, but which portrays the underlying personality?"[51] By glorifying the self and setting the individual apart from the mass, the close-up abetted the triumph of personality.[52]

In their realism and exploitation of personality movies only enlarged upon a trend well established in the commercial theatre. But the degree to which these traits were pursued enables one to say that motion pictures created a whole new image for its per-formers. While audiences outside of New York would be fortunate to see their stage favorites once a year, the movies' wide distri-bution allowed millions of Americans to become familiar with many actors. The public could study them in various moods and situations—in short, come to feel that they knew them thoroughly. Away from the movie house the public's insatiable appetite for de-tails of screen stars' private lives was fed by the fan magazines and fan clubs, the two accoutrements of celebrity truly original with the movies.

In a significant sense motion pictures fused the two contrast-ing modes of stage performance: the heroic and the realistic. Be-neath the veneer of the newer realism and its enticements of per-sonality lay an older histrionic lure, nearly discarded on the stage, but given new form and power in the movies. This was the appeal to the audience's sense of collective values. Though mass society presented the compelling problem of preserving individuality, the older need of mythic symbols never disappeared. The cinema was an apt medium for filling this need. Audiences viewed, after all, only images—silent and ethereal. The darkened theatre, the flick-ering figures on the screen, the dreamlike atmosphere constituted a Jungian exercise in collective myth making. The simile of dreams was in fact applied again and again to movies. To "see the people in life size moving before your eyes, and yet realize there is not a single person there—it seems like some phantom of the brain, an hallucination, and one is almost tempted to rush to the stage and grapple with the ghostly actors as one is moved to cry out in the vividness of a dream."[53] The camera could also magnify screen characters to heroic proportions, imparting a transcendent presence unknown to actors of earlier generations. Ironically, motion pictures restored what dramatic critics lamented the theatre had lost: the grandeur and power of the classic stage. The public's fascination with the movie actor was not just a function of greater exposure, then, but resided in the motion pictures' ability to impart both a personal identification with a screen personality and a collective sense of primeval awe toward the screen shamans.[54]

This attachment, however, was peculiarly double-edged. "As an emotional response, it was different in kind and fervour from that which greeted stage celebrities," noted Alexander Walker. "It was close and personal, yet dissociated and mob-like. It radiated love, yet turned the loved one into an object. It derived from a star's uniqueness, but was diffused by her ubiquity."[55] The celebrity of the movie star carried an intrinsic ambivalence. The same power that cast a congenial spell over the movie public could on occasion (as Nathaniel West brilliantly perceived in *The Day of the Locust*) be transformed into a frenzied obsession seeking to devour the venerated object. The ambivalence should perhaps be seen as a reflexive response of mass culture against the source of its manipulation, a resentful spasm of revolt against the impersonality of mass society and the helplessness to change it. Movie stars are adored for their ability to rise above the mass and resented for that very fact. Given their greater exposure, their heightened cinematic presence, and the progressively tighter constraints of urban-industrial life, movie stars naturally would surpass stage players both as recipients of adulation and as objects of exposé and scandal.

"The legitimate drama," said George Arliss in 1919, "has never known anything like the popularity which is the movies' priceless possession."[56] And indeed it had not. Pickford, Chaplin, and Fairbanks became America's first players, and from the teens onward the motion picture, not the stage, became the path to national acclaim. In one sense the Hollywood image of lascivious unrestraint benefited the Broadway actor. Many conservative Christians replaced their hostility toward the theatre with a suspicion of the cinema and its actors. Moreover, stage players came to represent the more refined and decorous element of the acting profession. They were not the ones involved in the notorious Hollywood scandals of the early 1920s. Such Broadway stars as Katherine Cornell, Alfred Lunt, and Lynne Fontaine became the aristocrats of the acting fraternity, having eschewed the glamour and riches of movies for the higher rewards of artistic satisfaction on the stage.

Yet film stars were fortunate to work in a medium that so well suited America's prevailing cultural desires. The stage had adapted to changing tastes as well as it could. But for a society increasingly oriented to the visual, live theatre could not compete with the movies.

∗   3   ∗

"It is important to realize," writes Susan Sontag, "that human sensory awareness has not merely a biology but a specific history, each culture placing a premium on certain senses and inhibiting others."[57] Commentators on American society have frequently noted that we live in a visual age, where appeals to the eye dominate. Marshall McLuhan made the point most forcefully in *Understanding Media*, where he dates the beginnings of a visual orientation back to the introduction of the printed word.[58] But one could argue more reasonably that the late nineteenth century marked the transition from one kind of sensory dominance to another: from an aural orientation that predominated in the mid–nineteenth century to a visual orientation of the turn of the century. Developments in the theatre and motion pictures illustrate this change.

The spoken word reigned supreme in Jacksonian America. "Words—the popular mind was intoxicated by words," said Constance Rourke. It was not simply the lack of other media that accounted for this; it was the demands of a new nation's search for self-identity. Oratory became the main form of public ritual, observed Daniel Boorstin. At all kinds of public gatherings an address was the featured event, the face-to-face encounter of speaker and audience sealing the democratic pact. American nationality was created largely on the pulpits and platforms of the land.[59] Public address served many functions. Before the age of textbooks and lending libraries the lyceum acted as a chief means of popular education. And speeches served as public entertainment. Tocqueville noted that debating clubs took the place of theatricals in some communities. The oratorical style also exerted profound influence on literary form. F. O. Matthiessen wrote: "To a degree that we have lost sight of, oratory was then the basis for other forms of writing, and its mode of expression left a mark on theirs."[60]

The American theatre shared this fond regard for speech making. Most plays were simply vehicles to display the tragedians' eloquence. The thin plots moved from speech to speech, highlighted by impassioned cries for justice, declarations of love, vows of revenge. This declamatory tradition (discussed above in greater detail) meant that, despite the occasional spectacle, the theatre appealed first to the ear. Booth, Forrest, Cushman, Davenport, and other stars captivated audiences through the beauty and power of their voices.

The predominance of the aural surrendered before the impact of nineteenth-century technology. The torrent of print in the mass-circulation newspapers and magazines, the ubiquitous halftone reproduction, and the camera made the last two decades of the nineteenth century an era of heightened visual awareness of society.[61] The camera was especially significant. Photographs of all classes and conditions magnified the variety of the American experience. The city, transformed by the dazzling illumination of electricity, found a new symbol in the Great White Way of Broadway (a phrase coined in 1901). Visual communication revolutionized the field of advertising, where the compressed image of the trademark became an immediately identifiable symbol to American buyers.

Evolving theatrical techniques revealed a similar stress on the visual. As noted earlier, theatrical realism implied lifelike stage settings. David Belasco, the master of the "Drama of Illusion," painstakingly worked over every detail of his productions, turning fairly ordinary melodramas into exciting theatrical events. *Girl of the Golden West*, *The Darling of the Gods*, *Heart of Maryland*, and *Peter Grimm* were among the many of Belasco's visually impressive productions. The introduction of electric lighting was critical for the advancement of theatrical realism. A brilliantly lit stage enhanced the colors of scenery and costume and focused the viewer's attention on the visual frame, encouraging him to scan each new scene for detail rather than just wait on the speeches of the actors. In addition to sheer intensity, electric lights offered flexibility and the possibility for special effects undreamt of in the days of candle and gas. Belasco considered lighting the key to a successful drama. "Lights are to a drama what music is to the lyrics of a song," he said. He selected the lighting for every scene to create the appropriate atmosphere, from brilliant sunlight to a somber mood of twilight.[62]

Theatre critics recognized the visual trend of their day. Drama's compound appeal to eye and ear had always existed, observed Clayton Hamilton in 1914, but in different ages the proportion of these appeals had varied. Drama began as principally auditory and had grown progressively visual, "until today, for the first time it makes its appeal mainly to the eye."[63] Motion pictures carried the trend toward a visually accurate realism to its logical conclusion. Not only did they offer the truthful portrayal of the camera, but they relied solely upon the eye—the spoken word disappeared completely. "These are golden days for the deaf," William Lyon Phelps penned in 1918, "the ear is losing its importance every hour. Millions visit the movies, where the deaf are on an exact equality with those blessed or cursed with acute hearing." [64]

Unintentionally, the theatre paved the way for its own decline by its attempts at extreme realism. The theatre's unique strength lay in its actors, who used their powers of gesture and speech to communicate directly to their audience. When stagecraft began to rival acting, the theatre fell into a vulnerable position vis-à-vis the movies, for in this realm the movies had an unalterable advantage. Statistics tell the doleful story of the legitimate theatre's helplessness before the motion picture. Between 1910 and 1925 the number of theatres available for legitimate productions outside of metropolitan centers fell from 1,549 to 674. The number of theatrical troupes on tour decreased from 339 in 1900 to 39 in 1920. [65] Rising production costs must be considered in explaining the theatrical decline, but primarily the blame must be laid at the door of the movie emporium, which gave the public more realistic thrills and at a cheaper price.

Observers fearing for the theatre's future advised stage producers to meet the challenge by specializing in forms the movies could not reproduce. The *Nation* acknowledged in 1915 that motion pictures might replace the theatre as provider of mass entertainment. It advised the theatre, therefore, to concentrate on the spoken word as its proper province, leaving action and spectacle to the movies. [66] In effect that was what happened. Musicals, America's contribution to the theatre, became the staple of road shows in the early 1920s, along with classic drama and costume extravaganzas, all forms the black-and-white silent movies could not emulate. [67]

But film proved unsurpassed for exploiting personality. The vividness of the movie image highlighted every nuance of expression. Silence was no handicap, for Americans read personality best through externals of dress, look, and mannerism. Indeed, concern was expressed in the early days of talking pictures that sound robbed actors of their distinct personality. In silent movies, the argument ran, actors had to appeal solely through visual expression of face and body, and in so doing they created personality. With the advent of sound, players returned to the conventions of stage acting, using what many considered artifical tones and mannerisms. Natural expression was replaced by stylization. "It is criminal to suppress the natural release of genuine emotion," lamented Ivah

Bradley, "and to cover it with a meaningless artificiality."[68] These fears, however, soon proved groundless, as the movie industry discovered that talking pictures in no way impeded the creation of stars.

* * *

One must conclude that the relationship of stage to movie acting is a complex one. In some respects the movies appeared to be the superior medium. Silent films enthroned actors in the public consciousness as stage actors had never been. Actors' personalities—their most vital element—shone most brightly when only their image was present on the screen. And movies created a closer bond between actor and viewer than had been true before. Yet for all of that, motion pictures actually removed actors from the center of their art. Onstage the player was the medium of the play. Of scenery, lighting, music, props, and all the other ingredients that went into the commercial theatre, only the actor was absolutely essential. But as Siegfried Kracauer observed, film was not exclusively human. Its medium was the film itself, its subject matter all things visible. Moreover, the actor's body lost its integrity on film. The camera dismembered heads, arms, and legs through close focus or by fusing them with the environment. And cameramen, editors, and directors became the final arbiters of the movie art, using actors as a raw material, first dissected and then reassembled as the finished piece of work.[69]

In a sense, then, the popularity and wealth the movies bestowed were gained at the cost of an artistic alienation. "The film actor feels as if in exile," wrote playwright Luigi Pirandello, "exiled not only from the stage but also from himself."[70] Though many actors might agree with the spirit of Pirandello's remarks, it was a trade-off many willingly made. Few screen stars deserted Hollywood for Broadway. Yet as virtually every actor confessed in his more reflective moments, the challenges and satisfactions of stage work—the chance to develop a character and play it before a live audience—remained the greatest expression of his art and the truest test of his craft.

Nine

Artists and Artisans

ured by Hollywood, lionized by the press, emulated by
the public—actors nonetheless remained discontented
within the theatre. The various problems described
above did not disappear as the nineteenth century gave way to the
twentieth; indeed, in certain ways players felt more aggrieved than
ever, particularly with the centralization of theatrical management.
In consequence, where the founders of the Actors' Society began
with a concern to advance players' professional status, leaders a
few years later began to aggressively demand changes in the theatrical system itself. Such a change of goals only further confirms
what sociologists have long observed: that an initial obsession with
winning the public's respect as a profession generally broadens to
include tangible efforts at protecting the group's interests.[1] The Actors' Society's multiple efforts on the players' behalf have already
been described. Though its achievements were modest, the ASA
paved the way for the less conciliatory and more effective Actors'
Equity Association, an actors' union.

The transition from professional society to union was a troubling one, however. For an occupation still insecure in its pretensions to professional standing unionization appeared demeaning,
a threat to its hard-earned status. As actors wrestled with this issue, they played out a conflict experienced by many other occupations similarly poised between aspirations to professional standing
on the one hand and a labor system that prompted union principles on the other. The middle ground that actors chose to occupy—
incorporating trade-union tactics within a continued self-definition
of professionalism—points up the inadequacy of rigid distinctions
between the two. The players' willingness to carry out an effective
strike in 1919 even while justifying such activity on the grounds of
professionalism resembled attitudes of musicians, athletes, nurses,
and teachers. In this as in so much else, actors were models for life.

* 1 *

The most important institutional change in the theatre of the 1890s was the formation of the Theatrical Syndicate.[2] The syndicate, which would restructure power relationships in the theatre, was formed in response to the haphazard business practices of the theatre, in particular the inefficient way in which combination companies booked their tours. Theatre managers or their agents annually descended on Union Square in mid-June to line up attractions for the coming season. Not infrequently touring companies booked several theatres on the same date, would then fill the most lucrative contract, and leave the forsaken theatre with an empty date; conversely, companies sometimes showed up for a one-night stand to discover that another troupe had preempted the house.

To alleviate this problem theatrical circuits began to appear as early as the 1870s, where groups of theatres in an area banded together to sign their attractions. Touring companies liked the idea because it simplified tour arrangements. By the mid-1880s local circuits flourished, the Kansas-Missouri Circuit, the Saginaw Valley Circuit in Michigan, and the Lone Star Circuit in Texas being just three of many. Theatrical centralization further progressed with the creation of booking offices in New York. The booking agent served as middleman for hundreds of theatres in arranging attractions. Charles Frohman and his partner, W. W. Randall, controlled the bookings for more than three hundred theatres in the 1880s, and by 1890 Frohman headed the biggest booking agency in the country. Only Marc Klaw and Abraham Erlanger's booking office rivaled Frohman's in size, with their business centering in the South.

The inexorable logic of nineteenth-century business dictated that the major booking agencies should consolidate. Their union produced the Theatrical Syndicate in 1896, an organization that virtually monopolized the booking of first-class theatrical attractions in America. Known in theatrical circles as simply "the trust," the syndicate shared in the trend toward consolidation and control that characterized American industry. Six men, three sets of partners, made up the syndicate: Charles Frohman and Al Hayman, Abe Erlanger and Marc Klaw, and Samuel Nixon and J. Frederick Zimmerman. They all contributed a share of theatres to the common pool. At its beginning the syndicate controlled or had an interest in thirty-three first-class theatres. In addition, Frohman, Klaw, and Erlanger controlled bookings in over five hundred theatres, which—though in smaller communities—were vital to the health of a tour, and Hayman's partnership with Frohman added the bookings in most of the important cities from the Missouri River to San Francisco.

The syndicate openly boasted of its intention to monopolize the booking business. Its attractions were required to play in syndicate theatres if there was one in the city. And since the syndicate had theatres in most major cities as well as in hundreds of smaller towns, stars and independent managers had little choice but to opt for syndicate management. In turn, independent theatre managers discovered that to get Broadway stars into their houses they had to climb on the syndicate bandwagon. Frohman and company had both performers and exhibitors at their mercy. In remarkably short order the syndicate controlled the American theatre, a dominance it retained until the Shuberts broke it in 1910.

The Theatrical Syndicate organized as a booking office pure and simple. Originally, Charles Frohman was the only member who also produced plays, and his supply of excellent attractions gave the syndicate an invaluable resource. Later, however, some of the other members tried their hands at producing or formed partnerships with other producers, and their shows received preferential treatment in their bookings, which caused independent stars to complain of discrimination. James K. Hackett, for example, after leaving Daniel Frohman's management and becoming an independent, complained that he had to pay a 5 percent fee for a route.

Despite these abuses, the Theatrical Syndicate brought efficiency and greater profits to almost everyone in the theatre. Theatre owners, glad to rid themselves of the headache of booking, willingly handed over the disposition of their stages. And actors were generally better off with the syndicate, because its managers paid the best salaries. John Drew, Nat Goodwin, Richard Mansfield, James K. Hackett, and even that archenemy of the trust, Francis Wilson, all agreed on the superiority of the syndicate to outside management. Rank-and-file players also enjoyed more security under the syndicate's dependable system of booking, which increased their chances for a full season of regular pay. The syndicate's bitterest enemies admitted that, in principle, a central booking agency was a good thing.[3]

Nevertheless, no theatrical institution has ever been as vilified as was the trust. Magazines and newspapers portrayed Klaw, Erlanger, and the rest as bloated, uncouth tyrants of the theatre. Fiske's *Dramatic Mirror* could scarcely find the words to describe the evil that the trust had wrought—a "hateful, corrupt and dangerous institution," it said, a "Shylock combination."[4] Texas, Indiana, and Massachusetts legislators unsuccessfully sought to curb the syndicate through antitrust legislation. Actors, even while performing in its theatres, continued sniping at the trust, accusing it of degrading the theatre's art.

Why the vilification? In part it was stimulated by the very idea of monopoly. In an age of reform Americans had grown antagonistic to the word "trust" and everything it stood for. There were the oil trust, the steel trust, the sugar trust, the tobacco trust, and now the theatrical trust, all the more heinous because it had invaded the sacrosanct realm of art. For the players themselves, though, and especially the stars, opposition to the syndicate sprang from their sense of having lost control of their profession to a group of commercial philistines. Unlike such English actor-managers as Irving, Forbes-Robertson, Tree, and du Maurier—who had their own theatres and remained influential figures on the British stage through World War I—the American counterparts found themselves subordinate to "the businessman in the theatre," as the phrase ran. Initial resistance to the syndicate came, in fact, from a group of actor-managers—Joseph Jefferson, Richard Mansfield, Nat Goodwin, James O'Neill, Mrs. Fiske, and Francis Wilson—who did not control a theatre of their own, but who wished to retain the right to book their own tours.[5] For them and for many other players, the trust symbolized the theatre's arrival as a big business. The term "producing managers" came into use, suggesting the large scale on which such people as Charles Frohman worked. Frohman's stable of stars, directors, and technicians resembled the film-studio organization of production. While Frohman himself was unobjectionable to his stars, he and other syndicate members represented a loss of autonomy for actors.

An early and short-lived actors' rebellion against syndicate control came in 1898. The participants' declaration of artistic freedom bowed before generous offers from the syndicate. Richard Mansfield, for instance, among the most energetic of the trust's foes, was also among the first to fall to the lure of the syndicate's pocketbook. His defection demoralized other actors who attempted to play only independent theatres. One by one, Goodwin, O'Neill, and E. L. Davenport capitulated. Francis Wilson came to heel only after his blacklist from syndicate theatres nearly ruined his career. The one major star who held out was the intrepid Mrs. Fiske. Backed by her husband's paper she quietly waged war on the syndicate, not through verbal assaults, but by refusing to play in its theatres. Turning down enticing offers from the syndicate, she performed in second-class theatres, dance halls, and on one occasion a skating rink. But Mrs. Fiske's solitary stand only accentuated the weakness of the players' organized resistance.

Clearly actors had to show a united front if they were to deal effectively with the syndicate. One attempt at solidarity was the Actors' Society, incorporated the same year as the Theatrical Syndicate. The professional aims of the ASA have been explored previously, but even in that organization's brief lifetime its leaders considered affiliation with organized labor. Soon after the society's founding, its leaders recognized their limitations in dealing with unscrupulous managers. Consequently, in the fall of 1897 the ASA leadership began talking of reorganization and affiliation with the American Federation of Labor. Joseph Wheelock, ASA president, promoted the idea diligently, circulating a letter to all members urging them to support affiliation. Alliance with organized labor, the argument ran, would give actors leverage in dealing with managers.[6] Wheelock found many supporters among the rank and file. Journeyman player Charles B. Poor called upon his fellow craftsmen to support the ASA in this venture:

> This is not anarchy. It is the voice of the oppressed crying out for justice, and will go ringing throughout this land of theatregoers, and will no longer be silenced. . . . I appeal to all members of the theatrical vocation, to their spirit of honor, pride and self-respect, and to the respect in which they hold their noble calling, come and join your issues with us for the betterment of our profession.[7]

Another actor, identified simply as "Damon," scoffed at the idea that because actors were artists they should not join a labor union. Musicians and scenic artists did not let their art stand in the way of unionization, he pointed out. Affiliation may not be necessary for the stars, but it would benefit "men and women who can only hope to reach honorable mediocrity, and they are the majority."[8] "Damon's" concern focused on the competition graduates of acting schools posed for experienced thespians. He urged that skilled players be given protection from "feather-brained aspirants anxious to 'strut and fret their brief hour on the stage,' with little thought about remuneration for their labor."[9]

But the issue of unionization nearly tore the ASA apart. A letter to the editor from "Pythias" countered "Damon's" enthusiasm for unionization, warning that the trade union issue was a divisive one for actors and that such a move might strangle what little art was left onstage.[10] The influential *Dramatic Mirror* opposed affiliation from the start. It argued that an occupation depending upon—even glorifying—individuality was inimical to union principles of uniformity. The ASA's board of directors itself was split on the issue. By February of 1898 the controversial issue had reduced previous membership of the ASA to one-half. The remaining members favored unionization and voted to affiliate with the National Association of Theatrical Stage Employees, which held a charter from the AFL.[11]

But the proposed affiliation with the Stage Employees never went through, and as the ASA returned to its original concept of a professional association, free from any taint of unionism, membership rebounded to its highest level. For the first time it attracted many stars who were not ready for so radical an expedient as a trade union. But the ASA was doomed to ineffectiveness concerning the most fundamental grievances of players. It settled into a program of moderate reform without questioning the theatrical power structure. The ASA stood aside in the battle with the syndicate, giving no aid to the independent stars who fought it. In its final few years of existence, as its membership dropped and its influence waned, the ASA made several more unsuccessful attempts to obtain a charter from the AFL. By the end of 1912 a number of actors decided to form a new organization concerned strictly with the economics of acting. Though the ASA lingered on until 1916, it had effectively given way earlier to a new organization: Actor's Equity.[12]

* 2 *

Organized by 112 players in May of 1913, Actors' Equity Association represented a new departure for actors. It offered neither the social aspects of the ASA nor the financial benefits of the Actors' Fund. Instead, as President Francis Wilson said in his dedicatory address, it was a "business association, established for the purpose of securing a 'fifty-fifty,' open-and-above-board contract as between actor and manager."[13] Actors partook of the prevailing American prejudice against labor unions, and the persistent animosity toward unionism among many players was reflected in Wilson's careful statement: "The Actors' Equity Association is not per se a labor union, and it never will become one unless, which is not likely, flagrant injustice on the part of managers compels it to ally itself with organized labor."[14]

Equity attracted leading performers to its council, evidence that even Broadway stars had become concerned about the need for a strong actors' organization. Elected as president was musical-comedy star Francis Wilson. A veteran of the wars against the syndicate, the diminutive comedian's spirited attack on the big businessmen of the theatre made him a logical choice in the fight for equity. Henry Miller was elected vice-president on the strength of his good name as an actor-manager. Members of the twenty-one-man council included George Arliss, Digby Bell, Holbrook Blinn, Jefferson De Angelis, Robert Edeson, and Wilton Lackaye.[15]

Equity did not restrict itself to New York's acting fraternity. Francis Wilson and Howard Kyle visited the Chicago chapter in 1917 to rouse enthusiasm among the popular-priced performers for Equity's work. They had to counteract suspicions among these actors that Equity would only work for the Broadway performer and that the 10–20–30 players would be second-class members. "Snobbery has no place here," Howard Kyle assured them, "the true actor shows his merit in one theatre as well as another." Equity also made a special effort at encouraging actresses to join. For a time after its founding in 1913, Equity admitted only male players, this policy from a belief that actresses ought to be spared the anticipated backlash of hostilities from managers. But the membership campaign went so well that by July of that year the bylaws were changed to include actresses. By 1918 liberation had proceeded to the point where three women were elected to the council: Helen Ware, Katherine Emmet, and Florence Reed.[16]

Equity's major concern was the theatrical contract or, more properly, the problems that commonly arose from contracts. Traditionally, if a manager or actor felt aggrieved, he had to seek redress in court, a long and generally fruitless procedure. To replace that cumbersome process Equity pressed for binding arbitration of contractual disputes. The informal beginning of Equity's arbitration came in September of 1913 when Mrs. Grace Thorne Coulter complained of mistreatment by Al Woods. The New York manager had hired her to take over a part in his production. She spent over two hundred dollars for dresses in anticipation of the role, only to be given a summary dismissal two days before she was to begin. Mrs. Coulter felt she ought to be reimbursed for the dresses, but Woods ignored her request. An Equity lawyer, Nathan Burkan, who was also Woods's attorney, acted as informal arbitrator, and he quickly secured a two-hundred-dollar check for Mrs. Coulter.[17] The principle of arbitration later became an integral part of Equity's contracts with producing managers.

Equity also thought that disputes would be less frequent if a standard contract form was adopted, and it pursued this goal diligently. Its journal, *Equity*, reflected this singleness of purpose. Some members complained that the magazine should be a "snappy news medium, containing general gossip." But in contrast to the *Actors' Society Monthly Bulletin*, *Equity* focused solely on the business side of acting. It eliminated the chatty features of the *Bulletin* in an attempt to convey a seriousness to its readers.[18] Every month

Equity ran a column telling how the organization had helped actors get that to which they were entitled. In one case a manager tendered an actor only half salary for the week preceding election day. Equity petitioned the manager, and, though the player actually had no written contract, succeeded in getting the balance of his salary paid immediately.[19]

The standard contract Equity desired contained seven major provisions. First, it would provide free transportation for players to and from New York during a tour, rather than have them pay their own way from New York to wherever the show opened and then back again from wherever it closed. Second, it would limit the period of free rehearsals. Traditionally, actors had donated two weeks of rehearsal before the start of the forty-week season. As productions became more elaborate in the twentieth century, rehearsals lengthened, often taking six to ten weeks, and for musicals, sixteen or eighteen were not unheard of. Even after that investment of time actors could never be sure that the show would not close after a few nights. Consequently, the contract's third point was to reestablish the inviolability of the two-weeks' notice clause. Equity also wanted, in its fourth point, to protect actors who had given more than a week's rehearsal from being discharged without pay. The fifth point would prevent an increase in the number of performances without pay. The eight-performance week was standard. But in some areas, where managers could add a Sunday evening show or a matinee on a local holiday, they would do so without giving their cast an extra cent. The sixth point stipulated full pay for all weeks worked, whether it be a holiday or Election Day. Finally, Equity asked managers to share with actresses the expense of their dresses.[20]

The grievances Equity set out to rectify were for the most part not new. The lengthening of rehearsal time was indeed recent, but the other items had been thorns in actors' sides for decades, and in its last two demands Equity actually sought to change theatrical custom. Consequently, one cannot say that Equity's founding in 1913 and full acceptance of trade-union principles in 1916 resulted from the immiserization of actors. Indeed, the Theatrical Syndicate's control of the theatre may have actually given journeymen actors greater security. Why, then, did Actors' Equity form when it did, and why did it evolve into a union?

The answers point back to the perception of Broadway stars, particularly the remaining actor-managers, that they no longer controlled the theatre. A few players had attempted to organize in the 1890s to protect their art from the "shopkeepers" of the theatre. But most stars opposed association, feeling it violated their independence and degraded their art. Broadway's biggest names came into the ASA only after its flirtation with organized labor had ended. By 1913, however, their decline in power vis-à-vis the syndicate led them to reconsider the need for effective association (though even then many actors conceded only grudgingly). On the other hand, the common players were more than ready to take collective action. They were the ones most at the mercy of unfair managers and of the ever-tenuous economics of the theatre. It had been the journeymen actors who voted for the ASA's affiliation with the AFL. But participation by the leading players was vital to the creation of a strong organization, for only the threat of their absence would bring pressure on the managers. Actors' Equity succeeded, then, through a coalition of two groups of actors, each with different aims: rank-and-file actors, to whom Equity promised alleviation of long-standing economic problems; and the stars, unbothered by the inequities of contract, but to whom Equity represented a reassertion of their professional status and dignity. This apparently conservative rationale for a radical measure was underscored by union organizer Francis Wilson. Actors' Equity, said Wilson, aimed "not at revolution, but restoration."[21]

* * *

Actors were by no means the first group in the theatre, or even the first artistic occupation, to unionize. They had several models to follow. Stage crews had been the first to organize in the theatre. In the late 1880s they united to demand that managers stop using actors as stagehands. Locals formed in the major cities, which then joined in 1893 in the National Alliance of Theatrical Stage Employees. Three years later the Protective Alliance of Scenic Painters formed. These unions gained full status as closed shops, successfully negotiating with managers on behalf of their members.[22]

Yiddish players also anticipated Actors' Equity with their Hebrew Actors' Union. Resentment against the domineering star-managers had brewed since the early days of the Yiddish theatre, and there had been a strike against Jacob Adler in 1887. Finally, Joseph Barondess, a Jewish labor leader, organized Yiddish actors in 1899. The Hebrews Actors' Union took on aspects of a guild—limiting membership and making admission difficult—in this respect going far beyond anything imposed by Equity.[23]

American musicians held up a final example of artistic unionization. The competition of contract musicians from Europe and native military bands prodded musicians to form local associations, which in 1886 joined to form the National League of Musicians.

The NLM attempted to combine the features of a professional association and trade union, as it was concerned with both artistic standards and economic benefits. Like the Actors' Society, the NLM
discovered the two purposes to be incompatible, and when the
American Federation of Musicians organized in 1896 with an avow-
edly trade-union philosophy, the NLM atrophied. The AFM used a
strict closed-shop policy and attention to practical issues to win for
musicians greater pay and security than they had ever known.[24]

Musicians were repeatedly held up to actors as exemplars of
protective action. As early as 1885 the *Dramatic Mirror* admired the
Musical Mutual Protective Union of New York's restrictions on foreign musicians and commented on its success in making sure its
members were faithfully paid, a claim, the theatrical journal chided,
which actors could not make.[25] In later years the *Actors' Society
Monthly Bulletin* printed many references to the work of the AFM,
such as its fining conductor Walter Damrosch one thousand dollars
for what it considered unfair labor practices.[26] When exhorting his
members to join the AFL, Equity leader Francis Wilson pointed to
musicians and stagehands: "Are we any less important as a profession, as a people, than the stage mechanics? They took the dare,
and they now have equitable contracts. Are we any less important
than musicians? . . . Yet these temperamental and hysterical musicians, from the snare drummer up to Paderewski, took the dare,
and they now have equitable contracts."[27] Where the founders of
the ASA consistently linked acting with law and medicine, Wilson's newfound paragons represented more modest occupations,
but offered a course of action more appropriate to players.

The players' conversion to unionism came after the managers
rejected all proposals for a standard contract. Producing managers,
theatre owners, and booking agents from New York and the rest of
the country had banded together in the United Managers' Protective Association, the body with which Equity tried to negotiate a
contract. The UMPA listened politely as Equity explained its position—then did nothing. Through 1914 and 1915, committees of the
two organizations met. Marc Klaw, president of the UMPA, acknowledged that Equity's demands were reasonable, yet he would
make no concessions.[28]

By February 1915, Equity's education in the realities of economic power led its council to appoint a committee to study the
organization of trade unions. Initially, only a few council members
favored such a drastic step, but within a short time a majority favored the action. In the spring of 1916 the Equity council began a
campaign to convince its members of the necessity for unionization. The clarion call came in Edwin Arden's article in *Equity* en-

titled "A Change of Heart." Arden recounted how Equity forsook radical measures in its beginnings, seeking to act firmly and with dignity. But in the conciliatory approach to obtaining a standard contract, Arden wrote, "we were either snubbed, ignored, paltered with or defied." Consequently, the Equity council decided that there was only one "Trail out of the Wilderness. THAT TRAIL IS AF-FILIATION WITH ORGANIZED LABOR." To those who objected that unionization violated professional standing Arden replied: "Pro-fession? Under present conditions ours is not a profession. It isn't even a trade. It hasn't the dignity of a vocation. It's only a job. And half the time we don't get paid for it." [28]

Still, in selling the idea of unionization to its members, Eq-uity's leaders had to reassure them that it entailed no loss of status. Unionization, to the contrary, was presented as the actors' only hope for retaining their artistic standing in the modern world of theatrical big business. Francis Wilson told players at the March 19 meeting that unionization was the only way to protect their profes-sional dignity. Equity leaders promised the restoration of tradi-tional status by means of a new expedient, thus reassuring mem-bers that the new departure served familiar ends.

This issue was of concern even to those outside the theatre. When Actors' Equity first organized in 1913 it had met a good-natured skepticism in the press. The clichés about actors' egotism and inability to work together were once again bandied about. "An incapacity for co-operation seems to be one of the traits of the artis-tic temperament," read the *Outlook*, "at any rate, all past attempts of players on the legitimate stage to organize have failed." [30] How-ever, when Equity not only survived but considered taking the plunge into unionism, observers had to reconsider. The issue then became whether unionization was proper for an artistic occupa-tion. A few writers ventured that it was not. But the liberal *New Republic* encouraged actors in their course. Author Hiram Moder-well recognized the dual nature of the actor's work: "In aesthetics he is beyond question an 'artist,' but in economics he is an artisan, a wage earner, a member of a trade." In the prevailing theatrical structure, Moderwell continued, actors would have no security un-til they overcame their fear of being thought "hod-carriers." [31]

In the midst of these debates Equity called simultaneous meetings in New York, Boston, Philadelphia, Chicago, and Los Angeles on March 10, 1916, to canvass members' opinions on the matter. The New York meeting, attended by nearly nine hundred, turned out to be a carefully planned propaganda session for affilia-tion with the AFL. Milton Sills spoke at the meeting in favor of af-filiation: "We have used every means, polite and diplomatic, to get the managers to accept our contract. They admitted the fairness of our demands, but refused to accede to them. What we have achieved so far we have attained by moral force, but moral force can only go so far."[32] Equity members in New York and other cities agreed that more than moral force was needed in dealing with managers and voted overwhelmingly to put the issue to referendum in May. Then at the annual meeting on May 29, members authorized the council to affiliate with organized labor when it saw fit. The 890 to 21 tally suggested that the term "union" had lost its fearful meaning.[33]

Yet even after members voted for AFL affiliation in 1916 they had one further hurdle to overcome. The White Rats, the vaudevillians' union, held the AFL's charter covering the amusement field, and if Equity wished to join, it would have to be as a branch of that organization. The vaudeville union had formed in 1900 as an offshoot of earlier organizations that had proven ineffective. The idea of becoming a part of the White Rats did not appeal to Equity leaders. The name itself was enough to make actors wince. Moreover, the White Rats' membership of some fourteen thousand far outnumbered Equity's twenty-five hundred, and the legitimate players feared their identity would be swallowed up in the organization. Further, it was rumored that the Equity council would not accept a coalition with the vaudevillians because of the persistent belief among legitimate players that they were superior to the White Rats' members. The council's avowed reason, however, for resisting union with the White Rats was its need for complete autonomy in dealing with the unique problems of the legitimate actors.[34] For whatever reason, Equity asked the White Rats to give up their charter so that the AFL might draw up a new one providing for separate action among the various groups of the amusement field. The White Rats, who were then engaged in a life-or-death struggle with the Vaudeville Managers' Protective Association, refused.

Affiliation had reached an impasse. But at that moment, in early 1917, the managers suddenly agreed to use a standard contract, and it appeared that recourse to the strength of the AFL would not be needed after all. The reason for the managers' change of heart was not apparent. Perhaps they thought conciliation was preferable to the chaos they saw in the vaudeville fight between performers and managers. At any rate, by October of 1917, Equity and the UMPA had agreed upon a standard contract that redressed the players' grievances.

The contract stipulated six major points: (1) after donating four weeks of rehearsals for a dramatic play and six weeks for a musical an actor was guaranteed at least two weeks of paid work; (2) a manager could close a play without notice at any time within the first four weeks, but if it ran longer he must give one week's notice; (3) managers would furnish all costumes of actresses earning less than $150 a week; (4) the eight-performance week became the standard, except in theatres where the custom was nine (actors also agreed to perform for free on eleven stipulated holidays); (5) actors were to be provided transportation for themselves and their baggage from New York and back again; (6) the UMPA promised to abide by arbitration in settling contractual disputes.[35] Players won nearly everything they asked for. Five hundred actors and managers dined together at the Hotel Astor on the evening of November 25 to celebrate the accord. Artist and businessman complimented each other's integrity and pledged faithful adherence to the terms of the contract.

The honeymoon ended soon after. A renewed rivalry between the Shuberts and the Klaw-Erlanger interests became the all-consuming concern of the producers, and in the heat of the battle the promised contract was overlooked. Frank Gilmore, an actor who had given up his career to become executive secretary to Actors' Equity, uncovered the disturbing statistic that well after the agreement had been made only one-fifth of UMPA's managers used the standard contract. Equity leaders finally realized that to reach their goal they would have to match strength with strength, and they began talking in greater earnest about the need for a closed shop backed by AFL muscle.

The closed shop was a disagreeable feature of unionism that Equity leaders had hoped to avoid. For many actors it represented a threat to the openness and accessibility that had always characterized their craft. The Equity council experienced its first major division over this issue, with Francis Wilson leading the more radical faction that was calling for the closed shop, while Howard Kyle advised moderation. Nevertheless, the council went ahead with its program of securing pledges from members to work only in companies where all the actors belonged to Equity. By the fall of 1918, 1,070 players had signed the pledge, 46 of whom were stars. Equity declared the pledge to be in effect at its November meeting, threatening noncompliant members with expulsion.[36] From its inception the organization had required two years of stage experience before an actor could join, but in 1918 it created junior memberships for beginners, restricting their right to vote or hold office, but giving them a chance to grow into staunch union actors. Actors' Equity boasted a membership of about three thousand by the end of 1918, including many important stars, without whom few shows could be produced.[37]

Theatrical managers had some tricks of their own, however. In an attempt to get out of the agreed (though repeatedly ignored) standard contract, the UMPA dissolved in late 1918 to be replaced by the Producing Managers' Association (PMA). The PMA disavowed the old standard contract and offered a new one, which would have extended the period of free rehearsals that actors must donate. Equity countered with its own demand of an eight-performance week, with all additional performances—be they on a holiday or not—to be paid for at one-eighth of a week's salary for each. Actors and managers were at loggerheads.

The Equity council decided once again that its only alternative was to turn to the AFL. At the annual meeting in May 1919 it sought another mandate from its members. The controversial issue attracted a huge crowd of twenty-five hundred actors to the Astor ballroom and several hundred more who could not fit in. Despite the overwhelming vote in favor of affiliation several years earlier, a serious division appeared within Equity's ranks at the meeting, as players who opposed affiliation were given a chance to voice their opposition.[38]

Blanche Bates, Belasco's "Girl of the Golden West," delivered the major address against affiliation with organized labor. She used a traditional argument, that trade union tactics degraded their artistic standing. Bates began her speech by extolling Actors' Equity, but also pointed to the theatre's difficult position:

> The theatre is the thing we live for and by; and are we actors going to be accused of putting the rock in front of them, that we are helping to wreck them? We are not in the condition of capital and labor—
>
> (Cries of "We are," "We are.")
>
> Oh, no, we are not; because we do not work with our hands; we work with the one thing God has given us, our hearts, our souls. We earn, of course, a return for our labors—we are not parasites; we love it and it is our glory, it is our world.
>
> (Cries of "Oh, oh, oh.")
>
> . . . When we do these things we are attacking the very things that are the essence of our lives, the glory of our lives, the thing we live by and for. We are not laborers with calloused hands; we use our hearts and our souls in this work, it is our life. We are not laborers, and what we have is something that cannot be capitalized. What

we give cannot be weighed or measured. Don't let us do something that we will regret doing.

(Expressions of disapproval.)

Isn't it dreadful to think that we, ourselves, are doing it to ourselves. The one thing that we have studied for, that we are not as other men—don't forget that—

(Cries of "We are; we are.")[39]

The open derision that met Bates's insistence on the incompatability of art and labor indicated that actors were broadening their notion of the behavior appropriate for professionals. Sociologists have noted that an overriding concern for professional status hinders unionization. Moreover, the exalted sphere of the artist, as Bates eloquently reminded actors, had always been thought to be above the mundane concerns of the laboring man. But actors were willing to bend their professionalism to harmonize with the economic situation they faced, as employees in a marketplace sometimes hostile to their interests. Collective bargaining seemed the only answer, and to achieve that end they redrew the boundaries of professionalism. Bates's final statement—that actors were not like other people—also brought disagreement from the audience. Actors' sense of distinctiveness had been tempered by a recognition of their similarity to other workers.

Another speaker opposing the path of affiliation was Charles Coburn, a member of the council. Coburn belonged to a group for whom the forthcoming strike presented a special dilemma: the actor-managers. He urged his fellow actors to move cautiously, encouraging cooperation rather than confrontation with managers. Louis Mann, another actor-manager, stated that a new class of young producing managers were emerging and Equity should move slowly and build up faith with them.[40] These actor-managers could not sit on the fence for long; they had to declare for one side or the other, and both Coburn and Mann ended up as foes of Actors' Equity.

The meeting concluded with members giving the council a vote of confidence to proceed as it saw fit. The council then asked the PMA if it would be willing to submit the dispute to arbitration. But the managers, who felt that they had the union on the defensive, answered that there was nothing to discuss. The season for engaging actors had arrived, and PMA managers tendered their own contracts, not the Equity contract. As always, players could turn down a job but with difficulty, and despite the pledge to sign exclusively with all-Equity companies, many players felt they had no choice but to sign. It was a critical time for Actors' Equity. In the June issue of *Equity* an article appeared entitled "Discipline," which reminded actors of their obligation to obey the pledge. It spared no words in telling its readers that the union was prepared to discipline members who compromised the principles of collective actions.[41]

At this crucial juncture Equity received the boost it needed: affiliation with the AFL finally materialized. The White Rats, whose ranks had been decimated in the war with vaudeville managers, agreed to give up its charter. The AFL then issued a new charter creating the Associated Actors and Artists of America, of which Actors' Equity became an autonomous branch. The move surprised PMA members, who thought that concern for tradition and dignity would ultimately prevail. But affiliation with organized labor only made the managers more determined to crush the experiment in collective bargaining. The stage was set for the great strike of 1919.

∗   3   ∗

The strike began inauspiciously for actors. On July 29 Equity ordered the actors in rehearsal for *Chu Chin Chow* to walk off the job. Although ten of the company's members belonged to Equity, only four obeyed the strike order. Managerial pressure induced the others to stay, and six of the players resigned from Actors' Equity, including leading lady Marjorie Wood, who became the first prominent thespian to desert the union during the strike, declaring that such actions degraded the player's art. Actor Wee Willie Deming wrote her expressing his regret over her action, once again invoking the example of musicians: "Do you think that Damrosch, Paderewski, Sousa, Victor Herbert and artists of the same ilk are any worse musicians because they have to carry a card in their pocket showing their dues have been paid to the musical union?"[42]

Equity's shaky start necessitated another general meeting to rally support for the walkout. On August 6, fourteen hundred of Equity's twenty-seven hundred members met at the Astor ballroom. A militant spirit filled the room. E. H. Sothern, one of the theatre's most respected figures and an actor-manager of the old school who was uncomfortable with talk of conflict and walkout, made an eleventh-hour appeal for one last attempt at conciliation with managers. But Sothern faced a more hostile and vocal audience than he had ever encountered in his thirty years on stage, and a chorus of hisses and noes roundly defeated the veteran's effort. In short order the members adopted a resolution stating that they would "not perform any services for any manager who is a member of the Producing Managers' Association, or who refuses to recognize our association or issue its contract." [43]

Needless to say, the PMA was not sitting idly by. It had embarked on a membership campaign of its own. Charles Dillingham, Florenz Ziegfeld, George Tyler, and Harrison Grey Fiske (the former champion of the actor's cause had been alienated by their trade-union tactics) were among the more prominent new members. It sought alliances in neighboring fields. Vaudeville, burlesque, and motion-picture managers (though filmmakers soon backed out) joined the crusade to crush the insurgent players by preventing strikers from turning to these fields. Without question actors faced a formidable foe.

The first successful walkout occurred in a play whose star stood to lose a great deal. Frank Bacon had been a journeyman actor for twenty years before finding fame on Broadway in *Lightnin'*. If the strike had failed, Bacon might have found himself back in the provinces. Nevertheless, he had always supported Equity and unhesitatingly closed his show. Altogether, twelve shows were shut down the night of August 7.

The managers and the public were both caught by surprise. Few thought the actors would actually carry out their threat. Long lines formed outside of theatres as patrons waited for refunds, while managers madly scrambled about trying to patch together a cast so that their shows might reopen. Players who had spent their entire careers on the road suddenly found themselves pursued by New York managers with promises of riches and fame. A few shows did reopen. Holbrook Blinn had closed his starring vehicle, *The Challenger*, on the first night. But the next evening Blinn announced that he had purchased an interest in the play and thus had an obligation to open it. This decision was followed the next day by his resignation from Actors' Equity. George M. Cohan also managed to open his show *The Royal Vagabond*. Yet despite the occasionally successful efforts of managers to put something on stage, sixteen theatres were dark by August 16, and by August 20 the curtain went up on only five shows. [44]

It was a strike such as New York had never seen. A carnival atmosphere pervaded midtown Manhattan. Actors formed picket lines around the theatres, engaging in good-natured banter with passersby who swarmed into the area to observe the spectacle. Players could not resist some spontaneous performing even while on picket duty, and their charm helped win public sympathy. A parade highlighted their demonstrations. From Columbus Circle to Madison Square stars, chorus girls, stagehands, and musicians, nearly two thousand in all, marched together down Broadway to rally support for their cause. Equity also put on a number of benefit performances at the Lexington Avenue Opera House to raise a strike fund. All-star casts, including Eddie Cantor, Eddie Foy, Jr., Ethel and Lionel Barrymore, Ed Wynn, and W. C. Fields as master of ceremonies, performed in a variety format to full houses.[45]

Although actors managed to maintain a tone of joviality throughout the strike, an undercurrent of bitterness and injured feelings was present. The strike polarized players, and the broken loyalties and sense of betrayal that accompanied it strained friendships to the breaking point. Actors used social pressure to bring recalcitrant fellows into the Equity fold. A list of members who failed to obey the strike order was posted at Equity headquarters. Eddie Cantor felt the sting of social ostracism before he joined the strike. "Mr. Ziegfeld and Mr. Erlanger are fine men," he said, "and they pay me a lovely salary, but they don't associate with me. The people who associate with me call me 'scab.'"[46] The strike threatened to split The Players, which had members on both sides of the issue.

The most celebrated disaffection was George M. Cohan's. Cohan was a self-made man of the theatre. As both a performer and a producer he insisted on full control of his shows, and the thought of Equity regulations impinging on that control infuriated him. From the very beginning he opposed Actors' Equity in no uncertain terms, and during the strike he made many rash statements, one being that he would lose every dollar he had before he would do business with Equity, even if it meant running an elevator for a living. Cohan also resigned from the Lambs and the Friars. He had been extremely popular with other actors, but his obstinate stand during the strike sadly damaged his reputation. Even so, the Friars marched from their clubhouse to the Cohan and Harris Theatre to plead, vainly, for their former abbott to reconsider.

Relations between players and managers, as would be expected, were tense. Producer George C. Tyler, always before known as the player's friend, wrote in a fit of disgust during the strike: "After the actors get through with their daily maudlin street display here in New York, I don't think they will be quite fit to do any clean plays. They are developing magnificently for 'get ta hell out of here' parts."[47] Although the strike was virtually free of physical conflict, a scuffle did break out once. When Harry Lamber, a deputy organizer for Actors' Equity, attempted to notify members of *The Royal Vagabond* company that a strike was on, manager Sam Harris grabbed him by the back of the neck and threw him out of the theatre.[48] Not all managers reacted so strongly. Even though opposing the strike, manager Al Woods brought his actors raincoats to make them more comfortable as they picketed his theatre during a downpour.[49]

The primary tactic used by managers to get striking actors back on stage was the injunction. Managers claimed that the walk-out violated contract agreements. Florenz Ziegfeld was the first to use the restraining order to keep his *Follies* before the public. The Shuberts went a step further, suing Equity officers and some two hundred members for half a million dollars in damages incurred in closing down the Winter Garden as well as seeking an injunction to keep the theatre open. The injunctions were an annoyance; they kept Equity lawyers busy contesting them. But they never suc-ceeded in keeping open a show for more than a few days.

Managers also attempted the ancient ploy of divide and con-quer. They encouraged disaffected actors to form a rival organiza-tion, the Actors' Fidelity League, which in effect was a company union. George M. Cohan offered a munificent gift of $100,000 to get the league started, and on August 23 Louis Mann called the or-ganizational meeting to order at the Biltmore Hotel. The tone of the meeting was openly hostile to Actors' Equity. "The person who de-liberately violates a bonafide contract, as Equity actors have done, is a dastard, and not a fit companion in such a great and glorious profession as that of the actor," Louis Mann said. Cohan was elec-ted president of Actors' Fidelity League (or, Fidos, as they came to be known), and Howard Kyle, who resigned as secretary of Equity, became secretary of the new organization that claimed 465 mem-bers, including David Warfield, Willie Collier, Mrs. Fiske, Hol-brook Blinn, and Lenore Ulric. In an effort to lure players away from Equity, the PMA offered Actors' Fidelity actors a contract that conceded everything Equity had asked for plus somewhat more. Yet in the crucial point of representation the contract did not allow for Fidelity's participation during arbitration of disputes; each actor would have to deal with his manager as an individual, making enforcement of even the most attractive contract difficult. The league's existence indicated that unionization continued to trouble many actors. But it failed to seriously cut into Equity membership or undermine the strike.[50]

Equity's affiliation with the AFL paid off handsomely during the strike. Labor leaders addressed mass meetings of actors, en-couraging them and giving advice on tactics. Samuel Gompers made a personal appearance at a meeting, the presence of the ven-erable champion of labor adding dignity to the actors' cause. Play-ers also received a show of solidarity from other theatrical workers. On August 16, when the strike was two weeks old, actors were joined in their walkout by the stagehands and musicians. Teamsters pledged not to handle baggage or scenery for managers whose names appeared on the unfair list. Billposters likewise refused to post bills for non-Equity theatres. The actors' eventual victory owed much to the support of the theatre's auxiliary workers.[51]

The actors' strike extended beyond New York City, as Chicago and Boston theatres were later drawn into the conflict. It took Equity longer to shut down operations in these cities because the managers, alerted to the New York walkouts, had armed themselves with injunctions against a strike. In Chicago, two plays closed a few days after the New York walkout. But uncertain Equity leadership in the Windy City prevented a full-scale strike, and only when Equity representative Berton Churchill arrived from New York on August 17 did a coordinated strike effort begin. Within a few days every legitimate theatre in the Loop was closed. Results were slower in Boston. Not until the beginning of September did Equity overcome the managers' intimidation of the touring players.[52]

By the close of August the managers could see that the end was near. None of their tactics for loosing Equity's hold on the theatre had worked. Every day that their theatres remained dark they lost thousands of dollars (by the end of the strike it was an estimated two to three million dollars). On September 3, the PMA agreed to sit down and talk with Equity leaders. It took a few days of negotiations to iron out an agreement, but on September 6 an accord was reached. A thirty-day strike that had closed thirty-seven plays and prevented sixteen others from opening was over.[53]

The actors won substantially all that they had fought for, primarily, of course, recognition of Actors' Equity as their representative and a standard contract that ran until June 1, 1924. Its provisions resembled the 1917 contract, but went even further in giving full pay for the rehearsal extensions and for Christmas and Easter weeks, establishing a strict eight-performance week as basis of pay, and guaranteeing that managers would pay for the complete outfitting of chorus girls. Final victory came in 1921 with the establishment of the "Equity shop," in which members pledged not to appear in any production on Broadway, on the road, in stock or tent-rep shows that was not all Equity. The closed shop solidified the actors' position and has defined theatrical relationships up to the present.[54]

During the strike actors received nearly unanimous public support. Despite the nationwide rail strike of the same year, which alienated the public from the railwaymen's cause and which might have disaffected it from any union militancy, editorials in newspapers and magazines proclaimed the actor's strike justifiable. Observers saw a greater significance in the actors' victory than simple economic benefit. It seemed to mark a new phase in the evolution of actors as social beings, indicating that they had overcome their storied egotism and inability to work together. The strike was an "eloquent assertion of cooperative endeavor and power," wrote one writer. Ethel Barrymore agreed with this judgment, testifying that the experience of the strike "is good for us. It is teaching us to depend on ourselves, and, even better, to depend on each other. The actor is growing up. He is becoming social." Rebecca Drucker of the *New York Tribune* perceived a "spiritual significance" to the conflict that would form a new bond between actor and society: "It is a democratic impulse to which the art of the theatre cannot fail to be sensitive. . . . Whether they win or lose, the strike will have served to take the actor out of the isolation in which he has lived so long; it will have given him a sense of common impulse with a larger and more struggling world than he had been aware of."[55]

Of course the applause was not universal. Unionization was seen by some as a betrayal of the artistic enterprise. Art was incompatible with collectivism. E. T. Vreeland of the *Nation* complained that actors had "developed a class consciousness, which leads one to the suspicion that some of them secretly indulge in the perusal of Karl Marx. The words 'capital' and 'labor' are frequently heard at their mass meetings, quite as though greasepaint were entirely compatible with the term. Art seems to have been sent to Cain's theatrical storage house."[56]

Art had indeed come to terms with labor. Most actors now accepted unionism. But it was unionism in the service of a higher ideal: professionalism. The once sharp distinctions between the two terms began to blur, and through the twentieth century more and more occupations combined the ideology of professionalism with the economic expediency of unionism.[57] This larger trend actors could not, of course, see. Their concern centered around the more immediate issue of reconciling economic grievance with occupational prestige. If actors did not fit the classic professional mold they nevertheless clung tenaciously to the label as a symbol of social achievement.

*   Coda   *

In 1885, as part of its campaign to ennoble the acting profession, the young Actors' Fund bought twenty lots in Brooklyn's Evergreen Cemetery for the burial of destitute actors. Since each grave was marked by only a plain marker, it was thought that a more elaborate monument ought to be erected in memory of these common players whose deaths had gone virtually unnoticed. As a result, the Actors' Fund mounted a drive among actors in 1887 to raise $4,500. The *Dramatic Mirror* encouraged players to give, as it would be a monument to the profession as a whole, combining "elements of reverence for the departed, honorable pride and respect of avocation." [58] On June 6 ceremonies were held at the cemetery to dedicate the monument, a simple granite shaft rising forty-five feet from a polished base. Some three thousand people attended the dedication, many of them members of the dramatic profession, but also many simply curious about a gathering of actors. The program included musical selections, a reading of an original poem by William Winter, and a few remarks by Edwin Booth. A. M. Palmer complimented actors for their contributions, a tribute, he said, to the memory of their departed colleagues and a witness to the "exalted dignity and worth" of their calling. Reverend Houghton of the Little Church around the Corner gave the benediction. [59] The *Dramatic Mirror* called the dedication "the most important event yet recorded in our theatrical progress." [60] As the speakers noted, the monument served as a visible statement of actors' efforts at social and professional advancement.

But progress did not mean complete achievement. Actors had to rely upon themselves to build the monument with little outside help. The public came and watched, but strictly as onlookers. Booth's and Palmer's insistence that social barriers were falling simply testified to the continued distance between actor and society. For the moment, actors had to depend upon self-help.

Thirty-two years later the Actors' Fund celebrated another event: the Actors' National Memorial Day. This was a public tribute to actors in late 1919 for their part in the war effort. During World War I over twelve hundred actors and actresses had performed for the troops in Europe; stateside they had given benefits for charities and helped sell over two hundred and fifty million dollars in war bonds. But their contributions meant the neglect of the Actors' Fund, and its persistent financial troubles mounted. To show America's gratitude for their efforts, a group of businessmen decided to sponsor a benefit to provide the Actors' Fund a permanent endowment.

The benefit followed the successful wartime tactic of the drive. Committees were organized to sell tickets systematically for the matinee performances of current attractions that would be given simultaneously in 221 cities and towns on December 5. Committee members included titans of American finance and industry: William Fellowes Morgan, William G. McAdoo, George W. Perkins,

John D. Rockefeller, Jr., Mortimer Schiff, and Felix Warburg. In smaller locales where no professional matinees were given, the plan called for amateur productions, benefit movies, ethical lectures, or ice cream socials as substitute fund-raising events. Local bankers were in charge of collecting the receipts and sending them to New York. Organizers hoped to sell as many tickets as possible at premium prices and devised gimmicks to that end, such as having tickets autographed by celebrities. A pair of tickets to *Declassee* with Ethel Barrymore, autographed by the Prince of Wales, brought five thousand dollars at auction. The Actors' Memorial Day was most vigorously promoted in New York, where forty-five theatres staged benefits. Mayor John Hylan called on New Yorkers to make it "a banner day of appreciation and generosity," and even clergymen exhorted their congregations to support the actors.[61]

The drive fell short of the million-dollar goal needed for the endowment, yielding the nevertheless sizable sum of $400,000. But more to the point here, the event signified society's complete embrace of the player. Where raising a few thousand dollars to erect a simple monument had been a major project in the 1880s, the Actors' National Memorial Day represented a nationwide effort involving hundreds of thousands of dollars. No longer did actors have to depend on their own resources. They had the support of America's business leaders and the goodwill of the public. By their participation in the war effort players had shown themselves loyal and useful citizens. Traditional suspicions were relaxed, and actors were welcomed into the fraternity of American society. "There never was a time when the claims of the profession were so widely recognized," editorialized the *New York Times*, "the sympathy between actor and public has a 'new strength and charm.'"[62]

The players' much-publicized war work offered the most vivid example of their new-found influence. Who else could present so persuasive a case for the purchase of war bonds? What other group could so cheer the boys in uniform? The root of this influence had little to do with the qualities of professionalism which had proven so elusive. The labored efforts at establishing a professional organization, the hopes of systematizing stage training, while not without effect, were in a larger sense irrelevant to the actors' future. As it turned out, actors' social prominence was not bound to traits of respectability, training, service, or any other marks of the recognized professions. In an age that revered these values it should not be surprising that actors viewed their acquisition as the key to social status nor that they were slow to recognize the real basis of their appeal. But their legitimation had occurred on another level and was tied to a contradictory impulse. Not conformity to, but freedom from, conventionality made actors appealing and significant figures. They symbolized an escape from the very sorts of personal restraints that professional dignity demanded. Their license for nonconformity continued to mark actors as a people apart.

The forty years from 1880 to 1920 have long been recognized as the formative ones of modern American society, when Victorianism was dissolved by the solvent of urban culture. The legitimation of the players' work and life testified to the death of an older, unitary culture and to the shape of a new, pluralistic one. Victorianism described a culture based on convictions about work, character, and social respectability. Social recognition under the Victorian dispensation came through tight adherence to well-defined standards. But actors embodied a different ethic, one that harmonized with an urban society that was no longer convinced of the older virtues. Mass society created personal needs that could not be filled solely by the ideal of social respectability. The stress on work and production gave way to pursuit of leisure and consumption. Development of character came to mean attention to the superficialities of personality. Concern about respectability devolved into the vagaries of image. Actors—as celebrities, as paragons of freedom, as models of lifestyle—epitomized the shift from an ethic of strict moral demands to one of permissive self-fulfillment.

Yet transitions from one cultural epoch to another are never complete, and vestiges of a fractured Victorianism would persist as a part of the twentieth-century order (seen, for example, in the continuing importance of professionalism as a means of ascribing status). Once again, though, actors point up with singular clarity the ambivalence of modernism. The distinguishing features of modernism—its pluralism of values and competing networks of cultural authorities—offered actors unprecedented opportunities for social influence. On the stage and off actors displayed the entire spectrum of social habits, from the greatest rectitude to utter dissolution. By their unique capacity to take on a role, to portray virtue and vice, to exalt the old while embracing the new, actors reflected the larger dialectic of American life. Domestic virtue and flaming passion, each had its place, the former reassuring in its restatement of traditional values, the latter provocative in its suggestion of liberation. In his embodiment of both lies the paradox of the actor, a contradiction rooted in the mysterious social drama of which he is a part.

Notes

INTRODUCTION

1. Recent examples include Albert F. McLean, Jr., *American Vaudeville as Ritual* (Lexington: University of Kentucky Press, 1965); David Grimsted, *Melodrama Unveiled* (Chicago: University of Chicago Press, 1968); Robert Toll, *Blacking Up* (New York: Oxford University Press, 1974); Neil Harris, *Humbug: The Art of P. T. Barnum* (Boston: Little, Brown, 1973); Lary May, *Screening Out the Past* (New York: Oxford University Press, 1980).
2. Constance Rourke, *American Humour* (New York: Harcourt, Brace, Jovanovich, 1931), p. 108.
3. See Neil Harris, *Humbug*, chaps. 3 and 10.
4. *New York Dramatic Mirror* (hereafter *NYDM*), 24 Dec. 1898, p. 34.

CHAPTER ONE

1. Jefferson De Angelis and Alvia Harlow, *A Vagabond Trouper* (New York: Harcourt, Brace, 1931), pp. 52–55.
2. George Blumenthal, *My Sixty Years in Show Business: A Chronicle of the American Theatre, 1874–1934* (New York: Frederick C. Osberg, 1936), pp. 16–17.
3. William Lawrence Slout, "The Repertoire Tent Show from Its Beginnings to 1920" (PhD diss., UCLA, 1970), pp. 42–44.
4. William Lawrence Slout, *Theatre in a Tent: The Development of a Provincial Entertainment* (Bowling Green, Ohio: Bowling Green University Popular Press, 1972), pp. 49–51, 71–72; Robert Klassen, "The Tent-Repertoire Theatre: A Rural American Institution" (PhD diss., Michigan State University, 1969), pp. 98–99; *NYDM*, 1 July 1914, p. 7.
5. Slout, *Theatre in a Tent*, pp. 14–22; Neil E. Schaffner, with Vance Johnson, *The Fabulous Toby and Me* (Englewood Cliffs, N.J.: Prentice-Hall, 1968), p. 29; Klassen, "Tent-Repertoire," pp. 98–99.
6. Slout, *Theatre in a Tent*, p. 32.

7. Edward William Mammen, *The Old Stock Company School of Acting* (Boston: Trustees of the Public Library, 1945), pp. 13–18.

8. Quoted in Eleanor Ruggles, *Prince of Players, Edwin Booth* (New York: W. W. Norton, 1953), p. 117.

9. Mammen, *Old Stock Company*, p. 23.

10. Harry Edward Stiver, "Charles Frohman and the Empire Theatre Stock Company" (PhD diss., University of Illinois, 1960), p. 60.

11. Mammen, *Old Stock Company*, pp. 19–25.

12. *Boston Sunday Herald*, 9 May 1880, clipping in the Union Square Theatre Collection, box 1, The Walter Hampden–Edwin Booth Theatre Collection and Library, The Players; Pat Ryan, "A. M. Palmer, Producer: A Study of Management, Dramaturgy, and Stagecraft in the American Theatre, 1872–96" (PhD diss., Yale University, 1959), pp. 338–39.

13. For a discussion of the combination system's origins see Alfred Bernheim, *The Business of the Theatre: An Economic History of the American Theatre, 1750–1932* (New York: Benjamin Blom, 1964; first published New York, 1932), pp. 27–31.

14. Mammen, *Old Stock Company*, pp. 10–11.

15. Stiver, "Charles Frohman," pp. 61–70.

16. Harry Mawson, "Revival of the Stock Company," *The Theatre* 3 (Feb. 1903): 38–41; *NYDM*, 29 Oct. 1898, p. 14; Glenn Hughes, *A History of the American Theatre, 1700–1950* (New York: Samuel French, 1951), pp. 324–25; *New York Times*, 10 Sept. 1911, pt. 5, p. 12; Harry Mawson, "In Stock," *The Theatre* 18 (July 1913): 27–30.

17. *Six Years of Drama at the Castle Square Theatre, May 3, 1897–May 3, 1903* (Boston: Charles Elwell French, 1903), pp. 7–9.

18. Mary Henderson, *The City and the Theatre* (Clifton, N.J.: James T. White, 1973), pp. 44, 134.

19. Bernheim, *Business of the Theatre*, p. 33.

20. Clara Morris, *The Life of a Star* (New York: McClure, Phillips, 1906), pp. 4–5.

21. See Bernheim, *Business of the Theatre*, for the number of combinations from 1900 to 1920, p. 75.

22. Hughes, *History of the American Theatre*, p. 236; Jack Poggi, *Theatre in America: The Impact of Economic Forces, 1870–1967* (Ithaca: Cornell University Press, 1968), p. 6.

23. William Wood, *Personal Recollections of the Stage* (Philadelphia: Henry Carey Baird, 1855), p. 447.

24. *NYDM*, 17 Jan. 1880, p. 4.

25. Ibid., 25 June 1881, p. 6.

26. Ibid., 16 Feb. 1884, p. 6; ibid., 26 Sept. 1891, p. 5.

27. Mrs. Olive Logan, *Before the Footlights and Behind the Scenes* (Philadelphia: Parmelee, 1870), p. 387.

28. Morris, *Life of a Star*, pp. 253–54.

29. Theodore Dreiser, *Sister Carrie* (Philadelphia: University of Pennsylvania Press, 1981), pp. 447–58.

30. Lagare Rogers Lytton Diary, 13 Jan. 1905, Lytton Collection, New York Public Library (hereafter NYPL).

31. Richard Mansfield to Augustin Daly, 8 April 1892, quoted in Joseph Daly, *The Life of Augustin Daly* (New York: Macmillan, 1917), pp. 546–47.

32. Ibid.

33. *New York Times*, 12 March 1905, pt. 4, p. 4; "Soup! Soup!" by John L. Marsh, *Players* 47 (Aug.–Sept. 1972): 286–91; Roland Ashford Philips, "The Super," *Green Book Album* 2 (Dec. 1909): 1254–58.

34. "The Experiences of a Chorus Girl," *Independent* 61 (12 July 1906): 80–85; Brooks Atkinson, *Broadway* (New York: Macmillan, 1970), p. 314; Allen Churchill, *The Great White Way* (New York: E. P. Dutton, 1962), pp. 8–9; James S. Metcalfe, "The Why of the Chorus Girl," *The Theatre* 33 (April 1921): 248, 292.

35. Otis Skinner, *Footlights and Spotlights* (Indianapolis: Bobbs-Merrill, 1924), pp. 35–36, 58.

36. John Golden and Viola Brothers Shore, *Stage Struck John Golden* (New York: Samuel French, 1930), p. 40.

37. Billie Burke to William Seymour, 26 Jan. 1909, William Seymour Papers, William Seymour Theater Collection, Princeton University.

38. Henderson, *City and Theatre*, p. 134; *NYDM*, 6 May 1882, p. 8.

39. Nat C. Goodwin, *Nat Goodwin's Book* (Boston: Richard G. Badger, 1914), pp. 99–100.

40. *NYDM*, 1 May 1880, p. 6; ibid., 25 July 1885, p. 10.

41. *New York Times*, 19 Oct. 1890, p. 17.

42. James Silver to Colonel James Milliken, 21 Nov. 1893, Milliken Papers, NYPL.

43. E. A. Warren to Colonel James Milliken, 11 Nov. 1893, Milliken Papers.

44. Dreiser, *Sister Carrie*, pp. 380–84.

45. *NYDM*, 18 July 1885, p. 10.

46. Harrison Grey Fiske, ed., *New York Mirror Annual and Directory of the Theatrical Profession for 1888* (New York: New York Mirror, 1888), p. vi.

47. *NYDM*, 9 July 1910, p. 11.

48. Ibid., 5 July 1890, p. 1.

49. Hughes, *History of the American Theatre*, pp. 238–39.

50. William Seymour to Charles Frohman, 26 March 1906, Seymour Papers.

51. Hartley Davis, "The Actor and the Manager," *Everybody's Magazine* 18 (April 1908): 375.

52. Francis Wilson to Alf Haymal [sic (Haymen)], 22 Dec. 1916, Francis Wilson Papers, Cage File, Billy Rose Theatre Collection, New York Public Library at Lincoln Center (hereafter NYPLC).

53. *New York Times*, 18 July 1909, pt. 2, p. 6.

54. *NYDM*, 3 Sept. 1881, p. 7; ibid., 24 Sept. 1887, p. 6.

55. Davis, "Actor and Manager," pp. 378–80; *NYDM*, 20 Sept. 1890, p. 2.

56. Julius Kahn to F. F. Mackay, 5 March 1888, Millicent Reinold Folder, Cage File, Billy Rose Theatre Collection, NYPLC.

57. *NYDM*, 30 May 1885, p. 7.

58. Ibid., 11 April 1885, p. 11.

59. Ibid., 8 Aug. 1891, p. 2.

60. Ibid., 9 Nov. 1889, p. 2.

61. Ibid., 10 Jan. 1891, p. 4.

62. Ibid., 1 Feb. 1896, p. 3.

63. Philip Hubert, *The Stage as a Career* (New York: G. P. Putnam's, 1900), p. 141.

64. *New York Clipper*, 17 Sept. 1881, p. 412.

65. The census category of actors and showmen included many people in addition to legitimate stage actors. It is conceivable that circus and vaudeville performers may have had a higher rate of unemployment and thus inflated the figures. Also it is unclear whether or not the census respondents included the summer layoffs as unemployment time. Probably they did not; the summer months were generally considered vacation time by actors. If actors had included the summer months, their occupation would have had an unemployment rate of nearly 100 percent!

66. Bureau of the Census, *Special Reports: Occupations at the Twelfth Census* (Washington: GPO, 1904), p. ccxxviii; *New York Times*, 7 Dec. 1913, pt. 8, p. 6.

67. Marcus Moriarty to Marion [Lester], 30 Oct. 1890, Malone Papers, NYPL.

68. Unidentified newspaper clipping (1903), in Owen Fawcett Scrapbook, "Fifty Years on the Stage," Fawcett Collection, University of Tennessee, Knoxville.

69. *New York Daily Tribune*, 31 March 1860, Clipping File, Billy Rose Theatre Collection, NYPLC; Mammen, *Old Stock Company*, pp. 25–29.

70. Mammen, *Old Stock Company*, p. 26; Wood, *Recollections*, pp. 449–51.

71. Franklin Fyles, *The Theatre and Its People* (New York: Doubleday, Page, 1900), p. 54; *NYDM*, 20 Dec. 1879, p. 4; ibid., 26 May 1915, p. 4.

72. *NYDM*, 1 Sept. 1894, p. 5; Bureau of the Census, *Historical Statistics of the United States, Colonial Times to 1970, Bicentennial Edition* (Washington: GPO, 1975), pt. 1, p. 168.

73. *NYDM*, 17 June 1882, p. 6.

74. Unidentified actress to Augustin Daly, circa 1880, quoted in *Life of Daly*, p. 342.

75. "What the Player Earns," *American Magazine* 69 (Dec. 1909): 264–72; Archibald Pollard, "What the Actors Really Earn," *Ladies' Home Journal* (Oct. 1911), pp. 19, 82.

CHAPTER TWO

1. The census category "actresses and professional show-women" included circus performers, dancers, and many other performers. Yet actresses and chorus girls would have made up by far the largest percentage of the category. The category "actors and professional showmen" would have included more performers outside the realm of the legitimate—professional athletes, balloonists, dancers, for example—meaning that there was probably greater divergence in the male category between the enumeration and the actual number of actors.
2. Bureau of the Census, *Special Reports: Occupations at the Twelfth Census* (Washington: GPO, 1904), p. cxlv.
3. In 1900 there were only 100 female architects against 10,581 men, 1,010 women lawyers versus 113,450 men, 463 women college professors in an occupation dominated by its 6,809 men, and 6,825 women physicians—a large number—but not large when compared to the 146,978 males practicing medicine. Altogether, women made up 34.2 percent of the professional service occupations in 1900, but this figure is as high as it is only because of the few professions which they dominated, significantly the less prestigous and lucrative ones: nursing, librarianship, music teaching, and elementary-school teaching. Figures are from Alba M. Edward, *Comparative Occupation Statistics for the United States, 1870 to 1940, in Sixteenth Census of the United States: 1940 Population* (Washington: GPO, 1943), pp. 119, 135–36.
4. *NYDM*, 11 July 1891, p. 4.
5. Michael Baker, *The Rise of the Victorian Actor* (London: Croom Helm, 1978), pp. 86–89.
6. Ronald Taft, "A Psychological Assessment of Professional Actors and Related Professions," *Genetic Psychology Monographs* 64 (1961): 362.
7. See Montrose Moses, *Famous Actor-Families in America* (New York: Thomas Y. Crowell, 1906).
8. Eleanor Ruggles, *Prince of Players, Edwin Booth* (New York: W. W. Norton, 1953), pp. 29–30.
9. Lewis Strang, *Famous Actors of the Day in America* (Boston: L. C. Page, 1899), pp. 70–71.
10. Ibid., pp. 205–7.
11. Ethel Barrymore, *Memories: An Autobiography* (New York: Harper, 1955), pp. 37–46.
12. Bureau of the Census, *Historical Statistics of the United States* (Washington: GPO, 1975) , pt. 2, pp. 379, 383.
13. Margherita Arlina Hamm, *Eminent Actors in Their Homes* (New York: James Pott, 1909), pp. 6–7.
14. Gustav Kobbe, *Famous Actors and Actresses and Their Homes* (Boston: Little, Brown, 1903), p. 295.

15. R. O. Loud, "Do Actors Read?—and What?" *Green Book Magazine* 10 (Nov. 1913): 856.

16. Franklin Fyles, *The Theatre and Its People* (New York: Doubleday, Page, 1900), pp. 24–25.

17. Philip Hubert, *The Stage as a Career* (New York: G. P. Putnam's, 1900), p. 186.

18. Arthur Hornblow, *Training for the Stage*, Lippincott Training Series (Philadelphia: J. B. Lippincott, 1916), p. 8.

19. Clara Morris, "A Word of Warning to Young Actresses," *Century* 60 (N.S., vol. 38, May 1900): 41; Clara Morris, *Stage Confidences* (Boston: Lothrop, 1902), pp. 12–15.

20. Clara Morris, *A Pasteboard Crown* (New York: Charles Scribner's, 1902).

21. Margaret Townshend, *Theatrical Sketches* (New York: Merriam, 1894), p. 12.

22. Maxine Elliott, "Maxine Elliott's Advice to Stage-struck Girls: 'Don't,'" *The Theatre* 8 (Aug. 1908): 202–3.

23. Elsie Ferguson, "Do You Yearn to Go on the Stage?" *Green Book Magazine* 9 (April 1913): 602.

24. Hubert, *Stage as a Career*, p. 24.

25. Yoti Lane, *The Psychology of the Actor* (Westport, Conn.: Greenwood Press, 1959), pp. 26–32.

26. Alfred C. Golden, "Personality Traits of Drama School Students," *Quarterly Journal of Speech* 26 (Dec. 1940): 564–75.

27. Ronald Taft, "A Psychological Assessment of Professional Actors and Related Professions," *Genetic Psychology Monographs* 64 (1961): pp. 309–83 passim.

28. DeWolf Hopper, *Once a Clown, Always a Clown* (Boston: Little, Brown, 1927), p. 2.

29. *Hartford Post*, 10 Nov. 1901, clipping in Robinson Locke Collection, vol. 277, p. 23, Billy Rose Theatre Collection, NYPLC.

30. Theodore Dreiser, *Sister Carrie*, pp. 157–58.

31. *New York Times*, 8 Feb. 1912, p. 1.

32. *NYDM*, 29 Sept. 1894, p. 12.

33. Edward William Mammen, *The Old Stock Company School of Acting* (Boston: Trustees of the Public Library, 1945), pp. 35–36.

34. Quoted in Hubert, *Stage as a Career*, p. 70.

35. Alexander Woolcott, *Mrs. Fiske: Her Views on Actors, Acting, and the Problems of Production* (New York: Century, 1917), p. 86.

36. Mammen, *Old Stock Company*, pp. 37–38.

37. David Belasco, *The Theatre Through the Stage Door* (New York: Harper, 1919), p. 40.

38. W. J. Meenagham to Colonel James Milliken, 18 May—, Milliken Papers. NYPL.

39. Joseph Daly, *The Life of Augustin Daly* (New York: Macmillan, 1917), p. 509.

40. Belasco, *The Theatre through the Stage Door*, pp. 16–17.

41. Juliet Everts, "The Study of Acting in Paris," *Century* 28 (July 1884): 472–74.

42. Barbara Whitehead, "Fancy's Show Box: Performance in the Republic, 1790–1866" (PhD diss., University of Chicago, 1976), pp. 93–121 passim.

43. See Alan Thomas, *Time in a Frame: Photography and the Nineteenth-Century Mind* (New York: Schocken Books, 1973).

44. Joseph Reed and William Walsh, "Beauties of the American Stage," *Cosmopolitan* 14 (Jan. 1893): 294.

45. Garff Wilson, *A History of American Acting* (Bloomington: Indiana University Press, 1966), p. 66.

46. Anne O'Hagan, "The Quest of Beauty," *Munsey's* 29 (June 1903): 406–9; Maggie Angeloglou, *A History of Make-Up* (New York: Macmillan, 1965), pp. 99–109; Rafford Pyke, "The Handsome Man," *Cosmopolitan* 35 (Oct. 1903): 627; Margaret Illington, "The Mad Search for Stage Beauty," *Green Book Album* 7 (May 1912): 952–60.

47. *NYDM*, 2 Oct. 1880, p. 6; George C. D. Odell, *Annals of the New York Stage*, 15 vols. (New York: Columbia University Press, 1927–49), 11: 248.

48. Odell, *Annals*, 11: 294–301; "Costly Dressing on the Stage," *The Theatre* 6 (Nov. 1906): 321–22.

49. Howard Kyle, Reminiscences of Henry Miller, Howard Kyle Papers, Billy Rose Theatre Collection, NYPLC.

50. Mammen, *Old Stock Company*, pp. 37–47.

51. It would be interesting to know the degree of occupational persistence among actors, but lack of information precludes even an estimated guess.

52. Felix Morris, *Reminiscences* (New York: International Telegram, 1892); *National Cyclopedia of American Biography*, s.v. Felix Morris, 11: 160–61.

53. *Dictionary of American Biography*, s.v. Bacon, Frank (by Edwin Francis Edgett).

54. *National Cyclopedia of American Biography*, s.v. Alberta Gallatin, 39: 71–72.

55. Ibid., s.v. Jessie Shirley, 18: 272.

56. Ibid., s.v. Robert Hardaway, 43: 31–32.

57. *Notable American Women*, s.v. Crosman, Henrietta (by Robert Dierlam).

58. *Dictionary of American Biography*, s.v. Lackaye, Wilton (by Edwin Francis Edgett).

59. *National Cyclopedia of American Biography*, s.v. Helen Ware, 31: 107.

60. Channing Pollock, "A Word about Shooting Stars," *Green Book Magazine* 10 (Oct. 1913): 599–607.

61. Eugene O'Neill, *Long Day's Journey into Night* (New Haven: Yale University Press, 1956), pp. 149–50.

62. Irving Howe, *World of Our Fathers* (New York: Simon and Schuster, 1976), pp. 472–73.

63. Hutchins Hapgood, *The Spirit of the Ghetto* (New York: Funk & Wagnalls, 1965), p. 149.

64. David Lifson, *The Yiddish Theatre in America* (New York: Thomas Yoseloff, 1965), p. 126.
65. Tytachony, First Yiddish School of Acting, Applications for enrollment, Cage File, Billy Rose Theatre Collection, NYPLC.
66. Hapgood, *Spirit of the Ghetto*, pp. 123–24, Lifson, *Yiddish Theatre*, pp. 128–29.
67. Howe, *World of Our Fathers*, pp. 473–76; Lulla Rosenfeld, *Bright Star of Exile: Jacob Adler and the Yiddish Theatre* (New York: Thomas Y. Crowell, 1977), pp. 305–7.
68. *Notable American Women*, s.v. Bertha Kalich (by H. L. Kleinfeld); Bertha Kalich to George Foster Platt (n.d.), Bertha Kalich Letters, Billy Rose Theatre Collection, NYPLC.
69. On the history of black entertainers see: James Weldon Johnson, *Black Manhattan* (New York: Arno Press and the *New York Times*, 1968; first published 1930), pp. 74–125; Robert Toll, *On with the Show* (New York: Oxford University Press, 1967), pp. 111–39; Langston Hughes and Milton Meltzer, *Black Magic* (Englewood Cliffs, N.J.: Prentice-Hall, 1967), pp. 20–60; Lindsay Patterson, comp. and ed., *Anthology of the American Negro in the Theatre*, International Library of Negro Life and History (New York: Association for the Study of Negro Life and History, 1967), pp. 3–10.
70. Toll, *On with the Show* p. 133.
71. *The Theatre* 1 (21 June 1886): 358.
72. Quoted in Toll, *On with the Show*, p. 129.
73. Ibid., p. 130.
74. Johnson, *Black Manhattan*, pp. 78–87; Yvonne Shafer, "Black Actors in the Nineteenth Century American Theatre," *CLA Journal* 20 (March 1977): 387–400.
75. Johnson, *Black Manhattan*, pp. 97–98, 170–73.
76. Lucie France Pierce, "The Only Colored Stock Theatre in America," *The Theatre* 8 (Jan. 1908): 109–10.
77. Johnson, *Black Manhattan*, pp. 175–77; *NYDM*, 5 May 1917, p. 5; Hughes and Meltzer, *Black Magic*, p. 106.
78. Johnson, *Black Manhattan*, pp. 183–85.

CHAPTER THREE

1. Henry Clapp, *Reminiscences of a Dramatic Critic* (Boston: Houghton, Mifflin, 1902), pp. 109–10.
2. Lew Benedict to William Seymour, —May 1918, William Seymour Papers, William Seymour Theater Collection Princeton University.
3. *NYDM*, 19 April 1884, p. 7.
4. On the history of New York theatres see Mary Henderson, *The City and the Theatre* (Clifton, N.J.: James T. White, 1973).
5. *The Theatre* 1 (23 Aug. 1886): 515–16.
6. *NYDM*, 22 Sept. 1888, p. 9.
7. Neil E. Schaffner, *The Fabulous Toby and Me* (Englewood Cliffs, N.J.: Prentice-Hall, 1968), p. 20.
8. Otto Fenichel, "On Acting," *Psychoanalytic Quarterly* 15 (1946): 144–

60; Conrad Chyatte, "Personality Traits of Actors," *Occupations* 21 (Jan. 1949): 245–50.

9. Erving Goffman, *The Presentation of Self in Everyday Life* (Garden City, N.Y.: Doubleday Anchor Books, 1959).

10. Ibid., pp. 1–22.

11. *NYDM*, 26 Jan. 1889, p. 6.

12. Michael Baker makes the same point about English thespians in *The Rise of the Victorian Actor* (London: Croom Helm, 1978), pp. 76–77.

13. Marvin Felheim, *The Theater of Augustin Daly* (Cambridge, Mass.: Harvard University Press, 1956), pp. 32–33.

14. *NYDM*, 2 Sept. 1882, p. 6.

15. Ibid., 7 July 1888, p. 9.

16. Philip Hubert, *The Stage as a Career* (New York: G. P. Putnam's, 1900), p. 165.

17. Jessie Busley, "Behind the Grease Paint," *Green Book Magazine* 8 (Sept. 1912): 408.

18. Germain Quinn, *Fifty Years Back Stage: Being the Life Story of a Theatrical Stage Mechanic* (Minneapolis: Stage Pub. Co., 1926) pp. 201–12; Judge Horton, *Driftwood of the Stage* (Detroit: Winn & Hammond, 1904), pp. 97–100.

19. *Actors' Society Monthly Bulletin* (hereafter *ASMB*) 5 (Dec. 1902): 8.

20. Rogers Legare Lytton Diary, 12–18 Dec. 1904, Lytton Papers, NYPL.

21. Frederick Warde, *Fifty Years of Make-Believe*, (New York: International Press Syndicate, 1920), p. 248.

22. *New York Times*, 8 Nov. 1885, p. 6.

23. *NYDM*, 10 May 1890, p. 2.

24. Ibid., 4 June 1887, p. 7.

25. Ibid., 8 March 1879, p. 4.

26. *New York Times*, 24 March 1912, pt. 9, p. 10.

27. Annie Russell, "What It Really Means to Be an Actress," *Ladies' Home Journal* 26 (Jan. 1909): 11.

28. *NYDM*, 13 April 1889, p. 2.

29. Bert Wheeler, Reminiscences, ser. 1, vol. 4, Oral History Collection, Columbia University, pp. 1106–8.

30. William Lawrence Slout, *Theatre in a Tent* (Bowling Green, Ohio: Bowling Green University Popular Press, 1972), p. 191.

31. James Kotsilibas-Davis, *Great Times Good Times: The Odyssey of Maurice Barrymore* (Garden City, N.Y.: Doubleday, 1977), p. 172; *New York Times*, 15 April 1906, p. 1.

32. Julius Kahn to F. F. Mackay, 5 March 1888, Millicent Reinold Folder, NYPLC.

33. *NYDM*, 18 Dec. 1886, cover.

34. Julie Opp Faversham, "The Lure of the Road," *Green Book Magazine* 8 (Dec. 1912): 1023.

35. Mary Shaw, "The Actress on the Road," *McClure's* 37 (July 1911): 263–71; Hubert, *Stage as a Career*, pp. 21–23.

36. *NYDM*, 10 Dec. 1913, p. 4; ibid., 14 Nov. 1908, p. 5; *Equity* 6 (Jan. 1921): 17–19.

37. *NYDM*, 8 Oct. 1881, p. 7; Edwin Booth to William Winter, 23 March 1881, in Daniel Watermeier, ed., *Between Actor and Critic* (Princeton: Princeton University Press, 1971), p. 238.
38. *NYDM*, 25 March 1899, p. 3.
39. Ibid., 17 July 1886, p. 6; ibid., 6 Aug. 1887, p. 7.
40. Ibid.; Susie C. Clark, *John Mccullough as Man, Actor and Spirit* (New York: Broadway, 1914), pp. 172–81.
41. *NYDM*, 21 April 1894, p. 2.
42. Unidentified newspaper clipping, 6 Feb. 1902, in Robinson Locke Collection, vol. 136, p. 38, Billy Rose Theatre Collection, NYPLC.
43. Ada Patterson and Victory Bateman, *By the Stage Door* (New York: Grafton Press, 1902), pp. 83–90.
44. Kotsilibas-Davis, *Great Times*, pp. 169–72.
45. Gustav Kobbe, *Famous Actresses and Their Homes*, (Boston: Little, Brown, 1905), p. 220.
46. Frances L. Garside, "The Honest-to-Goodness Truth about Me," *The Theatre* 30 (Oct. 1919): 244.
47. Clara Morris, "Should the Actress Marry," unidentified article in the Robinson Locke Collection, vol. 353, p. 17.
48. The percentage of single actresses ranked only thirty-seventh among other occupations.
49. Figures from the Bureau of the Census, *Special Reports: Statistics of Women at Work, 1900* (Washington: GPO, 1907), pp. 36–38.
50. Bureau of the Census, *Historical Statistics* (Washington: GPO, 1975), pt. 1, p. 19.
51. Bureau of the Census, *Special Reports: Occupations at the Twelfth Census* (Washington: GPO, 1904), p. ccxviii.
52. Ronald Taft, "A Psychological Assessment of Professional Actors and Related Professions," *Genetic Psychology Monograph* 64 (1961): 358, 367.
53. *NYDM*, 2 June 1883, p. 6.
54. Dora Knowlton Ranous, *Diary of a Daly Debutante* (New York: Duffield, 1910), p. 129.
55. Clara Morris, *The Life of a Star* (New York: McClure, Phillips, 1906), p. 26.
56. *Custer County Chief*, 30 Aug. 1895, p. 3.
57. Zoe Beckley, "The Theatrical Marriage," *The Theatre* 28 (Dec. 1918): 360–62.
58. *Twelfth Census*, p. ccxx.
59. Bureau of the Census, *Women at Work*, p. 38.
60. C. J. Bulliet, *Robert Mantell's Romance* (Boston: John W. Luce, 1918), pp. 140–97 passim.
61. "Divorce—the Fruit of the Stage," unidentified newspaper clipping, 1906, Billy Rose Theatre Collection, NYPLC.
62. *New York Times*, 26 May 1913, p. 6.
63. William L. O'Neill, *Divorce in the Progressive Era* (New Haven: Yale University Press, 1967), pp. 255–57.

64. *New York Times*, 23 Sept. 1900, p. 17; Helen Green, *At the Actors' Boarding House and Other Stories* (New York: Nevada Publishing, 1906).

65. *NYDM*, 25 Feb. 1914, p. 8.

66. See Kobbe, *Famous Actors*, and Margherita Arlina Hamm, *Eminent Actors in Their Homes* (New York: James Pott, 1909).

67. Hamm, *Eminent Actors*, p. 6.

68. Editor's note, *Good Housekeeping* 54 (Jan. 1912): 41.

69. Margaret Anglin, "Domesticity and the Stage," *Good Housekeeping* 54 (Jan. 1912): 41.

70. Mary Mannering, "The Home, the Stage and the Woman," *Good Housekeeping* 54 (Feb. 1912): 201–8.

71. Julie Opp, "The Actress and the Home," *Green Book Album* 3 (June 1910): 1265.

72. Ibid.

73. Ada Lewis, "Being an Actress," *Green Book Album* 4 (Dec. 1910): 1236–37.

74. Valerie Hope, "Actors and Matrimony," *Green Book Album* 3 (Feb. 1910): 315–18.

75. Virginia Tracy, "The Home Life of Actors," *Collier's* 48 (Oct. 1911): 19.

76. *NYDM*, 11 Jan. 1890, p. 6; ibid., 24 Dec. 1898, pp. 68–70; Emmett C. King, "The Club Life of Actors," *Munsey's* 43 (May 1910): 267.

77. James Nicholson, *History of the Order of Elks* (New York: National Memorial and Pub. Commission of the Benevolent and Protective Order of Elks of the U.S. of A., 1953), pp. 11–17, 29.

78. *NYDM*, 9 June 1900, p. 12; Otis Skinner, *Footlights and Spotlights* (Indianapolis: Bobbs-Merrill, 1924), p. 161; *NYDM*, 31 March 1915, p. 5.

79. King, "Club Life of Actors," pp. 264–65; DeWolf Hopper, *Once a Clown, Always a Clown* (Boston: Little, Brown, 1927), p. 209; *NYDM*, 28 Feb. 1891, p. 5; Kotsilibas-Davis, *Great Times*, pp. 165, 268–69; Allen Churchill, *The Great White Way* (New York: E. P. Dutton, 1962), pp. 115–27.

80. Hopper, *Once a Clown* p. 211.

81. Ibid., pp. 188–93.

82. *NYDM*, 1 May 1909, p. 11.

83. Ibid., 4 April 1891, p. 1; Arthur Hornblow, *Training for the Stage*, Lippincott Training Series (Philadephia: J. B. Lippincott, 1916), p. 44.

84. *NYDM*, 17 Dec. 1892, p. 3; ibid., 24 Dec. 1898, pp. 30–32; ibid., 20 May 1893, p. 12; King, "Club Life of Actors," p. 268; Hornblow, *Training for the Stage*, pp. 44.

85. For biographical information on Booth see *Dictionary of American Biography*, s.v. "Booth, Edwin (by Ernest Sutherland Bates); Eleanor Ruggles, *Prince of Players, Edwin Booth* (New York: W. W. Norton, 1953).

86. Margaret Townshend, *Theatrical Sketches* (New York: Merriam, 1894), pp. 15–18; Edwin Booth to Laurence Hutton, 8 Oct. 1885, Laurence Hutton Papers, Princeton University; Harrison Grey Fiske to Ed-

win Booth, 2 Dec. 1881, Edwin Booth Papers, The Players Library; *NYDM* 24 June 1882, p. 2; Edwin Booth to unknown,—1874, copy, Booth Papers.

87. Mary Anderson de Navarro, *A Few Memories* (New York: Harper, 1896), p. 214.

88. Charles H. Shattuck, *The Hamlet of Edwin Booth* (Urbana: University of Illinois Press, 1969), p. xiii.

89. Hans Gerth and C. Wright Mills, eds., *From Max Weber* (New York: Oxford University Press, 1946), pp. 14–17.

90. Ibid., pp. 302–11.

91. Francis Gerry Fairfield, *Clubs of New York* (New York: Henry L. Hinton, 1873), p. 7.

92. Fairfield, *Clubs*, pp. 66–70.

93. *NYDM*, 2 July 1887, p. 2.

94. The Century Association, *The Century, 1847–1946* (New York: The Century Association, 1947), pp. 3–10; Fairfield, *Clubs*, pp. 40–45.

95. John S. Phillips, *The Players* (Board of Directors, The Players, 1935), pp. 5–7; Richardson Wright, "The New Tenants at No. 16," in *The Players Book*, ed. Henry Wysham Lanier (New York: The Players, 1938), pp. 97–116.

96. The Players, *Minutes of the First Meeting*, 31 Dec. 1888 (New York: n.p., 1908), pp. 5–6.

97. Edwin Booth, quoted in Daniel Watermeier, ed., *Between Actor and Critic* (Princeton: Princeton University Press, 1971), introduction, p. 9.

98. Edwin Booth to William Winter, 8 June 1888, in ibid., p. 290.

99. Edwin Booth to Jervis McEntee, 28 May 1888, Booth Papers.

100. William Winter, *Life and Art of Edwin Booth* (New York: Macmillan, 1893), p. 133.

101. Brander Matthews, "The Players," *Century* 21 (Nov. 1891): 28–29; *NYDM*, 27 May 1893, p. 4.

102. Matthews, "The Players," pp. 29–30; Harrison Blake Hodge to George Foster Platt, 28 Oct. 1908, The Players Library.

103. King, "Club Life of Actors," pp. 261–62.

104. The two quotes are from Witter Bynner, "A Word or Two with Henry James," *The Critic* 46 (Feb. 1905): 146–48; Witter Bynner, "Some Reminiscences," in George Stewart Woodbridge, ed., *The Players after 75 Years* (New York: n.p., 1968), pp. 119–20.

105. Frank Conlan, Reminiscences, typed manuscript, Chicago Historical Society.

106. *Catalogue of Relics in Safes Belonging to the Players*, 23 April 1901, Billy Rose Theatre Collection, NYPLC; Matthews, "The Players," pp. 31–33.

107. Ruggles, *Prince of Players*, p. 363; "The Memoirs of Clarence Clough Buel, 1850–1933," unpublished manuscript, The Players Library, p. 122.

108. *The Players*, brochure, June 1959 (Marchbanks Press, New York).

109. Quoted in Ruggles, *Prince of Players*, p. 341.

110. Edwin Booth to Laurence Hutton, 5 June—, Hutton Papers, Princeton University.
111. Quoted in Churchill, *Great White Way*, p. 116.
112. Frank Marshall White, "New York's Clubs for Actors," *Green Book Album* 2 (Aug. 1909): 343–50.

CHAPTER FOUR

1. The literature on professionalization is enormous. Sociologists pioneered the study, and most works come from that discipline. Only in the past couple of decades have historians taken note of the importance of professionalization, but in this short time historical studies of the movement have become a veritable cottage industry. I shall list only the most enlightening works on the period I discuss. Burton Bledstein, *The Culture of Professionalism* (New York: W. W. Norton, 1976); Robert Wiebe, *The Search for Order, 1877–1920* (New York: Hill & Wang, 1967), pp. 111–13; Magali Sarfatti Larson, *The Rise of Professionalism* (Berkeley: University of California Press, 1977), pp. xvi-xvii; see also Laurence Veysey, "The Plural Organized Worlds of Humanities," in Alexandra Oleson and John Voss, eds., *The Organization of Knowledge in Modern America, 1860–1920* (Baltimore: The Johns Hopkins University Press, 1979), pp. 58–62; and John Higham, "The Matrix of Specialization," in Oleson and Voss, eds., *Organization of Knowledge*, pp. 3–18. On the professionalization of English actors see Michael Baker's fine study, *The Rise of the Victorian Actor* (London: Croom Helm, 1978), especially chap. 7.
2. William Wood, *Personal Recollections of the Stage* (Philadelphia: Henry Carey Baird, 1855), p. xvi.
3. Joseph Jefferson, *The Autobiography of Joseph Jefferson* (New York: Century, 1889), p. 111.
4. Frederick Warde, *Fifty Years of Make-Believe* (New York: International Press Syndicate, 1920), p. 296.
5. Garff Wilson, *A History of American Acting* (Bloomington: Indiana University Press, 1966), p. 17.
6. Alba M. Edwards, *Population: Comparative Occupation Statistics for the United States, 1870 to 1940* (Washington: GPO, 1943), p. 111.
7. Bureau of the Census, *Index to Occupations* (Washington: GPO, 1915), p. 395.
8. A. M. Palmer, "American Theaters," in Chauncey Depew, ed., *One Hundred Years of American Commerce*, 2 vols. (New York: D. O. Hayne, 1895), 1:164.
9. *NYDM*, 11 Jan. 1879, p. 4.
10. Ibid., 26 Nov. 1881, p. 6.
11. Jefferson, *Autobiography*, pp. 41–42.
12. David Grimsted, *Melodrama Unveiled* (Chicago: University of Chicago Press, 1968), p. 75.
13. Michael M. Davis, Jr., *The Exploitation of Pleasure* (New York: Russell Sage Foundation, 1911). Davis gives no explanation of his survey's method.

14. Ibid., pp. 30, 36–37.
15. Ben Graf Henneke, "The Playgoer in America (1752–1952)" (PhD diss., University of Illinois, 1956), pp. 75–86; *NYDM*, 27 Jan. 1883, p. 6.
16. *NYDM*, 18 Feb. 1882, p. 6
17. Joseph Daly, *The Life of Augustin Daly* (New York: Macmillan, 1917), pp. 104–5.
18. *NYDM*, 29 March 1879, p. 4.
19. Daly, *Life of Daly*, pp. 452, 454–55.
20. Louis Simon, *A History of the Actors' Fund of America* (New York: Theatre Arts Books, 1972), pp. 11–15.
21. *NYDM*, 22 July 1882, p. 7; ibid., 3 July 1886, p. 9.
22. Ibid., 21 Jan. 1882, p. 6.
23. Ibid., 14 Feb. 1882, p. 4; quoted in Simon, *Actors' Fund*, p. 16.
24. Simon, *Actors' Fund*, p. 17.
25. Ibid., pp. 26–37.
26. *NYDM*, 23 Feb. 1884, p. 7.
27. Simon, *Actors' Fund*, pp. 38–40; *NYDM*, 6 May 1882, p. 8.
28. *The Actors' Fund Association of American Annual Reports, 1882–1893* (New York: Actors' Fund, 1894), passim; *NYDM*, 15 June 1889, p. 2; ibid., 9 June 1888, p. 7; *Eleventh Annual Report of the Actors' Fund*, 3 June 1891 to 7 June 1892, p. 20.
29. Simon, *Actors' Fund*, p. 59.
30. William Rounseville Alger, *Life of Edwin Forrest*, 2 vols. (Philadelphia: J. B. Lippincott, 1877) 2: 850–52.
31. *NYDM*, 29 July 1882, p. 6; Richard Moody, *Edwin Forrest: First Star of the American Stage* (New York: Alfred A. Knopf, 1960), p. 391; *NYDM*, 26 Dec. 1885, p. 9; ibid., 4 June 1887, p. 6.
32. Simon, *Actors' Fund*, pp. 176–89.
33. Quoted in ibid., p. 43.
34. *NYDM*, 16 June 1883, p. 6; Simon, *Actors' Fund*, pp. 65–66.
35. *NYDM*, 7 June 1884, p. 7.
36. Ibid., 6 June 1883, p. 6; ibid., 9 June 1888, p. 3.
37. Ibid., 23 Jan. 1886, p. 6; ibid., 12 Jan. 1889, p. 6; *Actors' Fund Annual Report for 1900*, p. 20; Simon, *Actors' Fund*, pp. 63–64, 53–54, 72–73.
38. Simon, *Actors' Fund*, pp. 153–54.
39. Ibid., pp. 156–57.
40. Henry L. Taylor, *Professional Education in the United States*, 2 vols. (Albany: University of the State of New York, 1900), 2: 750, 956, 1: 154; Leo F. Smith and Laurence Lipsett, *The Technical Institute* (New York: McGraw-Hill, 1956), pp. 20–24; Charles Alphens Bennett, *History of Manual and Industrial Education, 1870–1917* (Peoria, Ill.: The Manual Arts Press, 1937), pp. 320, 351–85, 411–29, 507–08; Arthur L. Manchester, *Music Education in the United States*, U.S. Bureau of Education Bulletin, 1908: no. 4 (Washington: GPO, 1908), pp. 14–20; Henry Turner Bailey, *Instruction in the Fine and Manual Arts in the United States*, U.S. Bureau of Education Bulletin, 1909: no. 6 (Washington: GPO, 1909), p. 15.

41. Edward William Mammen, *The Old Stock Company School of Acting* (Boston: Trustees of the Public Library, 1946), pp. 39–70; Helen Ormsbee, *Backstage with Actors, from the Time of Shakespeare to the Present Day* (New York: Thomas Y. Crowell, 1938), pp. 141–42.

42. Mammen, *Old Stock Company*, pp. 66–70; Marvin Felheim, *The Theater of Augustin Daly* (Cambridge, Mass.: Harvard University Press, 1956), pp. 1–79 passim; Dora Knowlton Ranous, *Diary of a Daly Debutante* (New York: Duffield, 1910), p. 30.

43. *New York Clipper*, 17 Sept. 1881, p. 412.

44. *The Illustrated Dramatic Weekly* 1 (8 March 1879): 4–5.

45. *NYDM*, 26 Oct. 1910, p. 3.

46. Mary Robb, "The Elocutionary Movement and Its Chief Figures," in *History of Speech Education in America*, ed. Karl Wallace (New York: Appleton-Century-Crofts, 1954), pp. 179–80; Lester Hale, "Dr. James Rush," in Wallace, ed., *History of Speech Education*, pp. 219, 226–32.

47. Robb, "Elocutionary Movement," p. 198; Edith Renshaw, "Five Private Schools of Speech," in Wallace, ed., *History of Speech Education*, pp. 301–6.

48. Francis Hodge, "The Private Theatre Schools in the Late Nineteenth Century," in Wallace, ed., *History of Speech Education*, pp. 558–61; Clyde L. Shaver, "Steele MacKaye and the Delsartian Tradition," in Wallace, ed., *History of Speech Education*, pp. 202–18; Percy MacKaye, *Epoch: The Life of Steele MacKaye* (New York: Boni and Liveright, 1927) 1:270–72.

49. Hodge, "Private Theatre Schools," pp. 559–61; *NYDM*, 31 Jan. 1885, p. 7; Beverly Brumm, "A Survey of Professional Acting Schools in New York City: 1870–1970" (PhD diss., New York University, 1973), p. 43.

50. Hodge, "Private Theatre Schools," pp. 561–63.

51. *New York Times*, 24 June 1888, p. 13; *Dramatic Studies* 2 (Oct. 1898): 2; Mark Jerome Malinauskas, "The American Academy of Dramatic Arts: A History" (PhD diss., University of Oregon, 1950), p. 68; *New York Times*, 22 April 1894, p. 13.

52. Hodge, "Private Theatre Schools," pp. 564–67; source is *Dramatic Studies* 1 (Oct. 1898): 2.

53. *Dramatic Studies* 1 (Oct. 1898): 1.

54. *Annual Catalogue of American Academy of Dramatic Arts, 1914–15*, pp. 24–40; Bronson Howard, "Our Schools for the Stage," *Century* 61 (Nov. 1900): 28–37.

55. *Dramatic Studies* 2 (Jan. 1899): 3; Marianna McCann, "Two Schools of Acting," *Harper's Weekly* 35 (12 Dec. 1891): 999; Malinauskas, "American Academy," pp. 186–87; *Dramatic Studies* 1 (Oct. 1898): 3.

56. List of graduates at the American Academy of Dramatic Arts, New York City; *NYDM*, 28 May 1887, p. 6; Franklin Sargent to William Seymour, 25 July 1907, William Seymour Papers, William Seymour Theatre Collection, Princeton University.

57. Lawrence Barrett et al., "Success on the Stage," *North American Review* 135 (Dec. 1882): 587, 592, 596.

58. *NYDM*, 4 Nov. 1893, p. 12; ibid., 18 March 1899, p. 14.
59. *Notable American Women*, s.v. Jane Cowl (by Alan S. Downer); *New York Times*, 12 Sept. 1915, pt. 6, p. 3.
60. Bernard Beckerman, "University Accepts the Theatre: 1800–1925," in *The American Theatre: A Sum of Its Parts* (New York: Samuel French, 1971), p. 353; "Relationships between Educational Theatre and Professional Theatre: Actor Training in the United States," *Educational Theatre Journal*, special issue (Nov. 1966): 319–24.
61. *NYDM*, 10 Dec. 1892, p. 5.
62. The original name was Actors' Association of America. It was changed to Actors' Society of America in May 1896.
63. *Actors' Society Monthly Bulletin ASMB* 2 (Jan. 1900): 3; *NYDM*, 1 May 1909, p. 5.
64. Ibid. 3 (Jan. 1901): 2.
65. Ibid. 7 (July 1904): 7; *New York Times*, 25 May 1897, p. 7; *ASMB* 5 (Feb. 1902): 4–5.
66. *NYDM*, 22 Feb. 1896, p. 3; ibid., 16 May 1896, p. 11.
67. Ibid., 28 Nov. 1896, p. 3.
68. Ibid., 2 July 1881, p. 6.
69. Julius Kahn to F. F. Mackay, 5 March 1888, Millicent Reinhold Folder, Cage File, Billy Rose Theatre Collection, NYPLC.
70. *NYDM*, 31 Oct. 1896, p. 12; ibid., 28 Nov. 1896, p. 3.
71. Ibid., 19 Feb. 1898, p. 13.
72. *ASMB* 5 (April 1902): 3; ibid. 6 (July 1903): 2–3.
73. *NYDM*, 5 May 1888, p. 7; *ASMB* 5 (March 1902): 3–4.
74. Craig Timberlake, *The Bishop of Broadway* (New York: Library Publications, 1954), pp. 91–92.
75. William Lawrence Slout, "The Repertoire Tent Show" (PhD diss., UCLA, 1970), pp. 83–87.
76. *NYDM*, 13 June 1903, p. 12.
77. Ibid., 18 Feb. 1888, p. 6; ibid., 31 Dec. 1887, p. 7.
78. Ibid., 24 Dec. 1887, p. 7.
79. Ibid., 22 Feb. 1896, p. 17; ibid., 14 June 1902, p. 12; Gustav Kobbe, *Famous Actresses and Their Homes* (Boston: Little, Brown, 1905), pp. 175–76.
80. Germain Quinn, *Fifty Years Back Stage: Being the Life Story of a Theatrical Stage Mechanic* (Minneapolis: Stage Publishing, 1926), p. 29; *NYDM*, 25 July 1896, p. 2.
81. Lawrence Barrett et al., "Success on the Stage," pp. 594–95.
82. *NYDM*, 6 Feb. 1886, p. 6.
83. *ASMB* 8 (June 1905): 3–4.
84. *NYDM*, 27 Aug. 1898, p. 13; *ASMB* 5 (March 1902): 5.
85. *NYDM*, 25 Jan. 1902, p. 14; ibid., 13 June 1903, p. 12.
86. Ibid., 4 Dec. 1897, p. 14.
87. *ASMB* 5 (March 1902): 5.
88. Everett C. Hughes, *Men and Their Work* (Glencoe, Ill.: The Free Press, 1958), pp. 44–45.

89. George Herbert Palmer, *Trades and Professions* (Boston: Houghton Mifflin, 1914), pp. 32–33.

90. *Brooklyn Times*, 25 June 1892, quoted in *NYDM*, 2 July 1892, p. 4.

CHAPTER FIVE

1. Hornblow, *Training for the Stage*, Lippincott Training Series (Philadelphia: J. B. Lippincott, 1916), p. 25.

2. Quoted in Edwin Duerr, *The Length and Depth of Acting* (New York: Holt, Rinehart and Winston, 1962), p. 202.

3. Quoted in William Wood, *Personal Recollections of the Stage* (Philadelphia: Henry Carey Baird, 1855), p. xviii.

4. David Grimsted, *Melodrama Unveiled* (Chicago: University of Chicago Press, 1968), p. 86.

5. *Scot's Observor* quote in Drew Pallette, "The English Actor's Fight for Respectability," *The Theatre Annual* 7 (1948–49): 27–34; W. J. Reader, *Professional Men* (New York: Basic Books, 1966), p. 148; "Actors and 'Social Status,'" *Saturday Review* 59 (3 January 1885): 8.

6. Arthur Meier Schlesinger, *The Rise of the City* (Chicago: Quadrangle Books, 1971 [1933]), p. 79.

7. Joseph S. Zeisel, "The Workweek in American Industry, 1850–1956," in Eric Larrabee and Rolf Meyersohn, eds., *Mass Leisure* (Glencoe, Ill.: The Free Press, 1958), pp. 146–47. See also Daniel T. Rodgers, *The Work Ethic in Industrial America, 1850–1920* (Chicago: University of Chicago Press, 1978), chap. 4.

8. Foster Rhea Dulles, *America Learns to Play* (New York: Appleton-Century, 1940), pp. 201–2; Frank Luther Mott, *A History of American Magazines*, 5 vols. (Cambridge, Mass.: Belknap Press, 1938–1959), 4:369–82, 633–38.

9. Quoted in Mott, *American Magazines*, 4:369.

10. Dulles, *America Learns to Play*, p. 87.

11. Quoted in Allan Nevins, ed., *American Social History as Recorded by British Travellers* (New York: Henry Holt, 1923), p. 547.

12. Michael M. Davis, Jr., *The Exploitation of Pleasure* (New York: Russell Sage Foundation, 1911), p. 45.

13. Richard Henry Edwards, *Popular Amusements* (New York: Association Press, 1915), pp. 35–36.

14. "Christianity and Amusements: a Symposium," *Everybody's* 10 (May 1904): 695–701.

15. Howard Palmer Young, *Character through Recreation* (Philadelphia: American Sunday-School Union, 1915), p. 286.

16. For a brief survey of changing American attitudes toward amusements see Neil Harris, "Pastimes: From Threat to Therapy," in *American Pastimes*, Catalogue, Brockton Art Center–Fuller Memorial, Brockton, Mass.

17. Edmund Morgan, "Puritan Hostility to the Theatre," *Proceedings of the American Philosophical Society* 110 (27 Oct. 1966): 340–47.

18. Joseph P. Thompson, *Theatrical Amusements* (New York: Baker and

Scribner, 1847), p. 26; for a complete discussion of pre–Civil War clerical attitudes toward the theatre, see Grimsted, *Melodrama Unveiled*, pp. 22–34.

19. Examples are Rev. Herrick Johnson, *Plain Talks about the Theater* (Chicago: F. H. Revell, 1882); Josiah Leeds, *The Theatre* (Philadelphia: published for the author, 1884); J. M. Buckley, *Christians and the Theatre* (New York: Hart & Eaton, 1875); Rev. Perry Wayland Sinks, *Popular Amusements and the Christian Life* (Chicago: The Bible Institute Colportage Association, 1896).

20. Ellen G. White, *Testimonies for the Church*, 9 vols. (Mountain View, Calif.: Pacific Press, 1948), 4:652–53.

21. Buckley, *Christians and the Theatre*, p. 103.

22. Charles Booth Parsons, *The Pulpit and the Stage* (Nashville: Southern Methodist Publications, 1860), pp. 142–43.

23. Johnson, *Plain Talks*, p. 18.

24. Sinks, *Popular Amusements*, p. 79.

25. Louis Verneuil, *The Fabulous Life of Sarah Bernhardt*, trans. Ernest Boyd (New York: Harper, 1942), pp. 130–32.

26. *NYDM*, 9 March 1907, p. 14.

27. Ibid., 19 April 1890, p. 2.

28. Ibid.

29. "The Methodist Church and Amusements," *Outlook* 89 (2 March 1889): 9–10.

30. Frederick Warde, *Fifty Years of Make-Believe* (New York: International Press Syndicate, 1920), pp. 228–29.

31. "The Church and the Theatre," *Harper's Weekly* 48 (11 June 1904): 894.

32. Quoted in "The Methodist Amusement Ban," *Literary Digest* 44 (June 1912): 1260.

33. Ibid.; *New York Times*, 28 Nov. 1920, p. 20.

34. *Doctrines and Discipline of the Methodist Episcopal Church, 1924* (New York: The Methodist Book Concern, 1924), p. 280.

35. For a good discussion of liberal Protestant attitudes toward entertainment see Albert F. McLean, Jr., *American Vaudeville as Ritual* (Lexington: University of Kentucky Press, 1965), pp. 70–82.

36. *NYDM*, 27 June 1891, p. 8.

37. Washington Gladden, "Christianity and Popular Amusements," *Century* 29 (Jan. 1885): 388.

38. Alexander V. G. Allen, *Life and Letters of Phillips Brooks*, 2 vols. (New York: E. P. Dutton, 1900), 2: 560.

39. Otto Peltzer, "A Powerful Factor of Practical Christian Reform," *The Theatre* 4 (13 Feb. 1888): 56; Otto Peltzer, *The Moralist and the Theatre* (Chicago: Donald Fraser,1887), pp. 82–89.

40. Rev. Charles M. Sheldon, "Is a Christian Theater Possible?" *Independent* 53 (14 March 1901): 618.

41. *NYDM*, 7 July 1894, p. 5.

42. Ibid., 11 April 1896, p. 15.

43. *New York Telegraph*, 21 Aug. 1910, in Robinson Locke Collection, vol. 329, Billy Rose Theatre Collection, NYPLC.

44. *Variety*, 23 March 1917, p. 11.
45. Edward Wagenknecht, *Merely Players* (Norman: University of Oklahoma Press, 1966), pp. 206, 231; William Winter, *Other Days* (New York: Moffat, Yard, 1908), pp. 80, 195–96.
46. *NYDM*, 19 Feb. 1881, p. 6.
47. On the English organization, the Actors' Church Union, see Donald Hole, *The Church and the Stage* (London: The Faith Press, 1934), pp. 1–22; Pallette, "English Actor's Fight."
48. *NYDM*, 1 July 1899, p. 14; Magda West, "The Actors' Church Alliance," *Green Book Album* 1 (May 1909): 1016–20; George Wolfe Shinn, "The Actors' Church Alliance," *Arena* 28 (July 1902): 15–22.
49. Shinn, "Church Alliance," pp. 15–22; *NYDM*, 14 June 1902, p. 12.
50. *New York Times*, 19 Feb. 1900, p. 7; Shinn, "Church Alliance," pp. 15–22.
51. Rev. Walter Bentley, "The Coming Relation of Church and Stage," *The Theatre* 5 (Feb. 1905): 48–49.
52. Ibid.
53. *New York Times*, 16 Nov. 1902, p. 27.
54. Harold Frederic, *The Damnation of Theron Ware* (New York: Holt, Rinehart and Winston, 1958 [1896]).
55. Cleveland Amory, *Who Killed Society?* (New York: Harper, 1960), pp. 111–12; *NYDM*, 3 Feb. 1894, p. 7.
56. On the social status of English actors see Michael Baker, *The Rise of the Victorian Actor* (London: Croom Helm, 1978), pp. 86–94.
57. Edwin Booth to David Anderson, 9 Jan. 1881, Edwin Booth Papers, The Players Library.
58. W. H. Darlington, *The Actor and His Audience* (London: Phoenix House, 1949), p. 128.
59. *The Theatre* 4 (17 Nov. 1888): 413–14.
60. *NYDM*, 17 Nov. 1888, p. 10.
61. Parker Morell, *Lillian Russell: The Era of the Plush* (New York: Random House, 1940), p. 121.
62. Cornelia Otis Skinner, *Madame Sarah* (Boston: Houghton Mifflin, 1966), pp. 161–66; *NYDM*, 30 Oct. 1880, p. 6.
63. Edith Wharton, *The Age of Innocence* (New York: Charles Scribner's, 1968), pp. 102–3.
64. Neil Harris, ed., *The Land of Contrasts* (New York: George Braziller, 1970), pp. 17–19; Frederic Cople Jaher, "Style and Status: High Society in Late Nineteenth-Century New York," in *The Rich, The Well Born, and The Powerful*, ed. Frederic Cople Jaher (Urbana: University of Illinois Press, 1973), pp. 260–63.
65. *The Theatre* 3 May 1886, pp. 187–88.
66. Lewis A. Erenberg, *Steppin' Out* (Westport, Conn.: Greenwood Press, 1981), chap. 2; Jaher, "Style and Status," pp. 273–74.
67. Lawrence Reamer, "The Actors in Society," *Ladies' Home Journal* (7 Feb. 1901), in clipping file, Theater Collection, NYPLC; Burr McIntosh, "Actresses at Leisure," *Cosmopolitan* 31 (Oct. 1901): 591.
68. Kotsilibas-Davis, *Great Times Good Times* (Garden City, N.Y.: Double-

day, 1977), pp. 95–96; Philip Fordrall, "Following the Stars," *Green Book Album* 1 (Feb. 1909): 335; Ethel Barrymore, *Memories: An Autobiography* (New York: Harper, 1955), pp. 51–68 passim.

69. Elizabeth Hiatt Gregory, "From the Stage to Society," *The Theatre* 25 (March 1917): 156; Helen Ten Broeck, "Society and the Stage," *The Theatre* 31 (May 1920): 406, 476; Eleanor Robson Belmont, *The Fabric of Memory* (New York: Farrar, Straus and Cudany, 1957), pp. 65–148 passim.

It should be pointed out that society's acceptance of actresses who married into its ranks did not extend to its own daughters who married "down" to an actor. Katherine Harris's name was dropped from the *Social Register* when she married John Barrymore in 1910. Another of Barrymore's wives, Blanch Oelrichs, was similarly purged from the social canon in 1920. Both regained their standing upon divorcing the famous Hamlet of the hundred nights (Dixon Wector, *The Saga of American Society* [New York: Charles Scribner's, 1937], pp. 235–36).

70. Marguerita Arlina Hamm, *Eminent Actors in Their Homes* (New York: James Pott, 1909), pp. 5–6.

71. Quoted in Jaher, "Style and Status," p. 274.

72. Helen L. Horowitz, *Culture and the City* (Lexington: University of Kentucky Press, 1976); Neil Harris, "Four Stages of Cultural Growth: The American City," *Indiana Historical Society Lectures, 1971–1972* (Indianapolis: Indiana Historical Society, 1972), pp. 35–39.

73. Cleveland Amory, *Who Killed Society?* (New York: Harper, 1960), pp. 107–44 passim; Allen Churchill, *The Upper Crust* (Englewood Cliffs, N.J.: Prentice-Hall, 1970), pp. 217–20.

74. Erving Goffman, "Symbols of Class Status," *British Journal of Sociology* 2 (1951): 294–304.

CHAPTER SIX

1. Frank Luther Mott, *A History of American Magazines*, 5 vols. (Cambridge, Mass.: Belknap Press, 1938–1959), 4: 2–11; Neil Harris, ed., *The Land of Contrasts* (New York: George Braziller, 1970), p. 6; Neil Harris, "Iconography and Intellectual History: The Half-Tone Effect," in *New Directions In American Intellectual History*, ed. John Higham and Paul K. Conkin, editors (Baltimore: The Johns Hopkins University Press, 1979), pp. 196–209.

2. The *Reader's Guide To Periodical Literature* lists 63 articles on "actors and actresses" for 1900–1904, 96 for 1905–9, and 61 for 1910–14.

3. *NYDM*, 11 Jan. 1879, p. 4; ibid., 20 April 1889, p. 2.

4. William H. Crane, *Footprints and Echoes* (New York: E. P. Dutton, 1925), pp. 173–74.

5. *NYDM*, 11 Jan. 1879, p. 4.

6. John Ten Eyck, "Mr. Ten Eyck Calls on Miss Clark," *Green Book Magazine* 11 (March 1914): 395.

7. Alan Dale, "Acting off the Stage,"*Cosmopolitan* 45 (July 1908): 172–74; *NYDM*, 22 March 1890, p. 2.

8. *NYDM*, 4 Sept. 1912, p. 16; ibid., 16 Oct. 1912, p. 13; Channing Pollock, *Harvest of My Years*, pp. 48–89.

9. Albert E. Johnson and W. H. Crain, comps., "Dictionary of American Drama Critics, 1850–1920," *Theatre Annual* 13 (1955): 65–67; *NYDM*, 22 Feb. 1890, p. 2.

10. Michael Baker makes a similar point about the English theatre in this regard in his *Rise of the Victorian Actor* (London: Croom Helm, 1978), pp. 164–68.

11. William Winter, *The Actor* (New York: Burt Franklin, 1891), pp. 1–25.

12. Tice L. Miller, "John Ranken Towse: Last of the Victorian Critics," *Educational Theatre Journal* 22 (May 1970): 161–78.

13. For examples of all of the above critics' work, see Montrose Moses and John Mason Brown, eds., *The American Theatre as Seen by Its Critics* (New York: W. W. Norton, 1934).

14. Quoted in Tice L. Miller, "Alan Dale: The Hearst Critic," *Educational Theatre Journal* 26 (March 1974): 73.

15. Ibid., p. 71.

16. Richard Ludwig, "The Career of William Winter, American Drama Critic: 1836–1917" (PhD diss., Harvard University, 1950), pp. 166–67.

17. *The Theatre* 2 (24 Jan. 1887): 346.

18. John Emerson to Charles Bregg, 19 March 1908, Bregg Correspondence, Cage File, Billy Rose Theatre Collection, NYPLC.

19. Examples of photo albums are *Galérie théâtricale* (Paris: Bance, 1842); Howard Paul and George Beggie, *The Stage and Its Stars* (Philadelphia: Gebbie, n.d.); A. D. Storms, comp., *The Players Blue Book* (Worcester, Mass.: Sutherland & Storms, 1901); *The American Stage of To-Day* (New York: P. E. Collier, 1910); *The Marie Burroughs Art Portfolio of Stage Celebrities* (Chicago: A. N. Marquis, 1894).

20. *NYDM*, 1 Feb. 1908, p. 2.

21. *Stage Favorites* (New York: Will Rossiter, 1902); Ralph Stein, *The Pin-Up: From 1852 till Now* (Ridge Press/Chartwell Books, 1974), p. 61.

22. One example is John Joseph Jennings, *Theatrical and Circus Life* (St. Louis: M. S. Barnett, 1882).

23. *NYDM*, 2 June 1915, p. 9.

24. Ibid., 5 Sept. 1903, p. 15; George Kneeland, *Commercialized Prostitution in New York City* (New York: Century, 1913), pp. 102–3.

25. Robert Grau, *The Business Man in the Amusement World* (New York: Broadway Publishing, 1910), pp. 233–34; Daniel Watermeier, ed., *Between Actor and Critic* (Princeton: Princeton University Press, 1971), p. 160; *NYDM*, 22 Feb. 1879, p. 5; Frank Luther Mott, *A History of American Magazines*, 5 vols. (Cambridge, Mass.: Belknap Press, 1938–59), 3: 198–99; Byrne immediately started a new paper, the *Dramatic Times*.

26. *New York Herald*, 20 Nov. 1906, Brooks McNamara Collection of Dramatic Scrapbooks, New York City.

27. *NYDM*, 15 Oct. 1887, p. 7.
28. Kate Rankin to Clinton Stuart, 15 April 1881, Malone Papers, NYPL.
29. *New York Herald*, 28 Sept. 1902, McNamara Collection; ibid., 26 July 1912, McNamara Collection; unidentified clipping, 4 Feb. 1910, McNamara Collection.
30. *NYDM*, 11 June 1904, p. 11; ibid., 26 Nov. 1904, p. 12.
31. Ibid., 15 Jan. 1881, p. 2; ibid., 3 Sept. 1913, p. 8; ibid., 5 March 1881, p. 2.
32. Don R. Pember, *Privacy and the Press* (Seattle: University of Washington Press, 1972), pp. 8–14; Frank Luther Mott, *American Journalism* (New York: Macmillan, 1941), pp. 441–44.
33. E. L. Godkin, "The Rights of the Citizen—IV: To His Own Reputation," *Scribner's* 8 (July 1890): 65–67.
34. John Gilmer Speed, "The Rights of Privacy," *North American Review* 163 (July 1896): 64.
35. Samuel D. Warren and Louis Brandeis, "The Right to Privacy," *Harvard Law Review* 4 (15 Dec. 1890): 193–220.
36. Ibid., p. 195.
37. *NYDM*, 7 Aug. 1880, p. 6.
38. Ibid., 22 Dec. 1888, p. 10.
39. *The Theatre* 1 (26 April 1886): 157.
40. Speed, "Rights of Privacy," p. 68.
41. *New York Times* 15 June 1890, p. 2; ibid., 18 June 1890, p. 3; ibid., 21 June 1890, p. 2.
42. Pember, *Privacy*, pp. 60–61.
43. Samuel H. Wandell, *The Law of the Theatre* (Albany: James B. Lyon, 1891); J. Albert Brackett, *Theatrical Law* (Boston: C. M. Clark, 1907).
44. David Riesman's *The Lonely Crowd* (New Haven: Yale University Press, 1950) and Daniel Bell's *The Cultural Contradictions of Capitalism* (New York: Basic Books, 1976) have made important statements on this problem.
45. The best discussion of celebrity is found in Daniel Boorstin, *The Image. A Guide to Pseudo-Events in America* (New York: Harper & Row, 1961), chap. 2.
46. *New York Times*, 26 May 1913, p. 6.
47. Craig Timberlake, *The Bishop of Broadway* (New York: Library Publications, 1954), p. 352.
48. *NYDM*, 29 May 1880, p. 6.
49. Leon Meyer, "The Actor and the Absent Voter's Law," *Equity* 3 (July 1918): 3.
50. Earl See, "The Political Image of American Actors, 1865–1920," (PhD diss., University of Missouri, 1974), pp. 223–28.
51. *NYDM*, 29 May 1880, p. 6.
52. Edwin Booth to David Anderson, 20 March 1880, Booth Papers, The Players Library.
53. See, "Political Image," pp. 238–39.
54. Lotta Crabtree's Will, Seymour Papers, Princeton Univ., Diana Belais to Dudley Digges, 23 Dec. 1911, Dudley Digges Papers, NYPL.

55. Israel Zangwill, "Actress Versus Suffraget," *Independent* 67 (2 Dec. 1909): 1248–50.

56. *Notable American Women*, s.v. Logan, Olive (by Albert E. Johnson).

57. See, "Political Image," pp. 124–37; *New York Times*, 28 Sept. 1915, p. 11; Marian Strohman, "Actresses and Woman Suffrage," *Green Book Album* 1 (April 1909): 817–21.

58. Gene Adam Saracen, "Herne and the Single Tax: An Early Plea for an Actor's Union," *Educational Theatre Journal* 26 (Oct. 1974): 315–18.

59. Ibid., pp. 318–23; see "Political Image;" p. 112.

60. Joan Bennet and Lois Kibbe, *The Bennett Playbills* (New York: Holt, Rinehart and Winston, 1970), pp. 41–51; Edward L. Bernays, *Biography of an Idea* (New York: Simon and Schuster, 1965), pp. 53–62.

61. See, "Political Image," pp. 185–88.

62. Ibid., pp. 189–98.

63. Gustav Kobbe, *Famous Actors and Actresses and Their Homes*, (Boston: Little, Brown, 1903), p. 4.

64. John Drew, "The Actor" *Scribner's* 15 (Jan. 1894): 40.

65. "The Actor at Leisure," *Equity* 5 (July 1920) : 14–15.

66. *New York Times*, 7 Jan. 1912, pt. 7, p. 7.

67. *ASMB* 3 (Feb. 1901): 3.

68. Quoted in Toby Cole, ed., *Actors on Acting* (New York: Crown Publisher, 1970), pp. 569–70.

69. Idah McGlone, "Temper and Temperament of the Actor," *Green Book Album* 5 (Jan. 1911): 214.

70. *NYDM*, 2 Jan. 1892, p. 8.

71. Henry De Halsalle, "The Actor: the Man, and His Art," *Contemporary Review* 91 (May 1907): 357–59.

72. S. H. Clark, "Elocution and Psychology," *Werner's* 18 (March 1896): 209.

73. Hartley Davis, "Whom the Stage Demoralizes," *Munsey's* 25 (April 1901): 86–91.

74. *New York Times*, 22 June 1884, p. 6.

75. *The Theatre* 4 (27 Feb. 1888): 83.

76. *NYDM* 4 Feb. 1888, p. 3; ibid., 7 Jan. 1888, p. 3.

77. Albert Parry gives a delightful account of American Bohemianism in *Garrets and Pretenders* (New York: Covici-Friede Publishers, 1933), esp. pp. 7–62 passim; on the French background see Cesar Graña, *Bohemian versus Bourgeois* (New York: Basic Books, 1964), pp. 16–27, 71–82; "What Is Bohemianism?" *Overland Monthly* 1 (Nov. 1868): 425.

78. John Higham, "American Culture in the 1890's," in *Writing American History* (Bloomington: Indiana University Press, 1970), pp. 73–102; T. J. Jackson Lears makes a similar argument about the age in *No Place of Grace: Antimodernism and the Transformation of American Culture, 1880–1920* (New York: Pantheon Books, 1981), pp. 4–5.

79. Higham, "American Culture," pp. 78–81; John Kasson, *Amusing the Million*, American Century Series (New York: Hill & Wang, 1978), pp. 6–9; Charles E. Funnell, *By the Beautiful Sea* (New York: Alfred A. Knopf, 1975).

80. Larzer Ziff, *The American 1890's* (New York: Viking Press, 1966); Christopher Lasch, *The New Radicalism in America, 1889–1963* (New York: Vintage Books, 1965), pp. 62–64.
81. Higham, "American Culture," p. 79.
82. Ibid.
83. Edwin P. Irwin, "In Quest of Bohemia," *Overland Monthly* 48 (Aug. 1906): 91.
84. Parry, *Garrets*, pp. 102, 92–106.
85. William Dean Howells, *The Coast of Bohemia* (New York: Harper, 1893).
86. Parry, *Garrets*, pp. 159–62.
87. On this point see Daniel Bell, *The Cultural Contradictions of Capitalism*, esp. pp. 54–76.
88. Studies include John Higham's aforementioned article, John Kasson's *Amusing the Million* (1978), Lary May's *Screening Out the Past* (1980), Lewis Erenberg's *Steppin' Out* (1981), Jackson Lears' *No Place of Grace* (1981), and Paula Fass's *Damned and the Beautiful* (1977). Books dealing with this change have often focused on forms of amusement. More than other facets of life, entertainment has become a key for analyzing twentieth-century culture.
89. Fass, *The Damned*, p. 292. In the ongoing historiographical battle over whether to bury Victorianism in the pre–World War I years or in the 1920s, Paula Fass clearly favors the latter, seeing the twenties' college students as the vanguard of modernism. James R. McGovern in "The American Woman's Pre–World War I Freedom in Manners and Morals," *Journal of American History* 55 (Sept. 1968): 315–333, argues for the earlier date. Ultimately historians will see this dichotomy as false.
90. Ronald Taft, "A Psychological Assessment of Professional Actors and Related Occupations," *Genetic Psychology Monographs* 64 (1961): 324–25.
91. In certain regards the demand for freedom was very real, for example, the movement for women's equality. But the very intensity of the struggle indicated the reluctance of society to accept sweeping change.
92. Roger Caillois, *Man, Play and Games* (New York: Schoken Books, 1979), p. 121.
93. Ibid., p. 122.
94. Francis Hackett, "The Actor's Dilemma," *New Republic* 3 (15 May 1915): 46.
95. Jean Duvignaud, *L'Acteur* (Paris: Gallimard, 1965), p. 22.

CHAPTER SEVEN

1. Alan S. Downer, "Players and Painted Stage," *PMLA* 61 (1946): 528.
2. Garff Wilson, *A History of American Acting* (Bloomington: University of Indiana Press, 1966), pp. 41–95, 206–19.
3. Ibid., pp. 22–23.

4. *Hamlet*, III, ii; Donald C. Mullin, "Methods and Manners of Traditional Acting," *Educational Theatre Journal* 27 (March 1975): 6–7.
5. Willa Siebert Cather, "New Types of Acting," *McClure's* 42 (Feb. 1914): 44.
6. George H. Lewes, *On Actors and the Art of Acting* (London: Smith, Elder, 1875), p. 125.
7. Mullin, "Methods and Manners," pp. 5–22; Downer, "Players," pp. 574–75.
8. *The Art of Acting, or, Guide to the Stage* (New York: Samuel French, 1850–), p. 16.
9. Quoted in Downer, "Players," p. 575.
10. E. J. West, "The London Stage, 1870–1890: A Study in the Conflict of the Old and New Schools of Acting," *University of Colorado Studies*, ser. B, Studies in the Humanities, vol. 2, no. 1 (May 1943): 73.
11. Quoted in Edwin Duerr, *The Length and Depth of Acting* (New York: Holt, Rinehart and Winston, 1962), p. 380.
12. West, "London Stage," pp. 31–55.
13. Lewes, *On Actors*, pp. 116, 147.
14. Quoted in West, "London Stage," pp. 62–63.
15. Joseph Frobisher, *Acting and Oratory* (New York: College of Oratory and Acting, 1879), p. 392.
16. Two examples among many are Milton Nobles, *Shop Talk* (Milwaukee: Riverside Printing, 1889), pp. 7–8, and J. H. Barnes, "The Drama of To-day and the Public's Attitudes Thereto," *The Living Age* 250 (7 March 1908): 601–5.
17. On Herne see Herbert J. Edwards and Julie A. Herne, *James A. Herne: The Rise of Realism in the American Drama*, University of Maine Studies, 2d ser., no. 84 (Orono: University of Maine Press, 1964).
18. Quoted in Edwards and Herne, *James A. Herne*, p. 103.
19. Ibid., pp. 129–130.
20. *Dictionary of American Biography*, s.v. William Gillette (by William Van Lennep), supp. 2, pp. 235–36.
21. H. Dennis Sherk, "William Gillette: His Life and Works" (PhD diss., Pennsylvania State University, 1961), pp. 197–99; Norman Hapgood, *The Stage in America, 1897–1900* (New York: Macmillan, 1901), p. 70.
22. William H. Gillette, *The Illusion of the First Time in Acting* (New York: Dramatic Museum of Columbia University, 1915), p. 115.
23. Quoted in Sherk, "William Gillette," pp. 197–99.
24. Wilson, *History of American Acting*, p. 224.
25. Elizabeth Lindsay Neill, "The Art of Minnie Maddern Fiske: A Study of Her Realistic Acting" (PhD diss., Tufts University, 1970), pp. 34–50, 68, 248; Lewis Strang, *Players and Plays of the Last Quarter Century*, 2 vols. (Boston: L. C. Page, 1902), 2:295–96; Wilson, *History of American Acting*, pp. 225–27.
26. Chester T. Calder, "Mrs. Fiske—Our Intellectual Actress," *The Theatre* 17 (June 1913): 182–84.

27. Quoted in Neill, "Minnie Maddern Fiske," pp. 243 and 12.
28. Quoted in Wilson, *History of American Acting*, p. 230.
29. Carlotta Nillson, "Realism as the Standard of Modern Acting," *The Theatre* 6 (Dec. 1906): 324.
30. Brander Matthews, *On Acting* (New York: Charles Scribner's Sons, 1914), pp. 89–90.
31. Warner Berthoff, *The Ferment of Realism* (New York: The Free Press, 1965), p. 1.
32. Quoted in ibid., p. 51.
33. Robert Bremner, *From the Depths: The Discovery of Poverty in the United States* (New York: New York University Press, 1956), pp. 186–91.
34. Morton White, *Social Thought in America*, 2nd ed. (Boston: Beacon Press, 1957), pp. 1–12.
35. Giles Wilkeson Gray, "Some Teachers and the Transition to Twentieth-Century Speech Education," in Karl Wallace, ed., *History of Speech Education in America* (New York: Appleton-Century-Crofts, 1954), pp. 430–32; S. H. Clark, "Elocution and Psychology," *Werner's* 13 (March 1896): 205.
36. Mary Margaret Robb, "The Elocutionary Movement and Its Chief Figures," in Wallace, ed., *History of Speech Education*, pp. 193–94.
37. Samuel Silas Curry, *The Province of Expression* (Boston: School of Expression, 1891), p. 350.
38. Ibid., pp. 40, 133.
39. Robb, "Elocutionary Movement," p. 196.
40. Ibid., pp. 196–97.
41. Curry, *Province*, pp. 188–92, 200.
42. Christine Edwards, *The Stanislavsky Heritage* (New York: New York University Press, 1965), pp. 158–59.
43. Nathan G. Hale, Jr., *Freud and the Americans* (New York: Oxford University Press, 1971), pp. 98–115; Henri Ellenberger, *The Discovery of the Unconscious* (New York: Basic Books, 1970), p. 277; H. Stuart Hughes, *Consciousness and Society* (New York: Alfred A. Knopf, 1958), p. 105; see also Donald Meyer, *The Positive Thinkers* (Garden City, N.Y.: Doubleday Anchor Book, 1966).
44. L. Edward Purcell, "Trilby and Trilby-Mania," *Journal of Popular Culture* 11 (Summer 1977): 62–75.
45. Walter Prichard Eaton, "Dramatic Fashions," *Green Book Album*, 1910, in Robinson Locke Collection, vol. 148, Billy Rose Theatre Collection, NYPLC.
46. Michael Goldman, *The Actor's Freedom* (New York: Viking Press, 1975), p. 102; Yeats quoted in ibid.
47. Alfred Emmet, "Head or Heart: The Actor's Dilemma," *Theatre Quarterly* 5 (June-Aug. 1975): 15–21; Edwards, *Stanislavsky*, p. 130.
48. William Archer, *Masks or Faces? A Study in the Psychology of Acting* (New York: Hill & Wang Dramabook, 1957), p. 191.
49. Quoted in Clark, "Elocution," p. 208.
50. Curry, *Province*, pp. 123–33.
51. *New York Times*, 2 April 1908, pt. 4, p. 4; *NYDM*, 18 Jan. 1911, p. 3.

52. Alan Dale, "Stage Folk Merely Puppets," *Cosmopolitan* 43 (June 1907): 198.
53. William Collier, "Personality, the Thing You've Got to Have," *Green Book Album* 7 (March 1912): 652–59; George W. Lederer, "What You Need to Score a Hit," *Green Book Magazine* 8 (Dec. 1912): 953–59.
54. Walter Prichard Eaton, *Plays and Players* (Cincinnati: Stewart & Kidd, 1916), p. 388.
55. Lewis Strang, *Famous Actors of the Day in America* (Boston: L. C. Page, 1899), pp. 86–87.
56. Quoted in John Drew, *My Years on the Stage* (New York: E. P. Dutton, 1922), p. vii.
57. Curry, *Province*, pp. 45, 64–67.
58. *New York Times*, 1 Nov. 1914, pt. 4, p. 8 (interview with William Gillette).
59. Gillette, *Illusion*, p. 45.
60. Ibid., pp. 45–47.
61. Eaton, *Plays and Players*, pp. 381–82; Walter Prichard Eaton, "Some Popular Errors in the Judgment of Acting," *American Magazine* 70 (July 1910): 408–14.
62. *New York Times*, 8 Oct. 1905, pt. 3, p. 9.
63. Ibid., 1 Nov. 1914, pt. 4, p. 8.
64. William Winter, *The Wallet of Time*, 2 vols. (New York: Moffat, Yard, 1913), 1:173, 176.
65. Quoted in Richard Moody, *Edwin Forrest: First Star of the American Stage* (New York: Alfred A. Knopf, 1960), p. 398.
66. Mullin, "Methods and Manners," p. 7.
67. Robert E. Park, "The City: Suggestions for the Investigations of Human Behavior in the City Environment," *American Journal of Sociology* 20 (March 1915): 608.
68. Warren Susman, "'Personality' and the Making of Twentieth Century Culture," in John Higham and Paul K. Conkin, eds., *New Directions in American Intellectual History* (Baltimore: The Johns Hopkins University Press, 1979), pp. 212–25.
69. Ada Patterson, "The Inner Life of the Actress," *The Theatre* 22 (July 1915): 21.
70. Elizabeth M. Gilmer, "The Art of Wooing" *Cosmopolitan* 38 (Feb. 1905): 441–47.
71. See especially Erving Goffman, *The Presentation of the Self in Everyday Life* (Garden City, N.Y.: Doubleday Anchor Books, 1959).
72. Philip Rieff, *The Triumph of the Therapeutic* (New York: Harper & Row, 1966), pp. 14–25.
73. Richard Sennett, *The Fall of Public Man* (New York: Vintage Books, 1978); Christopher Lasch, *The Culture of Narcissism* (New York: W. W. Norton, 1979).

CHAPTER EIGHT

1. On the history of movies see Lewis Jacobs, *The Rise of the American Film* (New York: Teachers College Press, 1939); Benjamin B. Hamp-

ton, *History of the American Film from Its Beginnings to 1931* (New York: Dover Publications, 1970); Robert Sklar, *Movie-Made America* (New York: Random House, 1975); Edward Wagenknecht, *The Movies in the Age of Innocence* (Norman: University of Oklahoma Press, 1962); Garth Jowett, *Film: The Democratic Art* (Boston: Little, Brown, 1976); Lary May, *Screening out the Past* (New York: Oxford University Press, 1980).

2. Mary Anderson deNavarro, *A Few Memories* (New York: Harper, 1896), pp. 89–90.

3. Kalton C. Lahue, ed., *Motion Picture Pioneers* (South Brunswick and New York: A. S. Barnes, 1973), pp. 77–79.

4. Mrs. D. W. Griffith, *When the Movies Were Young* (1925; repr. ed. New York: Benjamin Blom, 1968), pp. 29–31, 53–54.

5. Ibid., pp. 108–14; Robert Windeler, *Sweetheart: The Story of Mary Pickford* (London: W. H. Allen, 1973), p. 42.

6. Frances Agnew, *Motion Picture Acting* (New York: Reliance Newspaper Syndicate, 1913), pp. 62–63.

7. Walter Prichard Eaton, "Actor-snatching and the Movies," *American Magazine*, 80 (Dec. 1915): 34, Robinson Locke Collection, NYPLC.

8. Alexander Walker, *Stardom* (London: Michael Joseph, 1970), p. 27; Anthony Slide, *The Big V: A History of the Vitagraph Company* (Metuchen, N.J.: The Scarecrow Press, 1976), pp. 34–36.

9. Gerald D. McDonald, "Origins of the Star System," *Films in Review* 4 (Nov. 1953): 449–58; Walker, *Stardom*, pp. 31–34; Slide, *The Big V*, pp. 34–36.

10. Mary Pickford, Reminiscences, ser. 4, vol. 1, pt. 2, Oral History Collection, Columbia University, p. 2720; Catherine Hayes Brown, *Letters to Mary* (New York: Random House, 1940), pp. 125–26.

11. Verne Hardin Porter, "It's like the Rush after a 'Strike' of Gold," *Green Book Magazine* 12 (Nov. 1914): 824–25.

12. McDonald, "Star System," pp. 452–58; Mrs. Griffith, *When the Movies Were Young*, p. 209.

13. Jacobs, *American Film*, p. 91.

14. George Arliss, *My Ten Years in the Studios* (Boston: Little, Brown, 1940), pp. 9–10.

15. Kalton C. Lahue, *Dreams for Sale* (South Brunswick and New York: A. S. Barnes, 1971), pp. 73, 134; DeWolf Hopper, *Once a Clown, Always a Clown* (Boston: Little, Brown, 1927), p. 141.

16. Ada Patterson, "Mr. Sothern in the Movies," *The Theatre* 24 (Nov. 1916): 292.

17. Pauline Frederick, "Why I Forsook the Stage for the Screen," *The Theatre* 22 (Nov. 1915): 237.

18. *Macbeth*, V, v; *New York Times*, 30 Jan. 1916, pt. 2, p. 8.

19. M. Michelson, "Immortality in the Films," *Collier's* 51 (12 April 1913): 11.

20. *Variety*, 16 July 1915, p. 10; David Belasco, *The Theatre Through Its Stage Door*, (New York: Harper, 1919), p. 213.

21. Robert McLaughlin, *Broadway and Hollywood* (New York: Arno Press,

1974), pp. 41–42; *New York Times*, 13 July 1915, p. 11; ibid., 18 July 1915, p. 18; ibid., 1 Aug. 1915, pt. 6, p. 2.

22. *Variety*, 14 April 1916, p. 19.
23. Ibid., 11 July 1919, p. 3.
24. *NYDM*, 20 Jan. 1915, p. 4.
25. Ashton Stevens, *Actorviews* (Chicago: Covici-McGee, 1923), p. 162.
26. Rufus Steele, "The New Rialto," *Sunset* 34 (May 1915): 899–908; Paul Hubert Conlon, "Los Angeles Rialto a Rival Broadway," *The Theatre* 24 (Aug. 1916): 86; "In the Capital of Movie-Land," *Literary Digest* 55 (10 Nov. 1917): 82–89.
27. "In the Capital of Movie-Land," pp. 82–89; William C. de Mille, *Hollywood Saga* (New York: E. P. Dutton, 1939), pp. 77, 97–98; Charlton Lawrence Edholm, "In Filmland by the Pacific," *Technical World Magazine* 19 (Aug. 1913): 907–10.
28. "In the Capital of Movie-Land," pp. 82–86.
29. "An Apostle of Comstockery Finds that Motion Picture Studio-Life Has Been Slandered," *Current Opinion* 63 (Nov. 1917): 318.
30. Charles F. Dole, "What Shall We Do with the Millionaire?" *New England Magazine* 3 (Nov. 1890): 432–34; E. L. Godkin, "The Expenditure of Rich Men," *Scribner's Magazine* 20 (Oct. 1896): 495–501.
31. George Ade, "Answering Wild-Eyed Questions About the Movie Stars at Hollywood," *American Magazine* 93 (May 1922): 52–53, 76–82; Margaret Thorp, *America at the Movies* (New Haven: Yale University Press, 1939), p. 69.
32. Pickford, Reminiscences, pp. 2697–98.
33. Jean Bernique, *Motion Picture Acting for Professionals and Amateurs* (Producers Service, 1916); John Emerson and Anita Loos, *Breaking into the Movies* (New York: James A. McCann, 1921), p. 10; Inez Klumph and Helen Klumph, *Screen Acting, Its Requirements and Rewards* (New York: Falk Publishing, 1922), pp. 103–5.
34. Richard Savage, "Trying Out for the Movies," *The Theatre* 23 (Feb. 1916): 75.
35. William H. Crane, *Footprints and Echoes* (New York: E. P. Dutton, 1925), p. 218.
36. Otis Skinner, "The Celluloid Drama," *Journal of the National Institute of Social Sciences* 7 (1 Aug. 1921): 62–64.
37. Porter, "It's like the Rush," p. 825.
38. Anna Steele Richardson, "'Filmitis,' the Modern Malady—Its Symptoms and Its Cure," *McClure's* 46 (Jan. 1916): 14; Lahue, *Dreams for Sale*, pp. 73–74.
39. Lahue, *Dreams for Sale*, pp. 134–35.
40. *Variety*, 15 Sept. 1916, p. 11.
41. Lahue, *Dreams for Sale*, pp. 82–84.
42. Pickford, Reminiscences, p. 2681; Walker, *Stardom*, pp. 45–47.
43. Richard Griffith and Arthur Mayer, *The Movies* (New York: Simon and Schuster, 1957), p. 54.
44. Richardson, "'Filmitis,'" pp. 12–14, 70; Griffith and Mayer, *The Movies*, pp. 55.

45. Garff Wilson, *A History of American Acting* (Bloomington: University of Indiana Press, 1966), p. 270.

46. Griffith and Mayer, *The Movies*, p. 54; Geraldine Farrar, *Such Sweet Compulsion: The Autobiography of Geraldine Farrar* (1938; repr. ed. Freeport, N.Y.: Books for Libraries Press, 1970), pp. 165–66.

47. Katherine Fullerton Gerould, "Hollywood: An American State of Mind," *Harper's* 146 (May 1923): 689–96; Robert Grau, "From $15 a Day to $100,000 a Year," *American Magazine* 82 (Aug. 1916): 52–53; Klumph and Klumph, *Screen Acting*, pp. 7–10; Harry T. Brundidge, *Twinkle, Twinkle Movie Star* (New York: E. P. Dutton, 1930), p. 3.

48. Agnew, *Motion Picture Acting*, p. 31; Klumph and Klumph, *Screen Acting*, p. 32.

49. Ernest Lindgren, *The Art of the Film* (New York: Macmillan, 1963), pp. 156–57; Siegfried Kracauer, *Theory of Film* (New York: Oxford University Press, 1960), pp. 93–95; Arliss quoted in Lindgren, *Art of the Film*, p. 156.

50. Vachel Lindsay, *The Art of the Moving Pictures* (New York: Macmillan, 1916), pp. 27–28.

51. Emerson and Loos, *Breaking into the Movies*, p. 10.

52. Warrer Susman, "'Personality,'" p. 22.

53. Quoted in Montrose Moses, *The American Dramatist*, 2d ed. (Boston: Little, Brown, 1917), p. 205.

54. John Wayne best exemplifies this dual appeal. His characteristic drawl and walk make for immediate recognition and easy caricature. But beyond that Wayne summed up America's mythic view of itself. As frontiersman and soldier he embodied society's self-idealization in the same way that Forrest had a century earlier. Skeptics need only review the eulogies following his death.

55. Walker, *Stardom*, p. 47.

56. *Variety*, 11 July 1919, p. 3.

57. Susan Sontag, *Against Interpretation* (New York: Farrar, Strauss & Giroux, 1966), p. 302.

58. Marshall McLuhan, *Understanding Media* (New York: McGraw-Hill, 1964).

59. Constance Rourke, *Trumpets of Jubilee* (New York: Harcourt, Brace & World, 1963), p. vii; Daniel Boorstin, *The Americans: The National Experience* (New York: Random House, 1965), p. 312.

60. F. O. Matthiessen, *American Renaissance* (New York: Oxford University Press, 1941), p. 22.

61. Neil Harris, ed., *The Land of Contrasts* (New York: George Braziller, 1970), pp. 6–7.

62. Lise-Lone Marker, *David Belasco: Naturalism in the American Theatre* (Princeton: Princeton University Press, 1975), pp. 75–83.

63. Clayton Meeker Hamilton, *The Theory of the Theatre*, consolidated edition (New York: Henry Holt, 1939), p. 187.

64. William Lyon Phelps, *The Twentieth Century Theatre* (New York: Macmillan, 1918), pp. 8–9.

65. Jack Poggi, *Theatre in America: The Impact of Economic Forces, 1870–1967* (Ithaca: Cornell University Press, 1968), pp. 29–30.
66. "The Theatre Adrift," *Nation* 101 (28 Oct. 1915): 512.
67. Poggi, *Theatre in America*, p. 35.
68. Ivah L. Bradley, "Voice and Personality in the Motion Pictures," *Journal of the Society of Motion Pictures Engineers* 21 (July 1933): 210; Alexander Bakshy, "The Shrinking of Personality," *Nation* 132 (27 May 1931): 590.
69. Kracauer, *Theory of Film*, p. 97.
70. Luigi Pirandello, quoted in Walter Benjamin, "The Work of Art in the Age of Mechanical Reproduction," in *Illuminations*, ed. Hannah Arendt (New York: Harcourt, Brace & World, 1968), p. 231.

CHAPTER NINE

1. Alexander Carr-Saunders and P. A. Wilson, *The Professions* (Oxford: Clarendon Press, 1923), pp. 302–3.
2. On the history of the Theatrical Syndicate see Monroe Lippman, "The History of the Theatrical Syndicate: Its Effect upon the Theatre in America" (PhD diss., University of Michigan, 1937), pp. 29–54; Alfred Bernheim, *The Business of the Theatre* (1932; repr. ed. New York: Benjamin Blom, 1964), pp. 34–59.
3. Lippman, "Theatrical Syndicate," pp. 169–72.
4. *NYDM*, 23 Oct. 1897, p. 15.
5. Alfred Harding, *The Revolt of the Actors* (New York: William Morrow, 1929), pp. 10–11.
6. *NYDM*, 2 Oct. 1897, p. 14; ibid., 16 Oct. 1897, p. 17.
7. Ibid., 27 Nov. 1897, p. 10.
8. Ibid., 16 Oct. 1897, p. 14.
9. Ibid., 4 Dec. 1897, p. 14.
10. Ibid., 11 Dec. 1897, p. 22.
11. Ibid., 5 Feb. 1898, p. 17.
12. Harding, *Revolt of the Actors*, pp. 10–12.
13. Francis Wilson, "Our Dedicatory Address," *Equity* 1 (Dec. 1915): 1.
14. *NYDM*, 20 Aug. 1913, in Robinson Locke Collection, vol. 329, Billy Rose Theatre Collection, NYPLC.
15. Harding, *Revolt of the Actors*, p. 15; Howard Kyle, Recollection of Henry Miller, typescript, Howard Kyle Papers, Billy Rose Theatre Collection, NYPLC.
16. *Equity* 2 (Sept. 1917): 7; Harding, *Revolt of the Actors*, pp. 17–18; *Equity* 3 (April 1918): 3.
17. Harding, *Revolt of the Actors*, pp. 16–18.
18. *Equity* 2 (March 1917): 1.
19. *Equity* 2 (April 1917): 7.
20. "Our Seven Aims," *Equity* 1 (Dec. 1915): 6; Harding, *Revolt of the Actors*, pp. 7–8; Francis Wilson, *Francis Wilson's Life of Himself* (Boston: Houghton Mifflin, 1924), pp. 248–50.

21. *NYDM*, 20 Aug. 1913, in Robinson Locke Collection, vol. 329, NYPLC.

22. *NYDM*, 30 April 1887, p. 6; Germain Quinn, *Fifty Years Back Stage* (Minneapolis: Stage Publishing, 1926), p. 148.

23. David Lifson, *The Yiddish Theatre in America* (New York: Thomas Yoseloff, 1965), pp. 130–31; Louis Lipsky, *Tales of the Yiddish Rialto* (New York: Thomas Yoseloff, 1962), p. 130.

24. Abram Loft, "Musician's Guild and Union: A Consideration of the Evolution of Protective Organization among Musicians" (PhD diss., Columbia University, 1950), pp. 281–311, 352–87; John R. Commons, "Types of American Labor Unions—The Musicians of St. Louis and New York," *Quarterly Journal of Economics* 20 (May 1906): 419–21, 427–38.

25. *NYDM*, 21 Nov. 1885, p. 2.

26. *ASMB* 8 (June 1904): 15.

27. "Proceedings of a Meeting of the Actors' Equity Association Held in Belvidere at the Hotel Astor New York—March 10, 1916," *Equity* 1 (April 1916): 5–6.

28. Harding, *Revolt of the Actors*, pp. 19–26.

29. Edwin Arden, "A Change of Heart," *Equity* 1 (March 1916): 1–2, quoted in Harding, *Revolt of the Actors*, pp. 28–30.

30. "An Actors' Trade Union," *Outlook* 106 (3 Jan. 1914): 12.

31. Hiram Moderwell, "Acting as a Trade," *New Republic* 6 (22 April 1916): 310–11.

32. *NYDM*, 18 March 1916, p. 7.

33. Harding, *Revolt of the Actors*, pp. 30–31; Paul Gemmill, *Collective Bargaining by Actors*, repr. from the *Bulletin of the United States Bureau of Labor Statistics*, no. 402 (Philadelphia, 1926), pp. 4–5.

34. Paul N. Turner, "White Rats—Federated Labor—Managers," *Equity* 2 (Jan. 1917): 1.

35. Harding, *Revolt of the Actors*, pp. 38–39.

36. Ibid., pp. 47–49.

37. Ibid., pp. 46, 52–53.

38. Ibid., pp. 53–58.

39. *Equity* 4 (June 1919): 13.

40. Ibid., p. 16.

41. Ibid., pp. 6–7.

42. Wee Willie Deming to Marjorie Wood, 30 July 1919, Deming Folder, Cage File, Billy Rose Theatre Collection, NYPLC.

43. Harding, *Revolt of the Actors*, pp. 78–80.

44. Ibid., pp. 74–89, 93–94.

45. Ibid., pp. 148, 151–52.

46. F. T. Vreeland, "The Actors' Strike," *Nation* 109 (23 Aug. 1919): 243.

47. George C. Tyler to Charles Bregg, 13 Aug. 1919, Bregg Correspondence, Cage File, Billy Rose Theatre Collection, NPYLC.

48. *Variety*, Daily Bulletin no. 1, 9 Aug. 1919, p. 27.

49. Charles Ruggles, Reminiscences, ser. 2, vol. 1, Oral History Collection, Columbia University, p. 13.

50. Gemmill, *Collective Bargaining*, p. 12; Harding, *Revolt of the Actors*, pp. 173–75.
51. Gemmill, *Collective Bargaining*, p. 11; Harding, *Revolt of the Actors*, pp. 192–97.
52. Harding, *Revolt of the Actors*, pp. 240–74.
53. Ibid., pp. 222–39, 273–74; Gemmill, *Collective Bargaining*, p. 13.
54. Gemmill, *Collective Bargaining*, pp. 13–16.
55. All three quotes are taken from *Current Opinion* 67 (Oct. 1915): 234–46.
56. Vreeland, "The Actors' Strike," p. 243.
57. The coming together of these two roads to collective upward mobility in the twentieth century is discussed in Marie R. Haug and Marvin B. Sussman, "Professionalization and Unionism," *American Behavioral Scientist* 14 (March–April 1971): 525–40.
58. *NYDM*, 8 Jan. 1887, pp. 6, 10.
59. *New York Times*, 7 June 1887, p. 5: "The Actors' Monument," *Harper's Weekly* 31 (18 June 1887): 438.
60. *NYDM*, 11 June 1887, p. 1.
61. *Variety*, 27 June 1919, p. 3: "Actors' National Memorial Day," *Theatre Magazine* 30 (Nov. 1919): 296; *NYDM*, 11 Dec. 1919, p. 1902; "The Work of the Actors' Fund," *Drama* 10 (Dec. 1919): 98–99; Louis Simon, *A History of the Actors' Fund of America* (New York: Theatre Arts Books, 1972), pp. 169–70.
62. *New York Times*, 4 Dec. 1919, p. 16.

Notes on Sources

American theatrical history of the period 1880–1920, while by no means neglected, invites greater attention to the interplay between stage and culture, such as that undertaken for an earlier period by David Grimsted in *Melodrama Unveiled: American Theater and Culture, 1800–1850* (Chicago, 1968), or for England in Michael Baker's *Rise of the Victorian Actor* (London, 1978). My study moves in that direction, and the materials listed here could help further investigation by scholars with similar interests.

The literature is best approached through bibliographies and indexes. The *Guide to Reference Books*, 7th ed. (Chicago, 1976), compiled by Eugene P. Sheehy, offers an overview of bibliographies and reference aids. Blanch M. Baker's *Theatre and Allied Arts* (New York, 1952) is an older but still useful work. Manuscript sources are located in William C. Young's *American Theatrical Arts: A Guide to Manuscripts and Special Collections in the United States and Canada* (Chicago, 1971). For the indispensable periodical literature refer first to Carl Stratman's *American Theatrical Periodicals, 1798–1967* (Durham, 1970), then to the *Cumulated Dramatic Index, 1909–1949*, 2 vols. (Boston, 1965), and of course to *The Reader's Guide to Periodical Literature* for the years under study. An unpublished dissertation of particular help for my project was Ronald Moyer's "American Actors, 1861–1910: An Annotated Bibliography of Books Published in the United States in English from 1861 through 1972" (University of Denver, 1974). A work too recent to have helped my research but one that will probably become the standard bibliographic guide for players is *American Actors and Actresses: A Guide to Information Sources* (Detroit, 1983), compiled by Stephen M. Archer.

For my purposes the manuscript collections were often disappointing. Actors were not very reflective about their profession in their correspondence. Consequently, though the manuscripts make for entertaining reading, they cannot be the backbone of research. Of more help are scrapbook collections that bring together newspaper and magazine clippings otherwise scattered beyond recall. The Billy Rose Theatre Collection of the New York Public Library at Lincoln Center holds many collections of letters and scrapbooks. Refer especially to the Robinson Locke Collecton of Dramatic Scrapbooks. Likewise, the main branch of the New York Public Library has a number of actors' papers. The Players Club library holds a collection of Edwin Booth papers as well as those of other actors belonging to the club. The Oral History Collection at Columbia University contains transcriptions from the reminiscences of a few stage actors from my era. And finally, the William Seymour Theater Collection at Princeton University repays a visit to its rich holdings.

Another category of primary materials—actors' autobiographies—are in some ways akin to correspondence. They are largely chatty accounts of plays and actors, generally lacking in professional self-scrutiny. They are also a far cry from today's "bare all" celebrity memoirs, maintaining a Victorian propriety that would disappoint the scandalmonger. Nevertheless, with patience one can uncover a great deal about theatrical institutions and ways of life. Among the most useful are: George Arliss, *My Ten Years in the Studios* (Boston, 1940); Ethel Barrymore, *Memories: An Autobiography* (New York, 1955); Jefferson De Angelis, *A Vagabond Trouper* (New York, 1931); Mary (Anderson) de Navarro, *A Few Memories* (New York, 1896); Nat Goodwin, *Nat Goodwin's Book* (Boston, 1930); DeWolf Hopper, *Once a Clown, Always a Clown* (Boston, 1927); Joseph Jefferson, *The Autobiography of Joseph Jefferson* (the classic theatrical memoir) (New York, 1889); Clara Morris, *The Life of a Star* (New York, 1906); Kate Ryan, *Old Boston Museum Days* (Boston, 1915); Otis Skinner, *Footlights and Spotlights* (Indianapolis, 1924); Frederick Warde, *Fifty Years of Make-Believe* (New York, 1920); Francis Wilson, *Francis Wilson's Life of Himself* (Boston, 1924); William Wood, *Personal Recollections of the Stage* (Philadelphia, 1855).

Another category of contemporary sources which is especially good for filling in the portraits of actors are collections of interviews and brief sketches of players, such as Margherita Arlina Hamm, *Eminent Actors in Their Homes* (New York, 1909); Montrose Moses, *Famous Actor-Families in America* (New York, 1906); Helen Ormsbee, *Backstage with Actors* (New York, 1938); and Ashton Stevens, *Actorviews* (Chicago, 1923). A related kind or writing that devotes greater attention to actors' performances are books by the era's drama critics. These are vital sources for the historian of the stage: Henry Austin Clapp, *Reminiscences of a Dramatic Critic* (Boston, 1902); Walter Prichard Eaton, *Plays and Players, Leaves from a Critic's Scrapbook* (Cincinnati, 1916); Clayton Hamilton, *The Theory of the Theatre* (New York, 1939); Norman Hapgood, *The Stage in America, 1897–1900* (New York, 1901); Brander Matthews, *On Acting* (New York, 1914); Montrose Moses and John Mason Brown, eds., *The American Theatre as Seen by Its Critics* (New York, 1934); Lewis Strang's two works, *Famous Actors of the Day in America* (Boston, 1899) and *Player and Plays of the Last Quarter Century* (Boston, 1902); and the profuse writings of William Winter, among them *Other Days* (New York, 1908), *Vagrant Memories* (New York, 1915), *The Wallet of Time* (New York, 1913), and his several biographies; also consult Daniel Watermeier's fine edition of the Edwin Booth–William Winter correspondence, *Between Actor and Critic* (Princeton, 1971).

Without question the most valuable primary sources were contemporary newspaper accounts and magazine articles. A quick perusal of the notes will show that the foundation of this study was the *New York Dra-*

matic Mirror, especially between the years 1879 and 1915. Through these years it was really the paper of record for the theatre. Available on microfilm, it has a wealth of information for the historian. Another theatrical trade paper, the *New York Clipper*, supplements the *Mirror* and should be consulted. As would be expected, the *New York Times* thoroughly covered the events behind and before the footlights. Many magazines of the era devoted significant space to actors and the theatre. *Cosmopolitan, Ladies' Home Journal, McClure's, Munsey's,* and *Scribner's* are particularly worth noting. Theatrical periodicals should also be examined: *Actors' Society Monthly Bulletin, Equity, Green Book Album* (later *Green Book Magazine*), *The Theatre* (1886–1893), *The Theatre* (later *Theater Magazine* [1901–]), and *Variety*. With the exception of some of the trade papers, most of these periodicals are well indexed.

A wide range of secondary works on the theatre supplement the primary materials. General works include *The American Theatre: A Sum of Its Parts* (New York, 1971); Alfred Bernheim, *The Business of the Theatre* (New York, 1932); Allen Churchill, *The Great White Way* (New York, 1962); Marvin Felheim, *The Theater of Augustin Daly* (Cambridge, Mass., 1956); Mary Henderson, *The City and the Theatre* (Clifton, N.J., 1973); Arthur Hornblow, *A History of the Theatre in America*, 2 vols. (Philadelphia, 1919); Glenn Hughes, *A History of the American Theatre, 1700–1950* (New York, 1951); Edward William Mammen, *The Old Stock Company School of Acting* (Boston, 1945); George C. D. Odell, *Annals of the New York Stage*, 15 vols. (New York, 1927–1949); William Lawrence Slout, *Theatre in a Tent* (Bowling Green, Ohio, 1972); Garff Wilson, *A History of American Acting* (Bloomington, 1966). The best single source on the history of actor training and elocution is Karl Wallace, ed., *History of Speech Education in America* (New York, 1954).

Theatre historians have diligently chronicled the lives of renowned players. In some cases these are biographies of a high order. Not surprisingly, however, most theatrical biographies are markedly sympathetic and thus lack an edge of critical analysis. Among those on major figures are: Archie Binns, *Mrs. Fiske and the American Theatre* (New York, 1955); Joseph Daly, *The Life of Augustin Daly* (New York, 1917); James Kotsilibas-Davis, *Great Times Good Times: The Odyssey of Maurice Barrymore* (Garden City, 1977); Lise-Lone Marker, *David Belasco: Naturalism in the American Theatre* (Princeton, 1975); Richard Moody, *Edwin Forrest: First Star of the American Stage* (New York, 1960); Lulla Rosenfeld, *Bright Star of Exile: Jacob Adler and the Yiddish Theatre* (New York, 1977); Constance Rourke, *Troupers of the Gold Coast* (on Lotta Crabtree) (New York, 1928); Eleanor Ruggles, *Prince of Players, Edwin Booth* (New York, 1953); Edward Wagenknecht, *Merely Players* (Norman, Okla., 1966). Not all of Broadway's stars have found modern chroniclers, including some who merit them, such as Mary Anderson and John Drew. In their absence turn to such biographical dictionaries as the *Dictionary of American Biography, National Cyclopedia of American Biography,* and *Notable American Women,* which give competent summaries of the life and art of leading American actors. They are constantly adding to their list of subjects.

I have drawn on a diverse sampling of scholarly article literature. The *Social Science* and *Humanities* indexes key most of these journals. The major theatrical journals are *Theatre Journal* (formerly the *Educational Theatre Journal*), *Theatre Quarterly*, and *Theatre Survey*. But the *Quarterly Journal of Speech* also has published numerous articles on the elocutionary aspect of acting. Three articles of special importance which might be easily overlooked bear mentioning: Herbert J. Edwards and Julie A. Herne, "James A. Herne: The Rise of Realism in the American Drama," *University of Maine Studies*, 2d ser., no. 80 (1964); E. J. West, "The London Stage, 1870–1890: A Study in the Conflict of the Old and New Schools of Acting," *University of Colorado Studies*, ser. B, Studies in the Humanities, vol. 2, no. 1 (May 1943): 31–84; and Alan S. Downer, "Players and Painted Stage," *PMLA* 61 (1946): 522–76.

Historians of the American theatre should not neglect the wealth of information and opinion contained in the many doctoral dissertations produced in university theatre departments. One can find unpublished dissertations on aspects of the theatre discussed nowhere else. I found this source to be extremely useful. They are described in *Dissertation Abstracts*, which now has a subject index. I shall name only those of greatest interest: Clifford Ashby, "Realistic Acting and the Advent of the Group in America: 1889–1922" (Stanford University, 1963); Monroe Lippman, "The History of the Theatrical Syndicate: Its Effect upon the Theatre in America" (University of Michigan, 1937); Pat Ryan, "A. M. Palmer, Producer: A Study of Management, Dramaturgy, and Stagecraft in the American Theatre, 1872–96" (Yale University, 1959); Barbara Whitehead, "Fancy's Show Box: Performance in the Republic, 1790–1866" (University of Chicago, 1976).

Various works helped to give my study some theoretical grounding. The literature of professionalism is already vast and still growing. Many case studies of different occupations as they professionalized add a comparative perspective. One can approach the field through a recent and highly imaginative work by Magali Sarfatti Larson, *The Rise of Professionalism* (Berkeley, 1977). Another recent interpretive work is Burton Bledstein's *Culture of Professionalism* (New York, 1976). *The Professions in America*, ed. Kenneth Lynn (Boston, 1968), offers a more standard introduction of the issue. Erving Goffman's influential social analysis has been based on the metaphor of theatricality, most notably in his *Presentation of Self in Everyday Life* (Garden City, 1959). Elizabeth Burns's *Theatricality: A Study of Convention in the Theatre and in Social Life* (London, 1972) takes the metaphor even further. Other theoretical works deserving notice include Roger Caillois, *Man, Play and Games* (New York, 1979); Jean Duvignaud, *L'Acteur* (Paris, 1965); Michael Goldman, *The Actor's Freedom: Toward a Theory of Drama* (New York, 1975); Siegfried Kracauer, *Theory of Film: The Redemption of Physical Reality* (New York, 1960); Yoti Lane, *The Psychology of the Actor* (Westport, Conn., 1959); and Alexander Walker, *Stardom: The Hollywood Phenomenon* (London, 1970).

Finally, a resource not to be overlooked in completing a social portrait of the theatre is fictional literature. For my era Theodore Dreiser is unparalleled, but Edith Wharton and Harold Frederic's novels also are pertinent. Beyond these major novelists lies a wealth of theatrical novels and short stories, hardly great literature, yet replete with details about the stage and attitudes toward the theatre not found elsewhere.

Index

American Civilization
A series edited by Allen F. Davis